Marketing Knowledge

Dominic Twose

MARKETING KNOWLEDGE

Cutting Through the Rubbish

With case studies and database analysis from Kantar

In memory of Lucy

People have always given objects more meaning than their purely functional benefits. American Indians thought trees contains spirits. Hindus think the cow is sacred. Children derive comfort from blankets. Christians revere relics of Saints. Eye of newt has never been the same since Shakespeare.

It is this process that makes a pair of trousers worn by Elvis worth thousands, that helps gypsies sell lucky charms, that makes people believe the configuration of stars can foretell their future, that transforms a house into a home.

This is why brands work.

Contents

Introduction

A quick check on Amazon suggests there are over 60,000 books available on the topic of marketing. So why another?

As a young man I had the good fortune to spend a month in West Africa. I remember being invited into a hut in a village in Upper Volta (now Burkina Faso). They were delighted to have an English guest – years earlier they had bought some English tea and were keen to share it with their English visitor. So, we sat talking in this mud hut, drinking tea. With us was the blind grandfather. Tea was clearly new to him, and he sat supping it with a spoon, as if it were soup. No one felt they could correct him.

It was a useful lesson for a young man. If only the grandfather could have seen our actions. It can be valuable to observe the experiences of others.

For the past 15 years I've had the role of Global Head of Knowledge Management at Kantar Millward Brown, the world's leading brand and advertising research agency. My role was to collect case studies from across the world, to explore the databases (Kantar Millward Brown has the biggest brand and advertising databases), and to write papers around what I found. Prior to that I spent 14 years working with a variety of clients, from small to multi-national.

I had at my fingertips an enormous wealth of material covering practical, real examples of what does and doesn't work. Real examples of how people dealt with marketing problems.

In this book I've tried to distil that experience. This is not a book about theory. This is not a book about one brand. This is not a book designed to put forward a particular argument.

It is a book of examples and database analysis. Because they came from client-funded projects, many of the examples are debranded. But the lessons are clear.

We live in an age where marketing campaigns are more complex than ever; but research budgets are being stripped back, making it harder to assess what aspects of the campaign have been successful. Rather than make guesses, it is useful to know what can and will work – as well as what is unlikely to work.

I'm grateful to everyone who gave me a case study over the years I was in my role – you helped keep Kantar Millward Brown at the head of understanding brands and advertising, and you've made this book richer. I'd also like to thank Rimmelle Freedman, David Friedman, Andy Farr, Dale Smith, Daren Poole, Dav Singh, Tracy Williams, Ollie Reece and Duncan Southgate who helped with some of the chapters. I left Kantar Millward Brown last year so I must thank Kantar for allowing me to write the book using their data. And I'm particularly grateful to Gordon Pincott whose thoughtful comments on much of the contents were always appreciated; to Nigel Hollis for robust debates over the years; to Nic Short, for many late-night wine-fuelled discussions; and to Polly Wyn Jones, who helped with a lot of the analysis. And finally I'd like to thank Gordon Brown; a car journey with him on the way back from a presentation twenty-five years ago was my inspiration.

Dominic Twose, 2019

BRAND KNOWLEDGE

Growing Brands

Coca-Cola's I Lohas brand was launched in Japan in 2009 around an eco-friendly positioning. The brand tapped into an unmet need to disrupt the bottled water category: research revealed that consumers wanted to do something about environmental issues but acknowledged that their behaviour had not changed. Thin and lightweight PET bottles helped generate a ritual out of twisting the bottle and offered consumers the means to choose a brand with a lower carbon footprint. The brand topped $1 billion retail sales in 2014, showing 8% year on year growth.

Successful brands have many characteristics, but they can be distilled into three broad areas; being different, being meaningful and being salient. Brands that increase their salience are likely to grow; and if they are meaningfully different, they're likely to grow faster. Strong marketing activity can help brands grow across all three of these measures.

Salient

People will often buy the brands that quickly come to mind when a need arises – these brands are salient. One of the most salient brands in the world is Coca-Cola. Other examples of highly salient brands include: Sberbank in Russia, PZU Insurance in Poland, Aeroflot in Russia, Hyundai in Korea, Skoda in Czech Republic, and McDonald's in many countries.

Different

For many years it has been rare (although not impossible) for brands in most categories to be substantially different in function; however even a small difference can be enough to tip the balance in favour of your brand over the competition. The difference could be a feature, a feeling, an impression; or even residual associations from a prior functional advantage. And in markets where technologies are rapidly developing, substantial differences are not uncommon, but you need to ensure that potential customers recognize the difference or recognize that your brand has redefined category expectations and is setting trends for others to follow.

In the book Reality in Advertising, Rosser Reeves popularised the term USP (Unique Selling Proposition), a concept developed in the 1940s. Many now dismiss it: most products today are almost identical; few unique claims exist.

However, it is interesting to read what Rosser Reeves wrote back in 1961 (the year I was born as it happens); 'It is true that a good many products are identical,' he acknowledged. But he argued that you can tell the public something about the product that has never been told before. 'This is not a uniqueness of the product, but it assumes uniqueness, and cloaks itself in uniqueness, as a claim.' He went on to say that while competitors may make the same claim, if you've advertised first and heavily, the USP will remain 'your claim'. Differentiation was possible back in 1961 in a market of near-identical products; and it is possible today.

The Apple iPhone is a great example of a brand succeeding by being so different that it redefined the category. Launched in 2007, the iPhone established design precedents, like its button placement and screen size. While less expensive copies quickly appeared on the market, the iPhone has retained its perception as being different, and maintains a high market share despite premium pricing. In addition to being physically different, the iPhone also has a distinctive personality; being seen as idealistic, assertive, sexy, adventurous and desirable.

Other examples of highly different brands include: Tesla in Norway, Pampers, Ikea, Free mobile in France, and the Apple iPhone.

Meaningful

Marketing plays an important role in creating brand meaning and shaping the brand experience. A meaningful impression made by a brand on consumers can be a powerful influence, whether it's based on tangible or intangible aspects: an emotional affinity or a sense of functional needs being met. A brand's meaning for you might simply be that it's familiar when others aren't, or the design may look more distinctive; but most likely it will stem from personal experience of a brand: your mother may have used the brand, it may have been recommended to you by a friend, or you've found it meets your needs better than other brands.

Levis, a long-established brand in the US, is seen as both meaningful and salient in the women's apparel market. While not seen as particularly different, the brand is considered trustworthy and straightforward.

In China, the cooking oil market is dominated by established Chinese brands; but Western olive oil is establishing itself, notably through the Chinese brand Mighty. While still not particularly salient, the brand is seen as being meaningful and different.

Other brands considered highly meaningful in certain markets include: All Nippon Airways in Japan, Singapore Airlines in Singapore; Toyota in Thailand; Google in France; Samsung in China; Castrol in India, and Sberbank in Russia.

The benefits of being meaningful, different and salient

Faster growth

Brands can succeed by being meaningful, different or salient, or a combination of the three. But, are these three characteristics equally important? The analysis below examines if a brand is Meaningfully Different (top quartile for each) in one year, and overlays that with its change in salience over the next five years; and relates that to its change in survey-based market share over the same period. The analysis highlights that building saliency is an important thing to do: Brands that increase their saliency are likely to grow. But meaningfully different brands tend to grow more than twice as fast; and typically grow even if salience does not. If your brand is meaningfully different, growth can be accelerated.

Being Meaningfully Different amplifies Salience

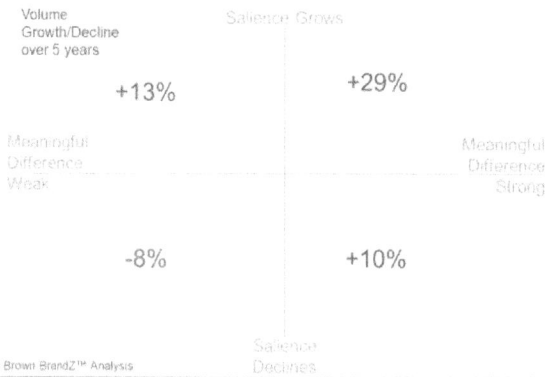

Volume
Growth/Decline
over 5 years

Salience Grows

+13%   +29%

Meaningful   Meaningful
Difference   Difference
Weak   Strong

-8%   +10%

Salience
Declines

Source: Millward Brown BrandZ™ Analysis

KANTAR MILLWARDBROWN

However, Hollis has pointed out that, among those that consider a brand acceptable, an average of just 18% agreed that it was different from others, and acknowledged that it is far easier to create differentiation when the product is tangible and consumer interest is high; e.g., in fields such as technology, automotive, or personal care ('It Is Not a Choice: Brands Should Seek Differentiation and Distinctiveness').

Premium pricing

There is a second valuable benefit of being meaningfully different. Being able to charge a price premium is an important but often overlooked component of brand equity. The ability to charge a higher price can have a far bigger effect on the bottom line than increasing volume share. And brands that are meaningfully different are more likely to achieve a premium status. The Purina and Chef cat food brands from New Zealand are examples of two very different business models but typical of their kind. Purina sells less volume than Chef but charges over twice as much per kilo, as a result Purina has the higher value market share. Purina is seen to be different from the alternatives and that difference is meaningful to many people. When people choose Chef they may recognise that Purina is different but that difference is not meaningful enough to justify the higher price. The fact that Chef is far cheaper is more meaningful to them, and the advantage it has in salience will help make many sales almost on auto-pilot.

Liking the brand

A third benefit of being meaningfully different is that people are more likely to like your brand.

The first thing to emphasise here is that most of the time, most consumers do not 'love' brands. At best they like them. Kantar Millward Brown's Emotional Priming research demonstrates that most brands evoke a mild, instinctive liking, not some more passionate response.

Kantar Millward Brown's BrandZ global brand equity study measures brand love through an Affinity scale; asking consumers to use a scale from -5 (hate it) to +5 (love it). Data from this confirms that most people do not love or hate brands (although there are country differences).

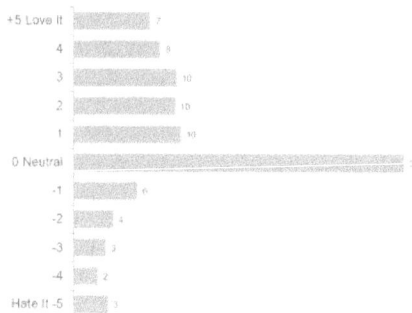

+5 Love It	7
4	8
3	10
2	10
1	10
0 Neutral	21
-1	6
-2	4
-3	3
-4	2
Hate It -5	3

KANTAR MILLWARDBROWN   Source: Kantar Millward Brown BrandZ database

There are also differences by category; for example in the US affinity is strongest for salty snacks and confectionery; weakest for banking and insurance.

Looking at the BrandZ database reveals a strong correlation between Affinity and brand usage: if you buy a brand you tend to like it. However, from this it is not clear whether people are buying the brands they like or liking the brands they buy. But there are brands that buck this trend; some discount brands are bought but not much liked; and some premium brands are admired more than bought.

Looking at brands that have relatively high Affinity compared with their level of usership, they index much more highly on being Different (170) and being Meaningful (143). Common examples include cars (Audi, BMW, Lexus, Mercedes), technology (iPhone, Amazon), as well as brands like Pampers and Lavazza.

This higher affinity is valuable. Analysis shows that affinity has an important role in encouraging repeat purchase. Combining data from Kantar WordPanel with BrandZ data shows that people are twice as likely to buy a brand again if they like it to start with.

Affinity supports repeat purchase

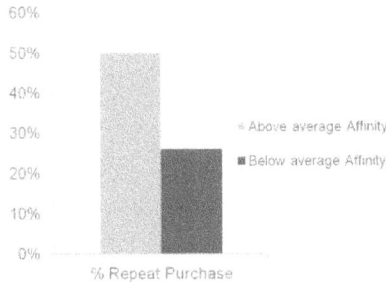

% Repeat Purchase

- Above average Affinity
- Below average Affinity

Becoming more salient

So how do brands improve their performance on these key measures? Strong marketing activity can have a powerful effect.

The UK airline easyJet launched its *Europe by easyJet* ad campaign to move on from its 'cheap and cheerful' positioning. The campaign, which highlighted the joy and human connection made possible by low-cost airfare, was highly impactful. Kantar Millward Brown's BrandZ data showed the brand enjoyed a huge increase in salience as well as an increased Power score (a measure of predisposition).

Becoming more meaningfully different

Capitalise on your difference

In some circumstances, it can be found that a difference is not being fully capitalised on. A few years ago Kantar Millward Brown conducted research for an OTC homeopathic brand in Poland, interviewing both doctors and patients, as well as conducting a pricing experiment in 18 pharmacies. The conclusion was that the equity of the brand was strong enough to withstand a substantial price increase. The client increased prices by 10%; and demand held steady.

In China, the premium toothpaste Yunnan Baiyao has been enjoying substantial growth despite strong competition from major global brands. The product contains Chinese herbs claimed to help bleeding gums and is increasingly noted as being different. Its digital advertising and content sponsorship, emphasizing its heritage and 'oral problem solved' message, positions the brand as increasingly meaningful; and its Power score is growing.

Innovate

Innovation can be exploited in several ways; through improvement of the core brand, through the introduction of premium variants, and through innovative customer experiences.

The Mahindra automotive brand launched a premium SUV in 2011, in a segment that was dominated by Sedans. This was seen as different, and the brand's Premium rating peaked in 2012 and 2013. The brand gained share. Since then, however, the segment has seen the entry of Hyundai, Renault Maruti and others, and the brand has lost its differentiation.

In 2007, Samsung's wide range of handsets and low pricing meant it was seen as meaningful by many consumers. Good distribution and heavyweight advertising kept the brand salient. Aggressive innovation in the form of the Galaxy (2009) grew perceptions of the brand's difference, which led to increased market share.

In 2009, the Buick brand underwent a complete product line overhaul, with many new models that were now unique and well-designed. During this period Buick completely re-vamped their positioning and communication programs. Their renewed product line has made them more Meaningful; they now have a product in most every luxury segment. And, they have really made an effort to be different from what they were; Buick has become a legitimate luxury brand.

Strong marketing

One of the most important ways advertising helps build brand value is by enhancing or framing the brand experience, making the experience more rewarding in either functional or emotive ways. In general, marketing can aid premium perceptions through both direct communication (using cues symbolic of a premium brand) and association (using retail, events, celebrities and media to create positive premium perceptions).

In 2010, the Spanish beer brand Estrella Galicia, realized they couldn't grow more based on their regional consumption and decided to go national. Their launch strategy consisted of a national TV advertising campaign building brand awareness and associations around taste and quality. This was aggressively supported below the line (many bars and pubs in main Spanish cities were re-decorated by Estrella Galicia) and by sponsorships. The national launch was very successful. Brand awareness increased from 54% to 94% in Spain. The Power score (the measure of predisposition) increased from 3.3% to 8.2%. The brand has become a well-known, meaningful brand for Spanish consumers, competing not only with local, traditional brands but also with international premium brands. When going national, it further defined its difference in taste and quality, amplifying the brand´s meaningful point of differentiation.

The Weave Your Magic campaign, with its beautiful shots of meal preparation, positioned the butter Lurpac as a recipe ingredient, and helped establish the brand as 'a champion of good food'; and Food Lovers were willing to pay more for the product.

In recent years in the UK, the Italian beer Peroni Nastro Azzurro has been supported by strong marketing activity including a series of high production value ads, with many premium cues, positioning the brand as a higher end beer. The beer now has very different perceptions in the UK compared to Italy; in Italy it is very salient, but in the UK it is seen as meaningfully different.

In the UK, the supermarket brand Aldi introduced the 'swap and save' challenge. While Aldi was known as a discounter, the campaign aimed to overcome perceptions of limited range, and the social stigma of shopping at a discount store. Through TV, print and digital, consumers followed aspirational people challenged to use Aldi for their main shop for four weeks. Market share increased, the brand was seen as increasingly different; and the Power score improved. The Aldi campaign won an IPA Effectiveness award.

In the US, Trader Joe's sells unusual foods at a good price in a characterful store environment. The brand had advertised on local radio, outdoor and social media, but largely ignored traditional marketing, relying on customer experience and word of mouth. Brand salience has remained low over the past few years but the store has been increasingly noted as being different; its indexed score rose from 158 to 196. Both its Power score (predisposition), and market share have also grown.

Aviva, a UK insurance company, used the well-known comedian Paul Whitehouse, playing a series of characters, to communicate messages about Aviva's value, service and innovations. Car quotes soared. BrandZ data showed that the brand was seen as more meaningful. The campaign won an IPA Effectiveness Award.

The Dove brand has become synonymous with its Real Beauty campaign, which began in 2004, but still benefits the brand, in this very aggressive category. In 2013 their Real Beauty Sketches drew attention to low self-esteem in a striking way, involving artists drawing sketches based on women's descriptions of themselves. The campaign won an IPA Effectiveness Award. Over the period in the UK, Dove grew in saliency and meaningfulness.

The Commonwealth Bank (CBA), a well-known brand in Australia, has had to fight off several competitive threats including the growth of new regional banks. To do so, Commonwealth doubled down on customer service with their CAN campaign. CBA invested over a

$1billion in technology enabling them to take the lead on innovation and customer experience. The launch of the CAN campaign was well executed with strong alignment across all touch points. This amplified the brand in-market, maintaining its leadership status. CBA equity grew strongly on all three measures and expanded its share of market both attitudinally and in terms of customers.

In 2011, Volkswagen China was losing its positioning and was increasingly seen as mainstream, sensible and utilitarian. The brand was facing falling market share. They launched the People's Car Project, a platform to inspire Chinese people to contribute their ideas for future car designs. In 2012, Volkswagen celebrated the people's ideas by turning them into reality. Volkswagen's design team took on an idea for a hover car and developed it using magnetic levitation technology which they depicted in a series of films. The brand has become more salient, meaningful and different. Its Power score has grown, and sales were up from 2.6million in 2012 to 3.4 million in 2014 (Wards Automotive Reports and Sterne Agee estimates).

Also in China, Blue Moon detergent has focused on an integrated campaign with heavyweight spend, except for 2012 when they stopped above the line to focus on in-store efforts; Blue Moon staff helped educate consumers about the benefits of the product. Over a four-year period the brand has become much more meaningful, different and salient. Power grew, and value share increased rapidly.

Brands that are salient and perceived as meaningfully different stand the best chance of growth; and strong marketing activity can help develop this equity. However, the effort required to increase perceptions of being meaningfully different for an existing brand should not be underestimated; and once those perceptions have been lost it is an enormous challenge to regain them.

Influencing Purchase Decisions

In the UK spirits market people are generally happy to buy the brand they bought last time; there is a clear relationship between preference and brand bought last. However the chart below shows that Famous Grouse was able to kick that trend; purchase levels were higher than its pre-existing demand. How did it achieve this?

Famous Grouse: Purchase outstrips demand

Logit Transformed rsqu = 0.79

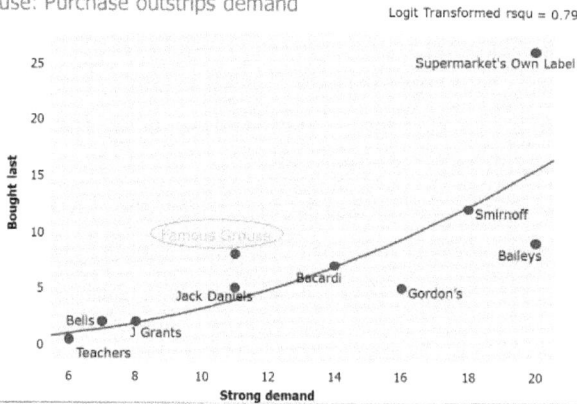

KANTAR MILLWARDBROWN

For the overwhelming majority of brands, both pre-existing demand and in-store activity are important for generating sales. Overall, the balance is around 70% in favour of pre-existing demand. However, the balance between the two varies considerably by country, category and brand. While price promotions are useful for generating short-term sales, packaging and display are also useful contributors to sales. Advertising is hugely important for stimulating brand demand, and TV remains a key component of this. There are clear benefits to ensuring consistency between advertising and in-store activity and this remains an underutilized opportunity for many brands.

Demand and Activation

Client marketing activities can be categorised into two main groups: long-term brand building and short-term persuasion.

Interaction with all brand connection points influences how we feel about brands, and it is these perceptions which shape how disposed we are towards buying brands. Call this Demand. But there is a difference between those connection points experienced outside the store, and those experienced inside the store.

The out-of-store experience can generate a certain level of interest in the brand, but actual purchase can be strongly affected by the in-store activity, as illustrated by the Famous Grouse example above, where in-store promotional activity had a strong effect.

Activity in-store can have a substantial effect on the brand actually purchased. This is Activation. Overall across the world, the balance between Demand and Activation has about a 70:30 ratio. However, the sales activation process is different for all individuals and can vary significantly.

Differences by country

The balance between the two varies across different countries; for instance, in China, in-store activity exerts a more powerful influence on the purchase of soft drinks than it does in Spain.

In general across Asian countries, in-store activity is more influential than it is in the West.

There is more of an opportunity for in-store activity for China in the Soft drinks category, than Spain

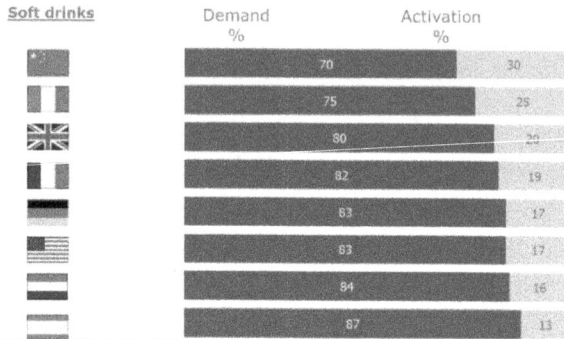

Soft drinks	Demand %	Activation %
	70	30
	75	25
	80	20
	82	19
	83	17
	83	17
	84	16
	87	13

KANTAR MILLWARDBROWN

Differences across categories

The Demand:Activation ratio also differs across categories. In longer-term purchase categories, the Activation phase is critical. For a car, the process begins the moment someone starts seriously considering their next purchase. Their consideration is influenced by many factors, including articles and web sites they read, TV and magazine ads they see, advice from friends, test drives they take and how responsive the local dealer seems. All these will play a role in converting their initial desire to buy a particular make or model into a sale. Overall, the Demand:Activation ratio for longer-term purchase categories is around 60:40.

For a typical packaged goods product, Activation will largely take place solely within the store environment. As people shop for the category, some brands will have more visible packaging, others will be running price reductions, others exciting promotions, and some will not even be on shelf. Overall, the Demand:Activation ratio for packaged goods is around 80:20.

Taking Germany as an example, the Demand:Activation ratio varies from 50:50 for hi-tech products to 83:17 for off-trade beer.

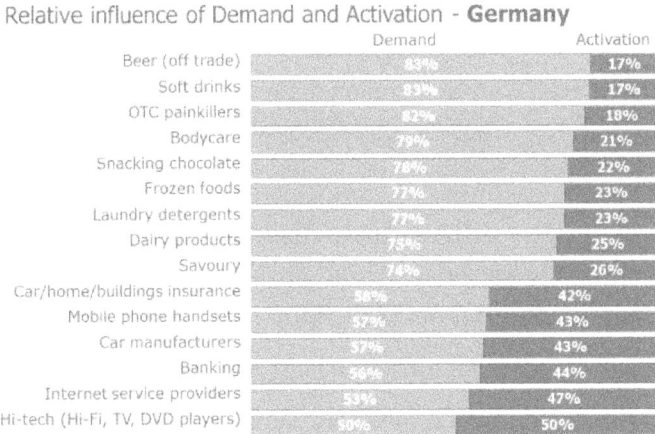

Relative influence of Demand and Activation - **Germany**

	Demand	Activation
Beer (off trade)	83%	17%
Soft drinks	83%	17%
OTC painkillers	82%	18%
Bodycare	79%	21%
Snacking chocolate	78%	22%
Frozen foods	77%	23%
Laundry detergents	77%	23%
Dairy products	75%	25%
Savoury	74%	26%
Car/home/buildings insurance	58%	42%
Mobile phone handsets	57%	43%
Car manufacturers	57%	43%
Banking	56%	44%
Internet service providers	53%	47%
Hi-tech (Hi-Fi, TV, DVD players)	50%	50%

A category such as soft drinks in the UK is driven mainly by Demand (80:20). People largely know which brand they want before they even get to the store, albeit choosing from a repertoire, so getting on their consideration list is the major part of the battle. However, special offers in-store may still have some impact on the final choice.

By contrast, the market for buildings and contents insurance is a category where the Activation phase is more significant (64:36). This is a category that people know little about, and the potential consideration set is very large; research is needed and advice sought. Despite this, pre-existing Demand for brands based on past experience and reputation is important too.

Differences by brand

Even within a specific country and category, there can be great variation between brands. The differences being due to the effectiveness of the activity at the different connection points. In the

UK in the deodorant market the proportion of Sure's sales decided pre-store is higher than that for other brands.

Which connection points are most important?

So, what are the connection points which have the biggest influence? Globally, prior product experience is the biggest driver of sales, having a huge effect on Demand. The majority of the time, consumers are happy to buy what they have bought previously, if it has met their needs.

However, in-store activity (increasingly online stores) and advertising also play important roles. As might be expected, in-store activity is particularly influential on Activation, while advertising is particularly influential on Demand.

The biggest influence in-store comes from price promotions (illustrated by its Power Score in the chart below); although these are not always beneficial for the brand in the long term. There are other elements of in-store activity which can also be beneficial, without having the drawbacks of price-promotions. The store is the one environment which the vast majority of consumers visit regularly, and this opportunity should be leveraged to communicate effectively with them. The packaging, the brand display, and special in-store displays can all exert a major influence.

The most appropriate displays will vary according to brand status. Launches will want to disrupt the category, and to question automatic choices. Brand leaders, by contrast will want to emphasise their familiarity, aiding quick recognition and routine, maybe by reminding the consumer of positive experiences or communications.

In Store influences

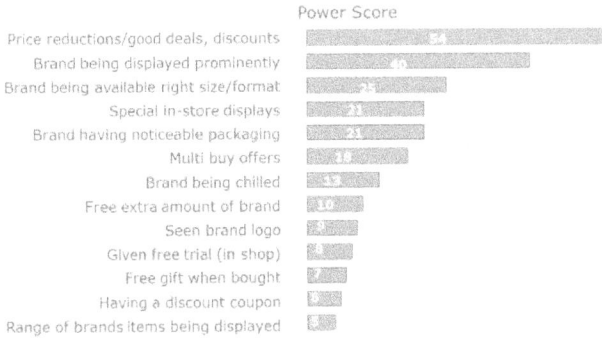

Power Score

Price reductions/good deals, discounts	
Brand being displayed prominently	
Brand being available right size/format	
Special in-store displays	
Brand having noticeable packaging	
Multi buy offers	
Brand being chilled	
Free extra amount of brand	
Seen brand logo	
Given free trial (in shop)	
Free gift when bought	
Having a discount coupon	
Range of brands items being displayed	

Total 247

KANTAR MILLWARDBROWN

A case study illustrates the importance of in-store activity. Brand A is the leading brand in its category across most markets in China. It focuses on TV advertising as a main driver of brand health and significantly outspends its main competitor — Brand B. However, in Guangzhou, Brand B made significant gains at brand A's expense, especially among the younger consumer group, using in-store activities, emphasising attractive displays, attention grabbing POS, and active sales staff. Over the course of this activity, consideration for Brand B, particularly among the younger target, improved dramatically, despite Brand A's TV dominance.

Consideration – Only/preferred brand

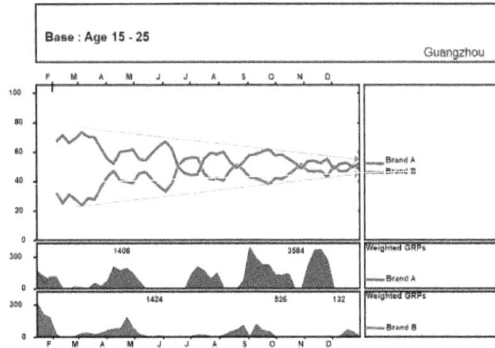

Base : Age 15 - 25

Guangzhou

The proportion of sales for brand B where salesperson recommendation influenced the sale rose from 14% in Q1 to 35% in Q3, while the proportion influenced by point-of-sale material rose from 16% in Q1 to 27% in Q3.

However, across the world, when it comes to advertising, TV still is the dominant power. While this reflects the proportion of the marketing budgets which continues to be spent on this medium, it is a useful reminder that TV still plays a major role for most brands.

Advertising - Global

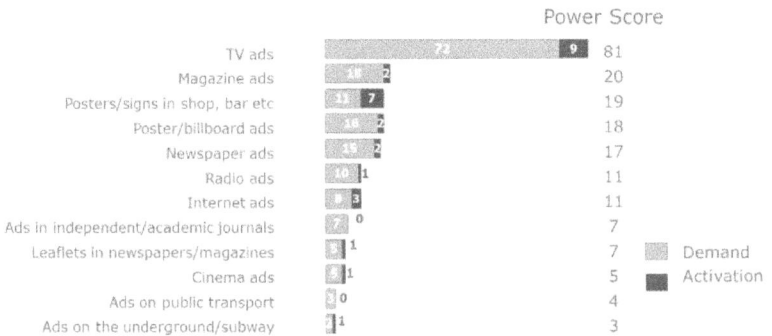

	Power Score
TV ads	81
Magazine ads	20
Posters/signs in shop, bar etc	19
Poster/billboard ads	18
Newspaper ads	17
Radio ads	11
Internet ads	11
Ads in independent/academic journals	7
Leaflets in newspapers/magazines	7
Cinema ads	5
Ads on public transport	4
Ads on the underground/subway	3

Demand
Activation

Total 213

Integration

So far I've talked about Demand and Activation as two separate elements of the marketing mix; which is how they are often treated. However, there are real benefits to be had by ensuring the two work together. In the UK, a few years ago the milk brand Cravendale, as part of a relaunch strategy, changed its in-store activity, including POS tastings, to be more consistent with its other marketing activity. On its own, the in-store activity had minimal effect, but when the in-store activity was tied in with the TV activity, the effect was greater than the two added together.

A second example comes from a brand with strong demand built on a heritage of clever, creative advertising. But the packaging and in-store presence was relatively weak, resulting in lost sales to competitors (including private label brands). Guided by research, they revised their packaging to build on the imagery that had been created through advertising and also focused more effort and resources on in-store activity. They continued to reinforce demand through TV and magazine advertising, creating a far more integrated message.

In-store experience can evoke associations from advertising, generating stronger interest in the brand. This can be a powerful tool and is a strong argument for fully integrated marketing.

Managing Multiple Brands

As a result of a merger, one major U.S. retailer found itself with a brand portfolio of six retail brands. This made no economic sense and it required massive marketing investment to support all six. Following a full brand positioning and architecture assessment for all the brands, a brand architecture solution was found, which focused on three brands with a differentiated positioning for each. Despite the retention of three brands, significant operational synergies were realized including common sourcing of products and materials for the different retail brands. Additionally, with only three brands to support, marketing spend was reduced by 20%. Profitability increased.

Many companies own multiple brands. This approach has undoubted advantages such as spreading risk, greater market share, and commensurate profit levels. However there are pitfalls to be avoided. Differentiation and clear targeting are essential, as well as an understanding of which brands are most likely to benefit from investment.

Cannibalization

The nightmare situation of multiple brand ownership is cannibalization. In the following example the client owned two brands in the ice cream market. Brand A was a well-established mainstream brand, while Brand B was a newer inspirational brand. Advertising for Brand B lead to a growth in consumption of Brand B, but at the expense of Brand A. When the support switched back to Brand A, the decline in usage was reversed, but at the expense of Brand B.

Consumers switch easily between the brands

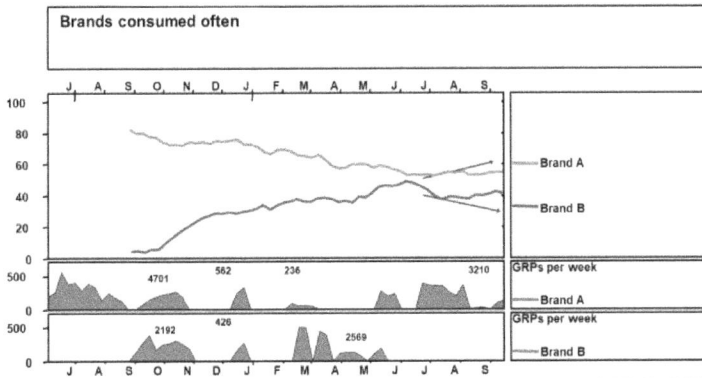

Differentiation and distinctiveness

The key to successfully manage several brands in a portfolio is distinctiveness. This can be differentiation at a rational level; a premium and a low-cost brand, for example.

However, even when the brands are functionally similar, there is still an opportunity to be distinctive. Brand A, a leading consumer electronics retail supplier in Canada with 20% market share, acquired Brand B, a relatively new entry to the Canadian market. The brands, despite having the same rational offering, were comfortably coexisting in the same territory and together generated a total market share of 30% (20% retained by Brand A, 10% growth achieved by Brand B).

Brand A and B occupied identical positions – both were seen as high-quality technology specialists. However, exploring the personality of the brands revealed very different positions. While Brand B had a fun positioning, Brand A was seen as complicated and rather intimidating. The two brands were attracting different audiences. This analysis also helped direct future activity. Although Brand B's position was strong,

Brand A needed to overcome the sense of intimidation associated with it, while capitalizing on perceptions of overcomplexity to generate a sense of expertise.

The brands clearly differentiate on personality dimensions

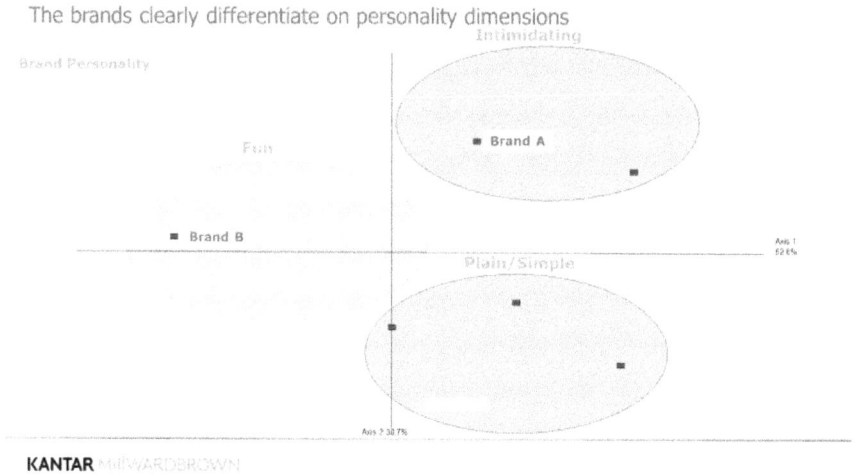

Targeting

The idea of differentiated positionings is inextricably linked to the idea of targeting and segmentation. In the above example, the key brands had different positionings, and so attracted different audiences. While basic demographic segmentations can be revealing, it is often more subtle attitudinal segmentations that reveal the underlying differences. In this example from an alcohol market, a cluster analysis based on a combination of category attitudes and lifestyle revealed that, while brands A and E were similar, they appealed to different audiences due to their different positionings. The risk of cannibalization was minimal.

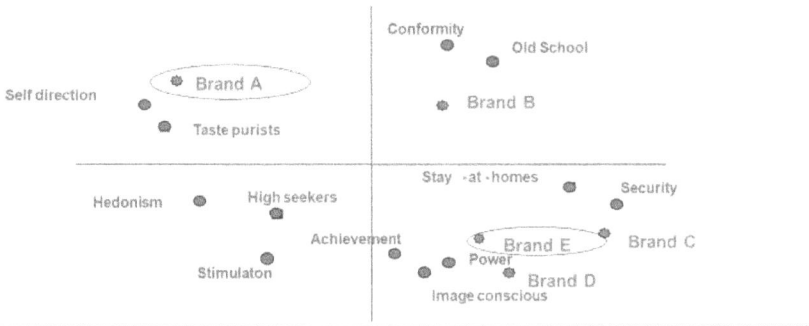

Conformity

Old School

Self direction

Brand A

Brand B

Taste purists

Stay -at -homes

Security

Hedonism

High seekers

Achievement

Brand E

Brand C

Power

Stimulaton

Brand D

Image conscious

KANTAR MILLWARDBROWN

Which to support?

There is also the question of which brands to support. How do you assess which brands in the portfolio will give best return on investment?

Size matters. Established brands with more than 10% market share are better positioned to gain market share than small brands. In addition to operational advantages, often large brands drive market share growth through strong brand equity built over years. The likelihood of increasing market share is much greater among large brands with high brand equity.

Big brands are better positioned to grow share

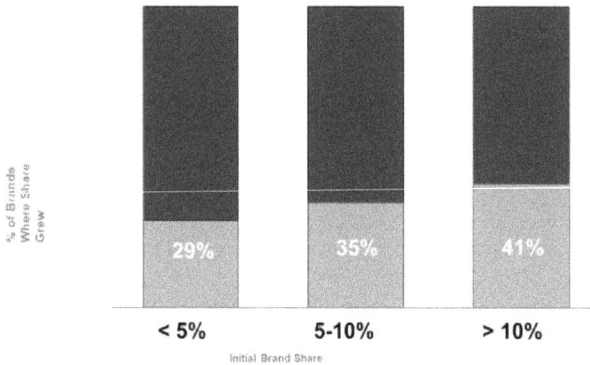

% of Brands Where Share Grew

29%	35%	41%
< 5%	5-10%	> 10%

Initial Brand Share

* Based on study of 366 brands from 31 categories measuring sales growth/decline of 5% over course of one year

KANTAR MILLWARDBROWN

However, funding each brand according to its size or current profitability may fail to capitalize on brands with potential. There are many factors that play a part in such decisions, including whether the category is in growth or decline, changing social trends, and demographic changes. The importance of particular brands to the company is also a factor which can't be underestimated. Linchpin brands, large dominant brands, brands with future potential, and those able to indirectly affect sales may all require support. Additional factors which need to be considered include forthcoming innovations, competitor threats, likely pricing levels, and the quality of upcoming marketing activity.

Brands with momentum are more likely to provide future profits, and equity analysis of your brands should be factored in when assessing which of your brands are worth investing in.

Stretching Brands

The diversity of the Amazon brand resulted in it becoming the largest internet retailer in the world. It is perhaps the best example of 'brand stretch'. The amazon.com website started as an online bookstore that moved into selling just about anything; and the brand now stretches into consumer electronics producing Kindles, Fire tablets/Fire TV and Echo.

It is common for brands to stretch into new categories. However, identifying the most appropriate categories can be a complex area. The issue at the heart of the matter is the double-ended question: Will the stretch benefit the parent, and can the parent benefit the stretch? There are many issues to consider when contemplating stretching your brand into new variants. Functional fit is naturally important, but so too is having the right brand personality, and a successful track record in diversifying.

Business basics

Strong business basics is one key requirement; can the product be produced and distributed in a cost-effective means? Economies of scale are difficult to achieve, particularly when relatively small variants are being considered. For example, one brand saw an opportunity to produce razors, a completely new category for it. However, while the concept appealed to consumers, the cost of production put on the product was too high for the brand to achieve profitable sales.

Functional fit

Consumers will allow brands to move more easily into new categories where there is a functional fit between the brand's identity and the needs of the new category. Starbuck's Verismo coffee machine was a new category for the brand but a great fit with the brand's identity.

Gillette successfully moved into male grooming products some years ago because its experience with one aspect of grooming — shaving — gave it credentials in other areas of male grooming, such as moisturizers and deodorants. Consumers can readily appreciate this. For instance, in one US study, the most appropriate stretch was seen to be AT&T making mobile phones, while one of the least appropriate stretches was Dell making liquor. Extremes highlight the potential problems: Johnnie Walker automobiles and Kentucky Fried Chicken skincare were both considered completely inappropriate.

Functional benefits

In Thailand, one of the leaders in the men's deodorant market, positioned as masculine, cool, with attractive fragrance, stretched into male grooming. Research suggested that the majority of men's personal care requirements were not being met and so men were forced to buy more typically feminine brands, which caused embarrassment. A facial foam, a body lotion and a shower cream were launched under the parent brand umbrella. However, while the brand had many emotional benefits, it lacked functional benefits in these new categories. These brand extensions have since been withdrawn.

Can the brand offer differential advantages? In most markets, a 'me too' brand is unlikely to succeed (however, it is possible. The spread I Can't Believe It's Not Butter was launched in the UK in 1991 with strong advertising. Utterly Butterly was launched in 1995. Its positioning was similar, but it adopted a quirky personality in its advertising, and the brand outperformed ICBINB in blind taste tests. Within a year its claimed usage levels were on a par with ICBINB).

In general, and as I've already covered, being seen as meaningfully different is a great benefit for a brand.

The right personality

However, there is more to consumer permission than this. Broader brand attributes than just functional competence play a role in determining the suitability of brand stretching. This was highlighted in one study where consumers were asked the appropriateness of brands stretching into new categories. The findings showed consumers allowed some brands to go further than others, even from the same category. For instance the concept of Sony automobiles was relatively well received.

One important factor here is the warmth of a brand's personality; more attractive brands tend to be more elastic.

In addition, the exact nature of the personality will also influence the perceived fit with a new category. For example, in the US, Gap offers a range of fragrances and some skincare products alongside its main offering of apparel. This seems like a good opportunity to exploit, as almost two-thirds of skincare buyers in the study regarded this as appropriate. In contrast, less than half that number said it would be appropriate if another apparel brand, Levi's, offered a range of skincare products. This difference can be traced in part to the difference in brand personality identified within the study. Gap has a more 'sensitive' personality than Levi's and sensitivity is a characteristic of skincare brands.

History of diversity

Besides personality, other brand values influence a brand's ability to stretch. In particular, brands based on broader benefits than simply product or service delivery are much more flexible and are allowed to go further by the consumer.

A history of diversity is also helpful. Brands which have previously stretched to new categories are allowed to do it again more readily. Sony is a good example of the influence of broad brand values. In the survey it was one of the more elastic brands in both the US and the

UK, and this seems likely to be driven by the values of quality and innovation identified by brand equity measures. In the UK Virgin is an excellent example, demonstrating both the effect of broad brand values, and a history of diversity. It was by far the most elastic brand covered by the study in the UK. The brand is far more diverse than an airline and music retailer in the UK — it also offers financial services, online automobile purchasing, mobile phone service provision, to name but a few. Its history of diversity seems to mean that consumers will allow the brand to go further than many others. At the same time, the unifying value that the brand promotes to consumers is one of a fairer deal, irrespective of the product field and this also seems to allow it to cross into new territory.

Advertising Variants

In the UK, a well-known spirits brand launched a variant in a relatively new alcohol category, one which was modern and appealed to a younger target. Around the variant launch, both the parent and the variant had TV advertising presence. Benefiting from the parent's strength in the market and the growth of a new category, the variant launch was so successful that it began to overshadow the parent. Shortly after the launch of the variant brand, saliency and communication awareness of the 'trademark' was being driven by the variant. Soon the variant was achieving as high levels of consumption as the parent brand. Consumption continued to grow for the variant while the parent's growth remained constant; the growth of the umbrella brand was being lead by the variant. The success of the variant was, in part, due to the established positioning of the parent brand and a well-timed launch into a new and exciting category.

There are benefits to advertising a new variant under an existing parent brand; values from the umbrella brand can be transferred by using similar branding devices, styles, or music. And when established or synergistic branding devices are included in the launch, the parent brand may also benefit. However, the danger is that the ad will be viewed as an ad for the parent brand. To prevent this occurring, the variant's name and its differences from the parent need to be highlighted within the ad.

The term 'variant' covers a range of scenarios, from the relatively minor, such as a new flavor, to the major, such as a launch that you intend will eventually overtake the parent brand. How you promote these launches will vary enormously. The scale of the activity will help ensure distribution, while the quality of the activity will have a substantial effect on the interest generated among consumers.

Using established campaign themes

It is common for variant launches to use umbrella branding devices to help launch the variant with the 'halo' benefits of the parent. In the UK, a chocolate brand launched a new round white chocolate variant, featuring the brand's spokesperson. The ad featured the celebrity skiing down a mountain. She tumbled and ended up wrapped in a snowball. Three quarters recalled her ending up in the snowball and this image helped cement the message; 84% understood that the brand was now available in a white chocolate format. The ad was hugely engaging, and consideration and sales responded well.

However, there are potential pitfalls to launching a variant using the themes from the umbrella brand advertising. Perhaps the most significant is that, without strong variant branding, advertising could be incorrectly linked to the umbrella brand or other variants. It is, then, critical that the variant's identity comes through clearly in the advertising. There is often an assumption that by communicating the variant's proposition and the parent brand name, viewers will realize it must be a new variant and listen out for the new variant's name; as a result the variant's name is often secondary within the ad. Instead, the ad needs to make it very clear to viewers exactly what the brand is called, what it is and how that differs from the parent, and that it's new. This is especially important when a well-established campaign is being used or when the new variant is the same product format as the parent, as consumers can easily fail to register what's new.

One variant launch suffered through poor variant branding. The objective was to gain trial by launching a variant using a high impact, pre-existing advertising campaign. The established campaign cued familiar brand associations, which were mainly linked to the parent brand. Playback of the ad focused strongly on campaign elements that did not link to the intended variant proposition. While 91% recognized the ad was for the parent brand, only 21% associated it with the variant. Although the parent brand, as a whole, received relatively good branded visibility, weak variant integration meant consideration for the variant remained static across the advertised period.

A launch is easier when a new variant can be demonstrated in a new context or environment, or a new distinctive pack is prominent. There is no evidence to suggest that existing branding devices are, themselves, a barrier to communication of news or to establishing a variant message. However, the scripts and ad structure need to be carefully reviewed to ensure that the dominant focus is the variant. If not, the consumer can take the easy option and simply keep on taking out the established parent brand and message. This was the problem an ice cream brand had to face when launching a variant in China. The ice cream brand was launched in Shanghai with a 30 second ad. Subsequently, a 15 second cut-down of the same ad was adapted to promote a new lemon-flavored variant. Tracking of the Shanghai market showed that, although the ad was well recalled overall, the intended message focus announcing the new lemon variant was recalled by only 11%. The variant launch failed.

Tag-ons

Tag-ons — five or ten second additions to ads — can work to launch relatively minor variants. If they are closely related to what was featured in the primary part of the ad, tag-ons can be effective in building awareness, especially if they feature the same brand and convey the same brand benefit but are announcing a new flavor or format of the product ('now available in strawberry flavor'). By repeating the theme from the main body of the ad, tag-ons can help enhance launch activity.

When a minor variant from a leader in the oral care category was launched, although the variant was supported by its own ad, the client quickly saw signs of news wear out. Given the strong relationship between the master brand and the new extension, the client decided to adapt the existing strong-performing master brand campaign to support the new variant. The ad used a pull-through banner, which ran along the bottom of the screen telling consumers of the new extension, together with a five-second tag. Brand equity for the launch continued to build throughout this airing.

However, the use of tag-ons is a challenging strategy to adopt, and one that only really has potential in some very specific circumstances, both in terms of their ability to get noticed and to communicate their intended message. This is related to both their brevity and their sometime disjointed attachment to the ad. Consumers will focus only on the most engaging and entertaining aspect of an ad and generally miss anything not central to that core idea (see the section on the Creative Magnifier effect elsewhere in this book).

We also know that consumers are likely to miss more than one or two messages in an ad, so adding an additional message within a tag will exacerbate the situation.

In general, tags added to previously aired ads are likely to be the least effective in getting noticed and delivering their news. This is because viewers generally shortcut their take-out of an ad based on what they remember seeing previously. So any messages added to a previously aired ad are most likely to be lost. For example, a tag-on was added to an existing successful 30 second ad. Interest plummeted when the tag-on was introduced. The product featured in the tag-on was not illustrated in the main ad, and its benefit was an entirely new concept. Only 9% mentioned the new ending when playing back the ad; the new variant was lost. The interest trace (where respondents record their level of interest throughout the ad) showed a sharp decline in interest when the tag-on was shown.

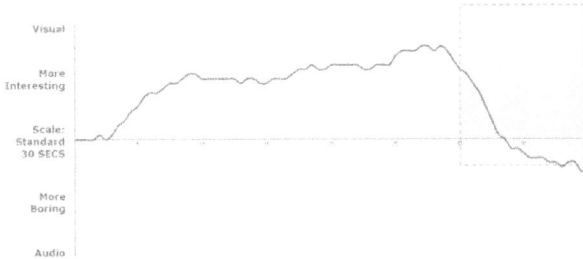

Visual

More
Interesting

Scale:
Standard
30 SECS

More
Boring

Audio

In contrast, it is possible for the variant to overshadow the parent. In a European ad, a creative showing the creation of a cup of coffee, made in chocolate, was used to communicate the launch of a new coffee flavored variant. Given budget restrictions, the client decided to integrate an additional pack shot to support the new raspberry variant too. However, the basic story and the metaphor were not clearly understood. Many respondents mentioned a cup without specifying that it was a cup of coffee. Because the creative idea was not understood, the coffee variant was not recalled from the story. Instead, the raspberry flavor became the first product attribute taken out from this ad due to its distinctive pink look — a sharp contrast between the brown and dark setting of the ad.

For tag-ons, the simpler and more self-explanatory the message the better. The tag's message should need no further explanation and should be able to stand alone. It is also important to retain viewers' attention right to the end of the ad, and so tags must be highly attention-grabbing, but simple given their brevity.

The Power of Umbrella Branding

A brand was launched into a European deodorant category — more removed from the core of the parent brand than its other categories — with very little direct above the line support. It lived off halo effects from brands under the same umbrella in other categories. Over the long-term, these halo effects were sustaining awareness of the brand, even building it. However, the brand's equity was still suffering due to heavy activity from competitor brands within the deodorant category. Analysis showed that the brand had the potential to grow. Eventually, funds were found to celebrate a consumer award given to the brand, and a campaign was aired. The response was strong, making a significant difference to the brand's equity and helping to boost sales.

Umbrella branding can be a successful marketing strategy. However, this depends on having a consistent and clear brand identity across the variants. But while this approach can help 'kick start' variant launches, halo effects are not guaranteed. Only around a quarter of variant ads benefit other variants within the portfolio so it is usually necessary to support individual variant launches. Additionally, while variant launches can help sustain the parent brand image, a constant focus on variant communication can dissipate the core brand image.

Consistency is key

Umbrella branding is a commonly used approach in portfolio management, where the parent brand name is used across a range of products. In such cases, there is an assumption that a halo effect will benefit the individual brands. A halo effect can often help 'kick-start' a new variant, through a sense of familiarity, credibility and associations. For this route to be successful, consistency is key. The chart below shows image profiling data (bars to the right indicate a competitive strength) for a highly successful skin care range in China.

The skin care brand has a clearly defined profile across its portfolio. In all formats it is seen as a modern brand with skin whitening properties, designed to enhance beauty and femininity.

The brand has established a consistent image

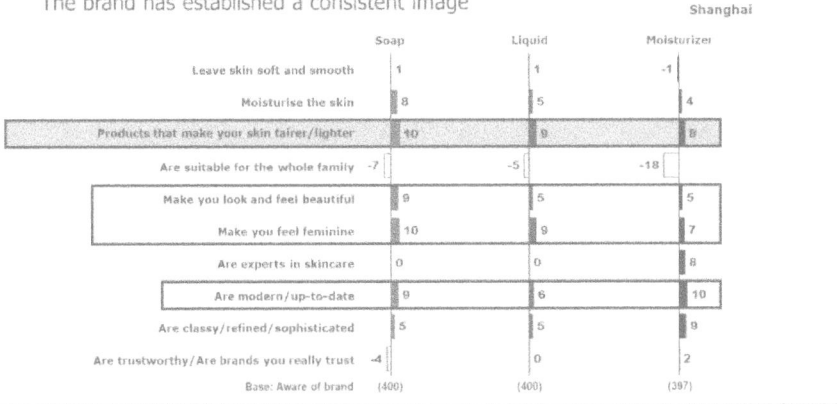

	Soap	Liquid	Moisturizer
Leave skin soft and smooth	1	1	-1
Moisturise the skin	8	5	4
Products that make your skin fairer/lighter	10	9	8
Are suitable for the whole family	-7	-5	-18
Make you look and feel beautiful	9	5	5
Make you feel feminine	10	9	7
Are experts in skincare	0	0	8
Are modern/up-to-date	9	6	10
Are classy/refined/sophisticated	5	5	9
Are trustworthy/Are brands you really trust	-4	0	2
Base: Aware of brand	(400)	(400)	(397)

Shanghai

Support is still needed

When the variants are functionally differentiated, it should not be assumed that advertising for the parent and some of the variants will necessarily support the other variants. When the variant is substantially different from the rest of the portfolio, it is more likely to require its own support.

This is well-illustrated by the deodorant example at the start of this chapter. Halo effects can keep a brand 'alive' in the mind of the consumer by providing reminders of the brand's existence. But the brand benefitted from bespoke category level activity. In an active category with specific category functionality, the brand needs to provide consumers with reasons to choose their brand over the others.

Halo effects on the parent brand

There are three possible types of halo effect where marketing activity for one brand in the portfolio benefits the others: sub-brand on parent, parent on sub-brand, and sub-brand on sub-brand. However, the reality is that, when they exist, halo effects typically work from variants up to the parent brand — less often vice versa.

For one established male deodorant, body spray variants, which are not antiperspirants, but deodorants (antiperspirants stop you sweating, deodorants mask any odour), constitute a high proportion of all its sales. Because of the body spray/deodorant product range and the young profile, the brand was seen as a fragrance brand, not a serious antiperspirant brand. The brand launched a true antiperspirant range. This made sense; it stretched the brand franchise, overcame credibility issues with the existing range and ensured the brand had something to offer groups of all ages and needs. The advertising also made use of the brand's established advertising style. As a result, the brand's efficacy images all responded positively.

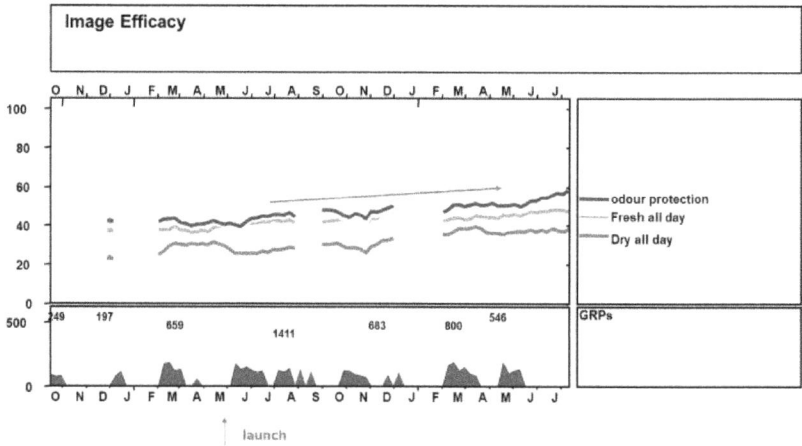

Image Efficacy

odour protection
Fresh all day
Dry all day

GRPs

launch

In another example, a new cleaning product was launched in the UK under an existing parent brand that already had a broad range of cleaning products on the market. It was supported by heavyweight TV spend in three TV regions, but with only light TV support in the rest of country. The product launch was also supported nationally in-store. The TV advertising was felt to provide new, different information, presented in a credible way, and was motivating. The new product's heavyweight advertising boosted brand image and created a new 'buzz' around the parent brand. In areas where the new product was not advertised heavily, awareness and image of the parent brand remained static or in slight decline.

New product advertising with heavyweight TV looks to have supported parent in boosted regions

	Pre-post shift Boosted regions %	Pre-post shift ROC %
Wide range of products	9	-13
Not messy to use	8	-5
Dedicated products for each task	5	-10
Good quality products	2	-7

KANTAR MILLWARDBROWN

Using variant news to support the parent brand can be very effective, revitalizing a brand's fortunes and making it seem more modern and progressive. If there are some exciting new sub-brands to show off, then it makes sense to do so, especially if the parent brand is in decline or perceived as old or less relevant. Parents may 'ride on the wave' of the new variants if they successfully rejuvenate the brand, as can be seen in the following example, where variant advertising made the parent brand seem more modern and up to date.

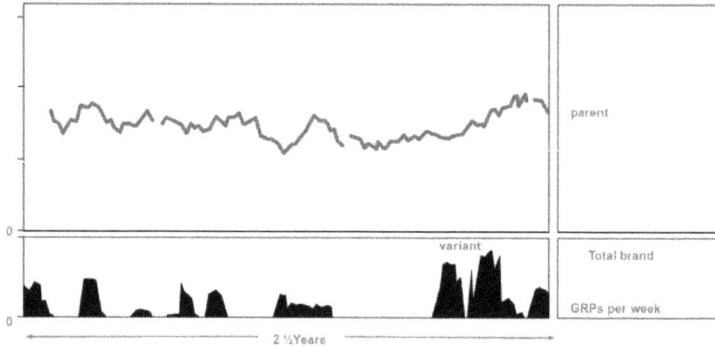

Are modern and up to date

Variant moved parent towards the modern end of the market

KANTAR MILLWARDBROWN

However, it is unwise to rely on halo effects. While halo effects from advertising are possible, they are rare. A review of 131 case studies shows that, when one variant advertised, only 23% demonstrated a positive halo effect on short-term sales for another variant. Of the cases that were positive, only 5 cases were 'highly' effective.

Variant support can dissipate the core

A balance needs to be struck between advertising the variant benefits and the core brand positioning. Variant advertising can generate a stronger rational response from consumers because it tends to advertise news, or communicate how the variant differs in a practical sense from established brands. However, there are dangers. Since variant advertising usually emphasizes differences between the parent and variant brand, a focus on variant advertising risks playing down the core brand values.

The graph below shows brand image data for a personal care brand that is the market leader in many countries around the world and stands for 'top performance' in many markets. It launched a variant in Europe which solved a category problem that was more 'cosmetic' than 'performance' related This was a genuine benefit in the market and represented a good chance for the brand to innovate and move forward. But, for several months the brand supported this variant and focused on its cosmetic benefit, at the expense of 'performance'. Without any reassurance on 'performance' from the brand over an extended period, the association between the variant and 'performance' started to erode.

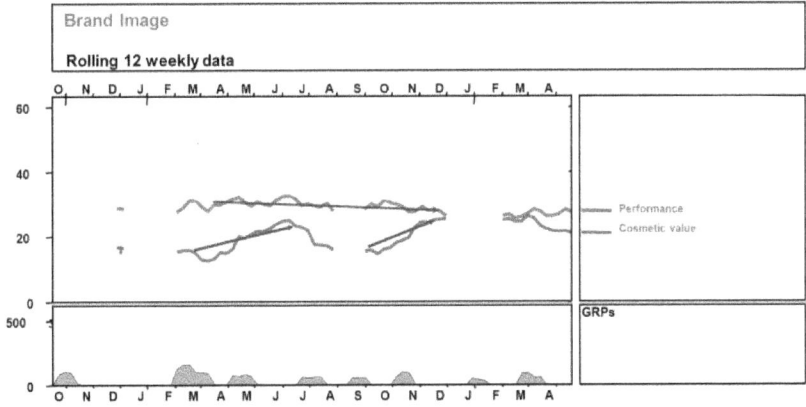

The core brand positioning is vital to the success of umbrella branding, and it must be sustained.

The Value to a Brand of a Satisfied Customer

A European telephone directory enquiry service enjoyed high levels of awareness and usage. New callers were attracted to the service by effective marketing communications, but poor service delivery meant that many of them were not retained. Research uncovered issues with service delivery; one in five who had called the service reported that they would not call again (compared to 1 in 20 for the main competitor). The company acted on these results. Higher quality control standards were imposed and training was rewritten. The improvement was dramatic. Within a few months, the rejection level had dropped from one in five to one in thirteen, and the brand went on to achieve the best score of the main providers in a subsequent government-funded study.

Negative impressions of the service declined

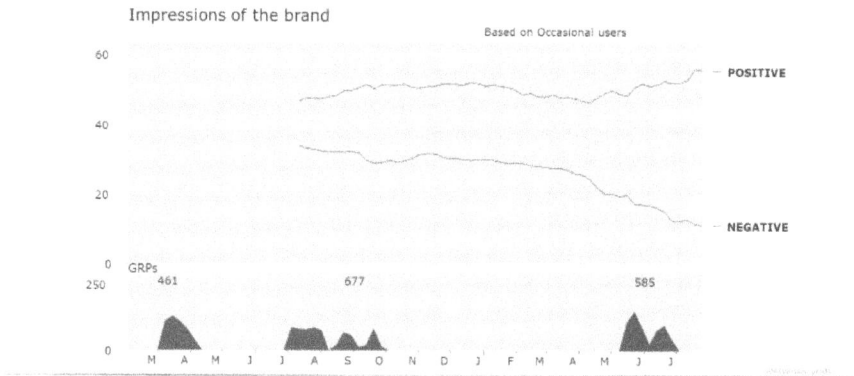

KANTAR MILLWARDBROWN

While customer satisfaction is a critical component of brand equity, many companies underdeliver on service. Improving the service element can be costly; often it requires the substantial reorganization of a business. However, if the benefits of doing so can be quantified, such investment may be justified. And when high levels of service delivery have been achieved, strong marketing can help to enhance perceptions of good service.

Customer satisfaction and brand equity

In most large organizations, one team handles customer satisfaction while another manages brand equity. When these teams don't collaborate or even communicate with one another, opportunities to increase brand value can be lost. This is an especially important issue for service-based industries.

To evaluate the relationship between service and brand equity for one mobile phone provider, a Customer Satisfaction Index was developed based on an amalgam of customer satisfaction questions. Three groups of customers were created: those with high satisfaction, those with medium satisfaction, and those with low satisfaction. The higher the customer satisfaction, the more likely consumers were to endorse key brand images such as 'are brands you want to be seen with' and 'are trustworthy and reliable.'

	CSI		
	High	Medium	Low
	%	%	%
Are brands you want to be seen with	87	88	66
Are trustworthy and reliable	96	93	77

Effective management of the customer experience across all touch points is the key to building customer commitment, retention, brand equity, and sustained financial success. However, to consistently deliver a quality customer experience is easier said than done. Senior management may be unwilling to buy in to the expense — in terms of both time and money— of reorganization and training.

The value of a satisfied customer

However, research can quantify the financial rewards of these investments and often they are substantial. For one bank, a sample of customers was interviewed about their satisfaction, and their behaviour was monitored over the ensuing 12 months. The research measured the number of products held prior to the start of the study, and then, using information on products that were open or closed in the subsequent year, the average number of products opened or closed was calculated for each point on the satisfaction scale. Likewise, by subtracting the number of products closed from products opened, the net product uptake was derived for each point on a satisfaction scale.

As an example, the following chart shows the top-level net gains in take-up of any product, indexing the results around 'fairly satisfied.' Those who scored in the top two boxes showed positive gains. If all customers could be moved from 'fairly satisfied' to 'very satisfied,' the number of new products opened would increase by 9.1%. If dissatisfaction could be completely eliminated, the increase would be 5.9%.

Top level net gains in take up of any product:
Top two boxes have positive gains

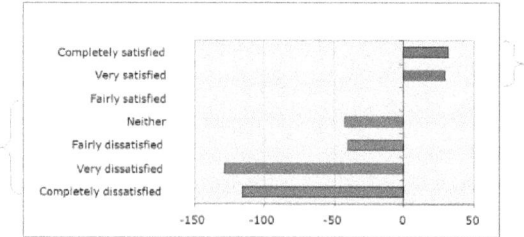

The results varied by product category. There was little to gain in moving customers to the upper levels of satisfaction to increase the uptake of checking or current accounts. (This was partly due to the small number of additional accounts that were opened during the period.) However, there was a strong potential for account closures among those customers who expressed dissatisfaction.

This type of analysis is a powerful tool that can allow clients to calculate potential future revenue if they move customers to higher points on the satisfaction scale, helping them to justify investment in customer satisfaction initiatives.

The role of advertising: enhancing the experience

Advertising has a very powerful role in 'framing' a customer's brand experience. By emphasizing the positive differentiated aspects of a brand, advertising can encourage users to focus on those things when they experience the brand, causing them to take less notice of other, weaker aspects of the brand.

This effect is due in part to the fact that people are unlikely to readily accept advertising claims about what a brand delivers until they've evaluated the claim themselves. For example, a retail store could claim to offer intelligent in-store customer support. This claim may register with consumers, but until they have had the opportunity to experience it themselves, they are likely to withhold judgment on it. While the brand's claim has been placed in people's minds, it will not be acknowledged as fact until people have tested it.

But when they do test it, they will focus on the helpfulness of the in-store staff; the advertising associations will draw their attention to specific aspects of their performance. This may cause them to overlook other things about the store, such as an outdated or unattractive décor, a relatively small selection of products, or limited shopping hours.

This highlights that just working to improve the marketing side alone isn't sufficient. The company must understand what's important to customers to develop a sufficiently appealing brand promise. The company must determine the financial viability of delivering on that promise by offering the required levels of performance. Finally, the company must ensure that each part of the operation knows how to consistently achieve the desired standard.

A simple example of the ability of marketing communications to enhance product perceptions can be found in an fmcg experiment looking at advertising for biscuits, confectionery, toothbrushes, and non-alcoholic drinks. When respondents saw advertising for a product and then tried the product, they were far more likely to consider buying the brand than if they had only tried it.

Advertising can frame the product experience in a way that stimulates sales

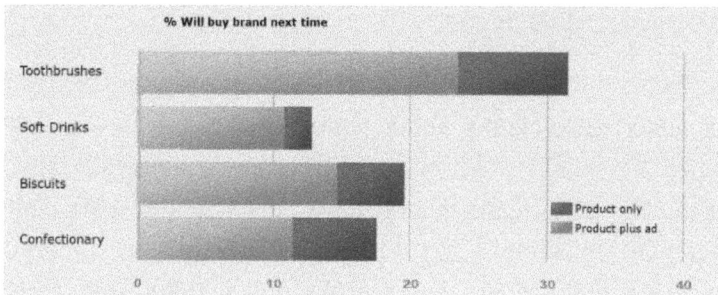

The graph below is a good example of this effect working in practice for a bank. A new campaign that started in March used a humorous approach featuring a comic actor. While there was no change in staff training over this period, there was an almost 10% improvement in the way customers viewed the bank's approachability. When advertising draws attention to some aspect of customer service, it becomes critical that the experience delivers on this. In this case, it did.

Advertising increased endorsement of 'Are more approachable than others'

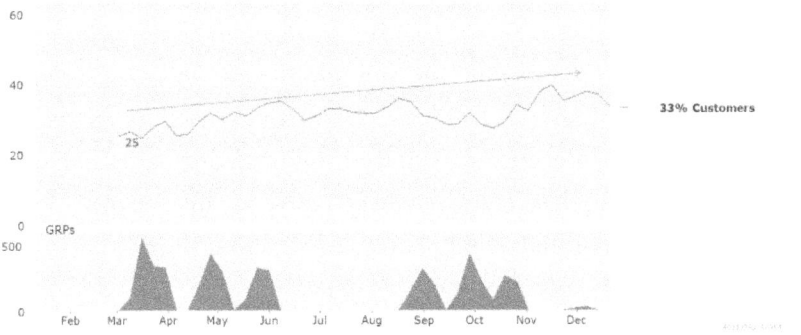

KANTAR MILLWARDBROWN

Passing on the word

An additional benefit of a satisfied customer is that they are more likely to recommend you to others. While brands in some categories are far more likely to be recommended than others, it is possible to buck the trend. For example, while financial services appear low down on the list of recommended categories, Internet banks are far more likely to be recommended than traditional ones. For more on this, see the chapter on word of mouth.

Managing the Brand as an Intangible Asset

Many of the world's biggest companies derive more than half their value from their brands. And building strong brands through effective marketing can have a very positive impact on share price. But the downside of building value on intangible assets such as brands is a higher degree of investment risk. Companies need to manage their brands like tangible assets to deliver optimal and sustainable value. And brand valuation is a powerful tool in this regard, enabling marketers to maximize on their investment and mitigate risk.

Understanding the value of intangible assets

Kantar Millward Brown's BrandZ study estimates the contribution of brands to company earnings. This varies widely between categories. In luxury goods, hair care and drinks a strong brand is very important. At the other end of the scale there are financial services, where personal relationships (particularly in the B2B space) play a greater part; and motor fuel, where factors such as price and location drive a high proportion of revenues.

The downside of valuable intangibles: greater volatility

Companies whose intangible assets account for a larger percentage of their value tend to be more volatile.

To measure the role of intangible assets in generating the value of the company, Kantar takes the total market value, subtracts the book value of tangible assets, and then divides that difference by the total market value of the company. Risk is gauged using a measure of the volatility of a company's share price, adjusted to eliminate the effects of the amount of debt the company carries.

Intangible assets include all the sources of competitive advantage that the company has in exploiting its tangible assets — including intellectual property, patents and technologies, distribution, operational processes, people, and brands.

Activities that are asset-intensive, such as manufacturing, are well-known and predictable in nature. Activities that heavily rely on intangibles, such as brand management, aren't as easy to grasp — and therefore tend to be riskier.

Coca-Cola and Pepsi are a good illustration of this. By spinning off their bottlers in 1986 and 1999 respectively, The Coca-Cola Company and PepsiCo got rid of their most capital-intensive and least profitable activities — allowing them to focus on their sources of competitive advantage: the management of their brands and their distribution net-works. As a result, The Coca-Cola Company and PepsiCo signifi-cantly improved their returns on capital. Yet the higher returns came at a cost. Their risk was also higher, because they focused on activities that were more volatile than manufacturing (e.g. brand management).

In general as companies refocus on activities that generate competitive advantage, they deliver higher returns to shareholders. But their risk profiles also change. On a risk-adjusted basis, these companies often don't deliver additional value to shareholders, because an increase in volatility has offset the increase in returns. The challenge is to better manage the intangible assets, to reduce the risk associated with them.

Mitigating risk through diversification

Companies need to find ways to more effectively manage their intangible assets, particularly brands, to mitigate the risk associated with such assets and better sustain their competitive advantage.

What does managing brand risk mean? The textbook answer to high risk is diversification. The Coca-Cola Company and PepsiCo again provide an interesting example. PepsiCo is more diversified than The Coca-Cola Company — Kantar has estimated that the Pepsi brand accounts for about 20% of PepsiCo's total revenues, whereas the Coca Cola brand accounts for over 40% of The Coca-Cola Company's sales. PepsiCo's risk level is less than The Coca-Cola Company's, because PepsiCo is more diversified. But PepsiCo's return on tangible capital tends to be lower than The Coca-Cola Company's. Diversification does mitigate risk, but it also sometimes reduces returns.

Brand valuation: the key to true marketing accountability

Brands and other intangible assets should be managed for shareholder value just like tangible assets. To this end, the first step is to assess their value. Then determine what drives that value, and identify how best it can be sustained and grown.

Brand valuation does exactly that. Putting a financial value on a brand transforms the role of marketing in the company — from being a cost centre to managing one of the company's most valuable assets. In many cases, that in itself is a major cultural shift. But brand valuation also determines *how* the brand creates value — making it a powerful way of identifying areas of strength and weakness for the brand, in relation to customers.

So brand valuation becomes a means for communicating about brand and marketing strategy in shareholder value terms, both internally and externally. It can also help optimize brand investments — taking into account not just short-term impact on sales, but also how the money you spend can generate longer-term revenues by changing customer perceptions.

Putting a financial value on your brand plan

There are clear benefits in putting a value on a brand plan. First, it allows for return on investment calculations to be based on a truly long-term perspective, not just on outcome within one fiscal year. And second, it enables testing of investment hypotheses — for example, to find out what happens if expenditure is reduced — within a framework both marketing and finance can understand.

A value that takes future profits into account

A brand isn't valuable because of the profits it has made in the past. When the City hold shares in a business, it does so because it expects the company's brands to deliver a stream of profits well into the future.

City analysts have a way of putting a present-day value on this long-term profitability, which they call Discounted Cash Flow (DCF). Of course, it's impossible to predict with any certainty what future events will have an impact on a brand's success; and the greater the uncertainty, the greater the risk facing potential investors — though they may be willing to accept this if the potential returns look attractive enough.

But, while several different factors may affect the degree of risk to performance and profitability over time, depending on the brand and category, there are two that remain constant: the strength of the current relationship between the consumer and the brand, and the commitment to investing in brand building.

Measuring brand strength to understand risk

Stronger brands are a less risky investment.

Earlier in this book I discussed the benefits of a brand being seen as meaningful, different and salient. The following chart, from the Kantar Millward Brown brand equity system, BrandDynamics™ illustrates that if a brand increases its salience, it is more likely to grow but if the brand is meaningfully different and grows salience, the brand growth is likely to be a lot stronger.

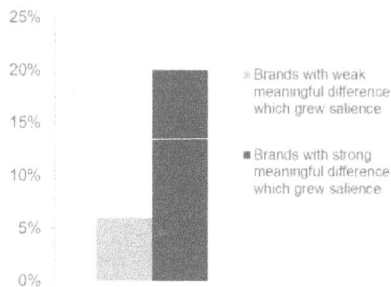

This relationship can help provide an objective, consumer-based measure of risk.

Brand investment: the key to long term value

Current brand strength is only part of the story. Risk to future profitability is also affected by investment in brand building. The following chart is based on analysis of over 350 brands from a range of categories.

The horizontal axis shows the extent to which brands were spending above or below their market size. The brands have been ranked and then grouped into 20 bands based on this measure. The vertical axis shows the proportion of each group that lost market share. Relative under-investment is clearly linked with a greater risk of decline in market share.

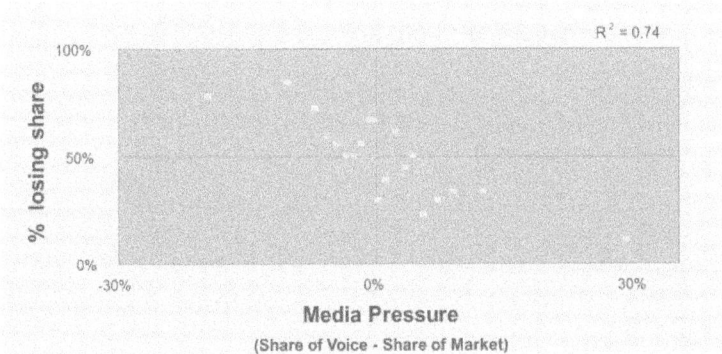

$R^2 = 0.74$

% losing share

100%

50%

0%

-30%   0%   30%

Media Pressure

(Share of Voice - Share of Market)

354 brands grouped on the basis of relative ad spend.

KANTAR MILLWARDBROWN

At every level of investment, there will be some brands that fail to deliver; but the greater the under-investment, the more likely this becomes. One reason for this is that advertising associations, images and memories help to define the brand, and shape consumer interactions with the brand. If these associations are not maintained and kept vibrant, then the relationship between the brand and the consumer is put at risk.

In one scenario, cutting advertising investment would have boosted profits by $0.5m in the first year. But it also increased the risk of future share loss, leading to a predicted reduction in overall brand value of over $3m.

Cutting advertising investment: a false economy

So brand investment and current brand strength are both contributors to the brand risk assessment. By factoring these into the brand plan, you can see what would happen to the brand's value if the advertising budget was cut. Generally speaking, a reduction in advertising investment produces an immediate increase in profit, but a significant decline in the brand's Net Present Value.

Managing the brand as an intangible asset helps the finance team see the value of investing in the brand; and it encourages a longer term view of brand management; both are advantageous to brand teams.

How to change a brand's name

An internet service provider in the UK was losing share and changed its name to that of its parent, a provider for other European countries. Unlike the UK brand it was seen as leading edge and dynamic. The launch campaign was weak on communication, and nearly a quarter of the UK brand's customers thought the name change was a bad idea. A new campaign, focused on the benefits of the parent, was well received by consumers. The ads were noticed, with ad awareness reaching almost 60%, and the ads conveyed more news value than the previous campaign. The brand began to establish a more distinct positioning. Following the earlier declines in market share, the brand's share held steady with the name change.

A brand may change its name for several reasons. The way in which the rebranding is managed will have a direct impact on the success of the name change. Name changes often result in a drop in sales, but when the process is done well, sales can hold steady. However, if a poor strategy is followed, a name change puts the brand at risk of losing equity, consumer loyalty and ultimately market share.

Brands change their name for several different reasons, including repositioning, merger, acquisition, globalization of brands, or to counter bad publicity or a negative image. The change can be major — a completely different name, such as Marathon to Snickers; minor — a slight modification to the original name, such as US Air to US Airways; or simply involve the addition of the parent brand name — Chicken Tonight to Knorr Chicken Tonight.

Brand health measures

While tracking measures usually suffer a significant decline with a brand name change, most measures show a steady increase back towards original levels after the new name is introduced. As would be expected, unaided brand awareness experiences the sharpest drop.

The biggest drop on average following a name change is for unaided awareness

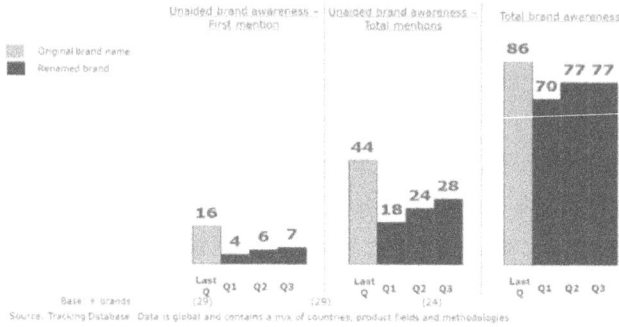

Unaided brand awareness – First mention | Unaided brand awareness – Total mentions | Total brand awareness

Original brand name
Renamed brand

First mention: 16, Last Q; 4, Q1; 6, Q2; 7, Q3
Total mentions: 44, Last Q; 18, Q1; 24, Q2; 28, Q3
Total brand awareness: 86, Last Q; 70, Q1; 77, Q2; 77, Q3

Base: # brands (29) (29) (24)
Source: Tracking Database. Data is global and contains a mix of countries, product fields and methodologies

Although, on average, total brand communication awareness actually increases following renaming, this is likely to reflect an increase in activity to communicate the brand name change.

Communication awareness increased on average following renaming

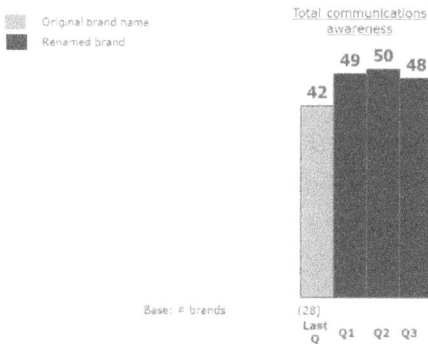

Original brand name
Renamed brand

Total communications awareness

42, Last Q; 49, Q1; 50, Q2; 48, Q3

Base: # brands (28)
Source: Tracking Database. Data is global and contains a mix of countries, product fields and methodologies

Levels of claimed usage decline less, with users naturally being less likely to be affected by the change in brand name.

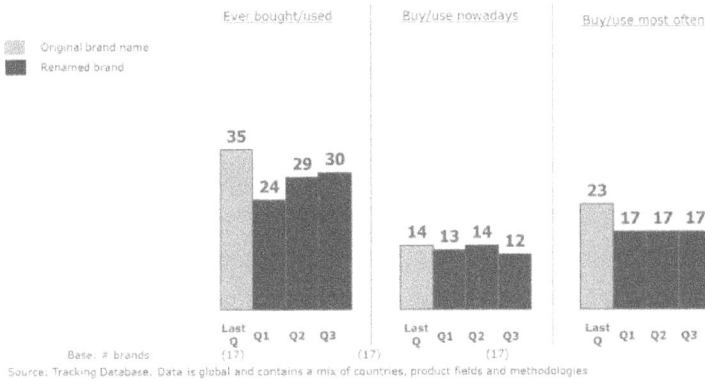

Ever bought/used | Buy/use nowadays | Buy/use most often

Original brand name
Renamed brand

35
29 30
24
23
17 17 17
14 13 14 12

Last Q   Q1 Q2 Q3   Last Q   Q1 Q2 Q3   Last Q   Q1 Q2 Q3

Base: # brands   (17)   (17)   (17)

Source: Tracking Database. Data is global and contains a mix of countries, product fields and methodologies

The impact of a name change

Some newly named brands are not picked up on or are overlooked, while some are flat-out rejected by consumers. Coco Pops, a Kellogg's cereal brand in the UK, changed its name after 28 years for global consistency, a decision that resulted in equity and market share declines along with strong public protest. Kellogg's responded with a television campaign that gave kids the opportunity to vote on which name they preferred — 90% chose the original name. The company listened and changed the cereal back to its original name. Sales increased 20% over the next year.

In my experience, many brands see an immediate 5–20% decline in sales, and can take years to restore levels, while others are negatively affected only in the short term. The sales response can be impacted by several things, including the amount of equity in the original brand name, how much is invested in communicating the name change, the strength of the advertising and the consumer reaction.

Successful transfers of equity

An Australian energy company was required to change its name after 10 years in the marketplace as the result of a sales deal. Prior to the name change it had maintained strong market presence, and it dominated media spend in the category to communicate the name change. It then returned to brand-based advertising as the new brand. It was successful in transferring its brand equity to its new brand name and protecting its previous investments in the brand. This was done via committed and clear communication about the name change followed immediately by a brand saliency-building campaign which communicated consistent and recognizable company values, including the same tone and slogan. Its introductory name change and follow-up ad were both well recognized and were very well branded.

Brand awareness and advertising awareness declined 15-20% initially but within one year were at parity with pre-name-change levels. The brand's share of the electricity market held steady during and following the name change.

A new beer brand in the Americas was forced, for legal reasons, to change its name after eight months of building strong awareness and a unique image associated with the beach, sun and fun. Qualitative research revealed that consumers thought it was unfair that the brand had to change its name. This led to a promotion inviting consumers to help choose the new name for the beer. To further attract attention during the period when the beer had no official name, the company created a no-name beer strategy, with advertising encouraging consumers to ask for the beer by describing how they thought of it. This further deepened the brand associations. A successful launch ad with the new name sustained the previous brand image and awareness, and usage levels were even stronger than before. The brand quickly achieved the second highest market share.

Top of Mind

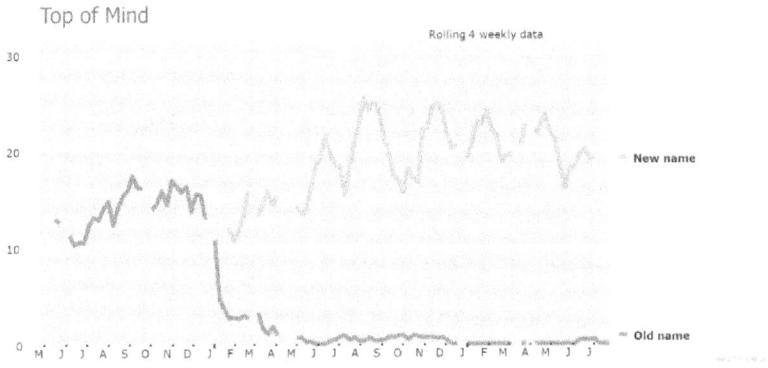

KANTAR MILLWARDBROWN

Drink Most Often

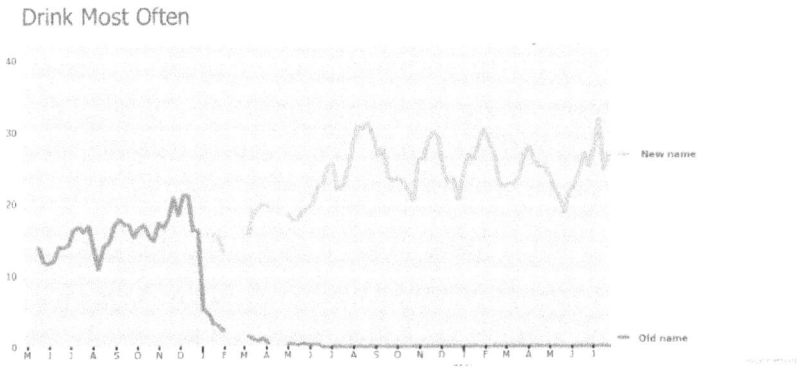

KANTAR MILLWARDBROWN

A margarine brand changed its name as part of a strategy to raise its profile by linking it to the name of a well-known and high-quality product line (owned by the same parent company). The change was announced through several communications activities — effective advertising (good cut through and strong message communication), in-store marketing, new packaging with a sleeve bearing the original name which when removed revealed the new name, as well as on-pack promotional leaflets with coupons. The name change was successful – awareness grew to 80% very quickly and consumers were confident that the product had not been changed and as a result the name change made no difference in their attitudes or usage of the product.

Steps to take towards success

Given the potential problems, and the total cost of the necessary surrounding activity, changing a brand's name should only be undertaken if clear financial benefits are anticipated.

It's important to understand the equity in the original brand name before starting the name change process. A full evaluation of the new brand name should be undertaken — checking it against strategic objectives, talking to target audiences and covering all relevant languages for linguistic issues. Packaging can also be used to make consumers aware of the upcoming name change, for example, both names can appear on the packaging for a time. Another option is to use packaging sleeves creatively, for instance, with the former name on an outside sleeve that can be removed to reveal the new name.

Considerable spend is likely to be needed to establish the new name. This should be seen as an investment in its future. One vital aspect is to communicate memorably that the new brand is exactly the same as the original named brand, or consumers are likely to assume changes have been made to the product as well as the name. An honest ex-planation of the reasons behind the name change is usually beneficial. Key elements of previous communications should also be maintained, such as the main message and tone. Ensure that advertising reaches both users and non-users of the brand.

Do not dwell on the change. Revert to brand advertising immediately following the name change to complete the transfer.

Expect spontaneous brand awareness to take longer to establish than other brand health metrics, and that the brand image will change and may not be as strong as it was before.

Managing a Brand in a Recession

Experience from recessions shows that it is common for marketing spend to be squeezed and emphasis placed on maximising short-term sales uplifts, through promotions, to help meet profit targets. However, brands need to be viewed as a long-term investment; a focus on short-term returns can have long-term repercussions.

During the U.K. recession of 1991/1992 the Renault Clio was launched and exceeded its first-year sales objectives. Andrex toilet tissue held its volume share at over 30%, despite its premium positioning. Gold Blend increased its market share, and Haagen-Dazs' sales figures grew almost 400% from 1991 - 1992.

With proper management, brands — even premium brands — can thrive in a recession. Recessions can present opportunities for the focused marketer.

The pitfalls of price promotions

While common, the use of price promotions to help generate consumer spending during a recession can damage the brand and make it hard to see how damaged the brand is.

One brand, with reduced media expenditure, reported increasing share in line with promotions. Analysis showed that the share increase was entirely down to the price promotions.

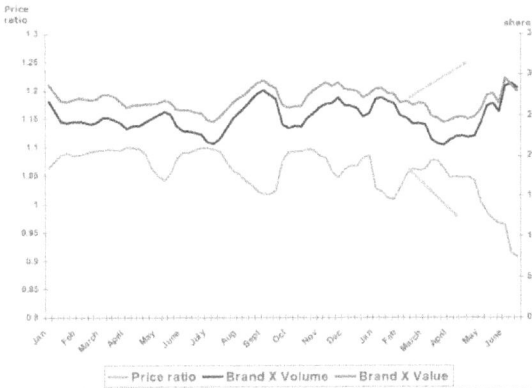

Share increases coincided with price reductions/promotions

Price ratio — Brand X Volume — Brand X Value

Moreover, the underlying base sales for the brand were in decline. This decline was matched by tracking study measures (illustrated here by claimed 'use nowadays'). Without this analysis, the brand team would not have been aware of the harm being done to the brand.

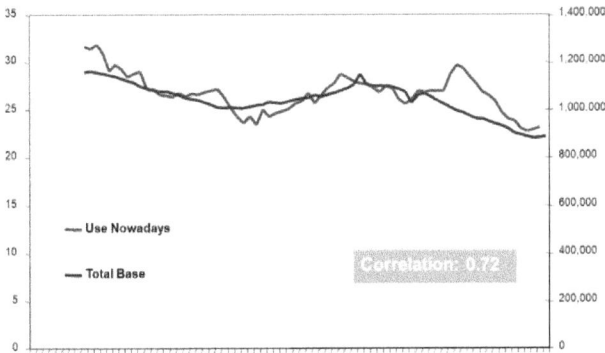

Strong correlation between base sales (IRI data) and tracking measures

— Use Nowadays

— Total Base

Correlation: 0.72

When others in your market are promoting on price, it can be hard to avoid joining in, but the results can be hugely damaging to all the brands. In the U.K., an OTC category was growing. However, as a result of a price war, the total volume sold on promotion increased by 15% across all brands in one year. Not only was value driven out of the market, but brand equity declined. Just half the consumers (55%) had a strong affinity to any one brand after the price war, compare to 81% before.

The dangers of reduced advertising spend

While reducing advertising spend can seem a logical way to increase short-term profitability during a recession, the consequences can be damaging. Brands can indeed 'go dark' for six months or so with little apparent deterioration in their health. But the problems come in the longer term and once decline sets in, it's hard to reverse. There is more on this in the chapter on brands going dark.

The need to take a longer-term view

Advertising has a long-term as well as a short-term effect on the brand. On average, there is about a 3:1 ratio of long-term to short-term sales (short-term here referring to first eight weeks), although this is variable across campaigns, and I've seen campaigns with a 5:1 ratio. Stopping advertising, or cutting ad spend may look like a short-term fix, but you are likely to be setting up problems for the future. Under-investment in advertising is clearly linked with a greater risk of decline in market share.

There is also this; at a time when other brands are cutting their spend, media costs are likely to go down, and achieving a strong share of voice can be achieved relatively cost effectively.

Compensating with copy quality

While ideally you should aim to maintain your spend, it is possible to grow your brand with lower budgets, provided the copy quality at least compensates for this. There is more on this in the chapter on the long term effects of advertising.

This can be seen in the examples given at the start of this article: Renault Clio ad awareness peaked at 65%; almost all consumers could recall something from the Andrex advertising; at peak, 63% were aware of the Gold Blend advertising; while Haagen-Dazs saw ad awareness grow from 1 to 23% among relevant readers — a strong performance for a print campaign.

The benefits of maintaining the presence of your brand during a recession and investing in great creative at this time is clear and important to fight for.

ADVERTISING KNOWLEDGE

Ways Advertising can Work

In 1993 a group of housewives were given a video of a TV programme to watch and later given a basket of products as a thank you.

Unknown to the housewives, this was part of a clever experiment to explore ways advertising might work.

The experiment used four brands and their ads. 1000 respondents were sent a video of a TV program to assess. It contained a few ads. The basic idea behind the experiment was straightforward — it used two matched pairs of cells. The first two cells measured what tends to be called Persuasion: one cell would see advertising, the other wouldn't. Both would then be asked their likelihood of buying the advertised brand in the future. The difference in scores would be the result of the advertising's persuasive effect.

The second two cells would measure the conditioning effect of advertising on product perceptions during trial. Both groups would be given the product to try under natural circumstances, but only one cell would have been exposed to the advertising first. Again, both groups would be asked their likelihood of buying in the future, but this time the difference would be due to what was called the Enhancement effect – the way advertising can frame experience.

For this to work properly, the housewives had to remain in ignorance of the nature of the test. This was not straightforward; they needed to be exposed to products as well as ads, and then complete a survey, all without giving the game away. Several steps were taken to ensure the disguise.

The results were published in 'Persuasion or Enhancement — An Experiment (1994)'. For all four brands, the Persuasive power of the ads were almost zero. Showing just the ad produced a more negative result than not showing the ad, but the effect was very small and not significant. However in all cases trying the product after seeing the ad produced a significantly more positive response than trying the product without seeing the ad. Additionally respondents were asked which of the brands they were 'most curious to try', and here there was a marked advertising effect; exposure to the advertising produced an average shift of +4% across the four products.

The experiment, taken alongside all the other evidence from tracking studies and sales modelling, suggested that traditional theme advertising — the repetition of relatively weak arguments, creatively presented — does not influence product perceptions at the time it is seen, but increases the likelihood of exploratory purchases — out of 'interest' — later. It also supported the idea that advertising memories can have a powerful influence on perceptions of the product when it is tried, increasing the chances that the advertised brand will be purchased subsequently.

It brought thinking about advertising into sharp focus.

Persuasion

Perhaps the most important finding was about persuasion. This is likely to surprise many who have read criticisms of Kantar Millward Brown, painting it as a strong proponent of persuasion. Nothing could be further from the truth.

Persuasion is often misunderstood, but is one of two fundamentally different functions of advertising. It happens when you communicate 'strong' news. What do I mean by strong? News that is relevant, believable, and differentiating. If the news is valuable, people take note of it, and it works immediately, so the effects are easily seen in improved buying and attitudes. However, the effect is more determined by the value of the news than the quality of the ad. To come up with relevant valuable news usually means improving the product offering, which requires substantial investment, so a strong persuasion effect is rare. The reality is, when the Kantar Millward Brown Link copy test was developed in 1989, it didn't include Persuasion questions; they were added a few years later when it was realised that, while not always relevant, they were sometimes useful, depending on the brand strategy.

When there is no news, viewers may still pay attention to ads, but they will take in most of what they see as a 'collage' of images and process those images only to the degree that they need to make sense of them. And if they are not actively thinking about the ad or the brand, it's very unlikely that their attitude towards the brand will be changed. There are two main opportunities for these associations to influence sales later when people think about the brand. This might happen when they are browsing supermarket shelves (and here there is a major role for packaging ad in-store activity to remind consumers of the advertising) or considering what car to test drive. Or it may be while they are actually using the product and deciding whether they like it.

Interest-Status

When you do your weekly shop, probably most things you buy, you buy almost on auto-pilot, with little thought. Decisions are made quickly, using what are now called 'fast and frugal heuristics' (where people accept choices that are 'good enough' for their purposes, based on very simple 'rules'); one of the most common is to choose the brand you bought last — in other words, most of the time you buy through habit. Gordon Brown, the co-founder of Millward Brown, said that most advertising was unlikely to upturn such habits.

But there are occasions when you are in the frame of mind to make an experimental purchase. Maybe your regular washing powder didn't get a stain out of your favourite shirt, and you want to try a new powder. Maybe you have a hot date coming for supper, and you want to get a better quality coffee than you buy for yourself. Maybe you fancy a chocolate bar but are in the mood for a change. When you are in the mood to try something different, a range of things can make one brand on the shelf seem more interesting than another: it might be on special offer; it might be new; it might be the most expensive brand (this can be taken as a sign of quality); or advertising memories may come to mind. These may be memories of a specific claim ('I wonder if it does taste as creamy as they say?'), or it might be that the advertising has left you with a positive emotional valence, making the brand 'warmer' than those around it. Or, indeed, it might just be that the advertising has given the brand salience, a sense of familiarity, a status that makes it seem a safer choice than those other brands you've not heard of. All these things can influence your purchase decision. And it may be that you are making such a rapid decision you're not even aware that the advertising associations have influenced your decision. This is what the experiment attempted to measure in the 'curious to try' question (I'd argue it wasn't a perfect question which is why it is rarely asked these days; most people are not likely to say they are 'curious to try' a major brand like Coca-Cola).

It is the way that previously seen advertising can affect purchase decisions which Gordon Brown called Interest-Status.

It is a useful concept for several reasons.

First, it explains why, even though you might not be persuaded by an ad at the time you see it, it can influence your later purchase decisions (so a strong persuasion score is not necessary for successful advertising).

It explains why advertising awareness relates to sales; the more impactful the ad the more likely the associations are going to be carried forward to a later point.

As an aside; some people have asked me if Interest-Status represents a particular advertising style. No. The ad might convey a functional message, or illustrate a relevant lifestyle, or be surprising, or just enjoyable. But as long as it is impactful, (and the strategy is a sensible one), it has the chance to affect purchase decisions.

The idea of Interest-Status, taken together with Enhancement, represent a useful understanding of how advertising can work.

Enhancement

A few years ago I was staying in a bed and breakfast in the west country. I had a full English breakfast which was delicious — apart from the bacon which had a strong, overpowering taste. I thought maybe it was a few months past its sell by date. When the landlady came to take away my plate, she said, 'I'm sorry you didn't like the bacon; it was cured locally by a traditional method; it's not pumped full of water like you get in the supermarkets.' I thought about this, and the next morning I ordered another full English breakfast and I tasted the bacon with a different mindset; I found myself thinking 'So this is the way bacon should taste, full flavoured'.

In a similar way, advertising can frame the way we experience brands. Gordon called the way that advertising affects product experience 'Enhancement.' It explained how, while advertising itself rarely seems to have a direct effect on brand perceptions (a view championed by Ehrenberg), in conjunction with product experience, it can be immensely powerful.

The effect can manifest itself in several ways. Akin to my bacon example, advertising can draw attention to one aspect of the brand experience and make it seem special. The way Lurpac has promoted its unique taste over the years is a good example. Or it maybe that warm advertising memories can make you more likely to want to like the brand, leading you to experience it through rose-tinted glasses.

Anyone who has conducted blind and branded product testing will know that extent to which brand associations can colour experiences.

There is instinctive resistance to accepting advertising claims, but this is neutralised when we are actually experiencing or investigating the product. So real attitude changes, and significant purchasing decisions, are delayed till people happen to try, re-try, or investigate the brand. For instance, one washing powder brand's advertising which emphasised specific functions failed to shift the relevant perceived pros and cons of the brand very much in tracking. Analysing by users and non-users confirmed that users of brands thought their brands were best in every important respect; the important attitude shifts happened when people decided to be users, not when they saw the ads.

This advertising effect can be very powerful, but its effects are hard to determine because they are smoothed across time. They are not easily observable in the short term, they show in long-term trends or the avoidance of downward trends.

Creative magnifier

The importance of advertising memories and associations, as opposed to immediate responses at the time of seeing the advertising, has some important consequences.

The key question is, what happens when people think about the brand? This may be days, weeks or even months after seeing the advertising. What they remember may range from detailed memories of the ad to a vague sense of having heard something about the brand. But if none of these come to mind when people think about the brand, the advertising is unlikely to influence their choice.

This presents a huge role for creativity. Ads which are creative are more likely to be remembered. This is why when we looked at ads which won Effie effectiveness awards, they were more likely than other ads to perform well on measures like uniqueness, involvement, different to other ads and enjoyment.

Effie award winning ads

INDICES	median	no of brands
Branding	106	16
Uniqueness	105	15
Involvement	104	15
Brand Different	102	15
Different To Other Ads	102	13
Enjoyment	102	16
Persuasion	101	12
Believable	100	14
New Information	100	15
Relevance	99	15
Appealing	98	16
Understanding	97	16

KANTAR MILLWARDBROWN

However, people don't remember TV advertising in a linear way, from the start through to the end. When Gordon Brown developed tracking studies, respondents were asked to describe ads they remembered, and a pattern seen across all ads was that the more creative, engaging elements of an ad were better remembered than other elements. People tend to remember only the parts that they find interesting or involving. Gordon Brown called this phenomenon the Creative Magnifier, because the creative elements of the ad are magnified in people's memories.

This has fundamental implications for the structure of advertising. It's essential that the brand, and the key messages to be communicated, are closely related to the interesting and involving parts of the ad. These must serve as a link between the brand and the any communication the ad is meant to convey. If the brand and the communication are not put across creatively, they are less likely to be remembered.

Sometimes, the whole creative hangs together so well that the entire ad will be remembered. Otherwise, it's usually helpful to consider which elements will *not* be recalled and make a judgement about how crucial these are. Slightly tongue in cheek, I used to talk about the Creative Cullender; you were OK if the water drained away, but if your pasta drained through the holes you were in trouble; what mattered was what was left in the cullender. In the same way, the question was – what of an advert was left in the cullender in people's heads? The trick is to look for which elements are *not* creatively highlighted and to think about whether it matters that these will not stick in the brain. When Link started, it originally had what was called a 'negative coding frame'; coders would record would code the elements which were not played back. This got dropped because it was too controversial with ad agencies but it does demonstrate the importance of looking for what gets forgotten.

Related to this is the key issue of branding. Some highly creative ads generate only weak advertising awareness for the brand. The reason is almost always a poor association with the brand. To function as 'ads' rather than mini-programmes, the entertaining material must associate with the brand. That's why, in the Effie analysis previously mentioned, Branding was so important.

Taking ads which achieved weak advertising awareness, generally whatever element in the ad is intended to integrate the brand into the story either does not register, or doesn't tie in with the other elements in the ad. Typical scenarios are the brand just popping up as a surprise at the end; that the 'bit which brought in the brand' is hard to comprehend, or is 'cut in' to the ad but gets by-passed by the flow of attention through the ad, the 'story line'. The findings were quite subtle. For example, viewers tend to direct their gaze to follow where the actor is looking (a fundamental component of the magician's misdirection) – which can completely by-pass the brand shot.

What implications does this have for making great advertising?

Firstly, the more persuasive the ad is, the more likely it is that immediate sales will be generated; and persuasiveness is about having a compelling message, one which is seen as new, relevant, believable and differentiating. This is covered in a subsequent chapter.

But this aside, other things being equal, the more likely people are to remember the ad when they think about the brand, the more likely it is that sales will be generated. Advertising memorability is about engaging the consumer with compelling creative; ads which are emotionally powerful.

Structure

While ads need to be engaging, it is vital that the most engaging elements should be clearly linked to the brand. Again, there is no simple scientific way of achieving this. Large pack shots or frequent repetitions of the brand name are not the answer. But there are a number of paths worth considering, which are covered later in the book.

But ultimately, it's a question of creativity. Great ads highlight the brand in a distinctive, enjoyable and involving way. If it's possible to describe what happens in the ad in a sentence without mentioning the brand (or an established brand cue), there's almost certainly a problem.

If it doesn't communicate, it won't work

Of course, successful advertising also depends on communicating effectively, whether that communication is functional or emotional, and causing consumers to respond positively.

But the ability of ads to deliver communication is incredibly variable. The crucial thing is for the communication to be related to the enjoyable, involving and memorable parts of the ad. Experience also shows that communication is most successful when ads dramatise their message; the guiding principle seems to be to show, don't tell.

Emotional Responses to Advertising

Dove adopted the Campaign for Real Beauty theme in 2004. Before this time, the brand communicated largely rational benefits, such as its moisturizing properties and mildness. It used mainly testimonial-style advertising, but, with little sense of a distinctive, dynamic or compelling personality, its growth was limited. The Campaign for Real Beauty aimed to build the brand at an emotional level by conveying a more democratic and celebratory vision of beauty. In doing so, Dove struck a strong chord with women who were tired of trying to live up to the idealized and unachievable standards shown by other brands. Almost overnight, Dove changed into a highly-distinctive, opinionated and admired brand — with a resulting huge uplift in sales across its entire range.

The generation of emotion is crucial for successful marketing. Many brands benefit from an association with positive emotions. However, the most successful brands tend to have a balanced set of emotional associations and functional strengths.

Advertising that generates a strong emotional response has two benefits. Firstly, it can help generate engagement and memorability. Secondly it can help the emotions transfer to the brand, shaping the brand perceptions. While advertising can generate negative emotions to help create drama, for most brand advertising this needs to ultimately result in a positive emotional takeout.

In their acclaimed monograph, *Marketing in the Era of Accountability*, Binet and Field report that 71% of campaigns in the IPA DataBANK (covering entries for the IPA Effectiveness Awards) consist of both rational and emotional elements. While emphasising the strengths of emotionally based campaigns, they report 'more complex' campaigns (most of which combine rational with emotional elements) as having the same 'Effectiveness Success Rate' as purely emotional campaigns; and report that campaigns using a Persuasion or information model have an Effectiveness Success Rate of 61%.

For the past ten years some commentators have reported that neuroscience has found the emotional content of advertising to be more powerful than any rational information. The neuroscientist Damasio has been interpreted as saying that when it comes to decision-making, feelings and emotions always dominate cognition. While some have regarded this as a new paradigm in advertising, it is worth reflecting on what Damasio actually wrote: 'I never wished to set emotion against reason, but rather to see emotion as at least assisting reason...nor did I ever oppose emotion to cognition since I view emotion as delivering cognitive information.' (Descartes' Error (New York: G. P. Putnam, 1994.), xix)

The reality is that a typical brand purchase decision for a consumer is trivial. They will take the minimum possible time to make their decision which, depending on the category, may be only one or two seconds. However, they will try to make the best possible choice, calling upon their memories of, and associations with, the brands being reviewed.

So what is the role of emotion in advertising?

Shaping perceptions

Emotion is important in marketing.

The U.S. telecom industry was known for advertising the rational 'value' benefits of their service: dependability, great price and special deals. The SunCom brand made major changes to their three-year-old marketing campaign, moving away from rational benefits in order to communicate more about the emotional benefits of connection. SunCom was the first US telecoms company to base its messaging on the emotions of being connected to the people who matter the most and on the feelings people get from talking to others whenever they want. Moving away from the rational campaign and focusing on the emotional benefits of the brand created stronger impact and communication. This led to stronger brand equity. The ads were more enjoyable and, by building on the strong branding created from the previous campaign, highly memorable. Additionally, communicating the emotional benefits of the brand in a credible way helped to increase the news value of the advertising. As a consequence, consideration of the service increased significantly. The re-launch enabled the emotional benefits of the brand to come through more clearly and the brand's equity grew.

Database analysis supports the idea that liking advertising relates to liking brands. If a brand has great advertising, it is likely to be liked (but it's important to note that some brands are liked without having great advertising).

Brand affinity relates to having great advertising

Affinity v Have great advertising (based on 16525 global brands r=0.68)

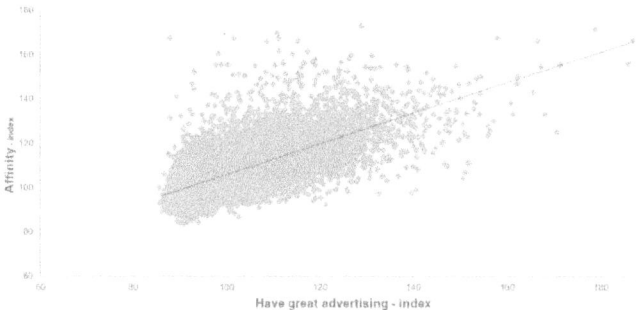

However, emotion should not be pursued at the expense of all else.

Kantar Millward Brown's Link™ copy testing database confirms this need for balance. Ads are routinely classified on their intended strategy; whether it is primarily an emotional appeal, or a focus on a rational message, or a mixture of the two (NB all ads will generate an emotional response of some kind; but here the emphasis is on whether the ad content is an emotional appeal or a rational message). Looking at the average sales effectiveness of ads in each category (defined as likelihood to observe a sales uplift of at least 0.5% of market share when the ad airs), the most successful ads are those which pursue a combined strategy of an emotional appeal with rational messages.

This is true across ads for all types of brands, but it is worth noting that for established brands ads focused on emotional appeals outperform those with a focus on rational messages; and for small/new brands those with a focus on rational messages outperform those focused on emotional appeals.

A balanced strategy is the most sales effective

Likelihood of sales effect*

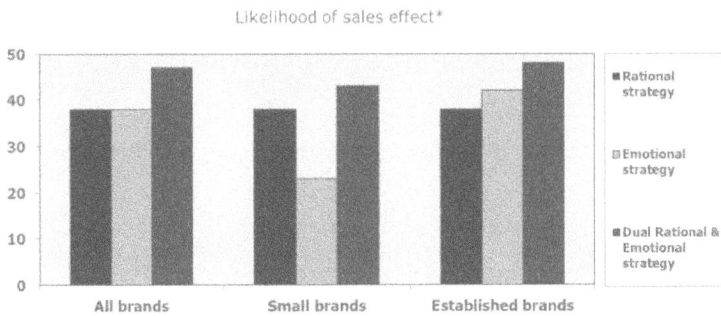

*>0.5% market share uplift

Base: 330 ads

KANTAR MILLWARDBROWN

The link with engagement and memorability

The other key role of emotion in advertising is to help generate engagement with the ad.

We pay more attention to emotionally-charged events, so we are more likely to get involved with emotionally-charged ads. The empirical evidence for this is very strong. The average involvement scores for TV ads in the Link global database clearly show that ads which focus on an emotional appeal are more involving to consumers than those with a focus on a rational message (those that pursue a combined approach fall in between).

Emotional ads have greater consumer involvement than purely rational ads

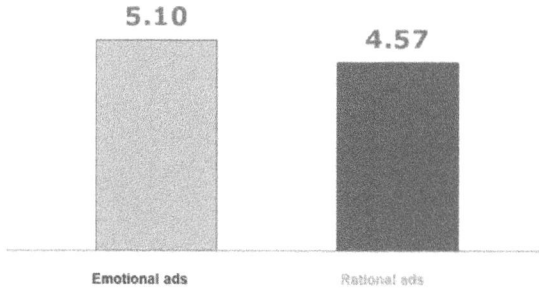

Ads which generate a strong emotional response are rated as more involving.

Ads which evoke stronger emotions generate greater involvement

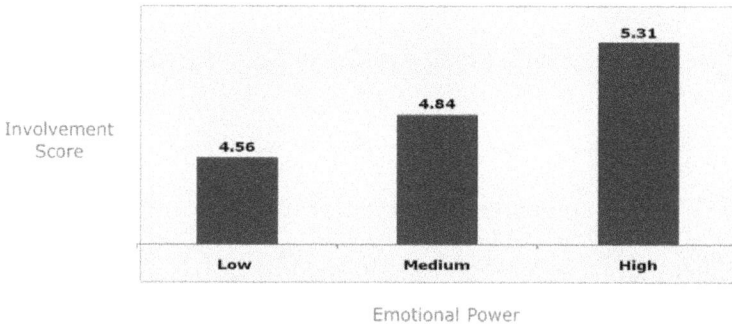

Emotional Power

1656 U.S English online ads, TV Link database

Unfortunately for advertisers, brands and advertising are not particularly important to people and so advertising is typically processed at a very shallow level. We usually watch TV to be entertained rather than to actively 'learn' about brands, so the chance of remembering ads, or what they say about brands, is generally low.

However, this is not to say that no processing of advertising takes place. An engaging commercial can evoke greater mental effort, and so boost its likelihood of being remembered. But the context of this is important: we are not in a deliberate learning mode, we want to be entertained, so advertising is largely processed as narrative. It is the narrative, rather than an explicit message about a product, that is likely to stick in the memory.

An important consequence of this greater engagement is that emotionally-charged ads are also more memorable. The more mental resources we devote to a stimulus, the more likely we are to remember it. In other words, if we are engaged with something, we are more likely to remember it than if we are uninvolved.

There is evidence that ads with emotional appeals perform better at generating ad awareness. Looking at some of the key countries in the Kantar Millward Brown Link database, and dividing them into ads where the focus is rational communication versus those with a focus on emotional appeal, shows that ads based on emotional appeals tend to be more memorable.

Rational ■
Emotional ▨

UK 5 7 · USA 4 5 · France 6 7 · Germany 4 5 · Italy 4 4 · Australia 5 5 · China (Shanghai) 6 9 · Russia 7 7 · Mexico 7 8 · Poland 6 7

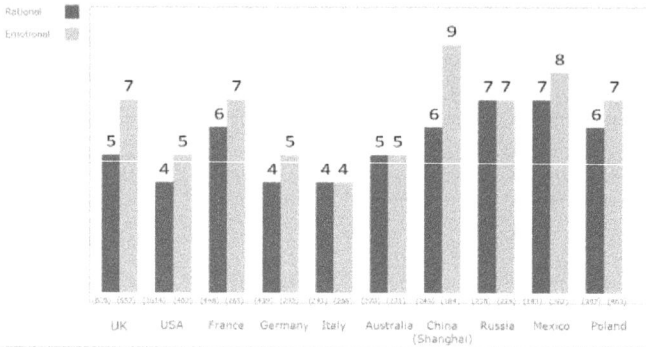

KANTAR MILWARDBROWN

Enjoyment is one measure of the emotional response of consumers to an ad — it tells us whether consumers experienced positive or negative feelings during the ad. Sorting ads into five groups based on how much consumers said they enjoyed them, and plotting this against their ability to generate ad awareness, reveals that the relationship between enjoyment and memorability is tick-shaped. The ads that evoke the least positive response (i.e., are disliked) are more memorable than those which fall into the middle ground, and those which elicit positive emotions become progressively more memorable.

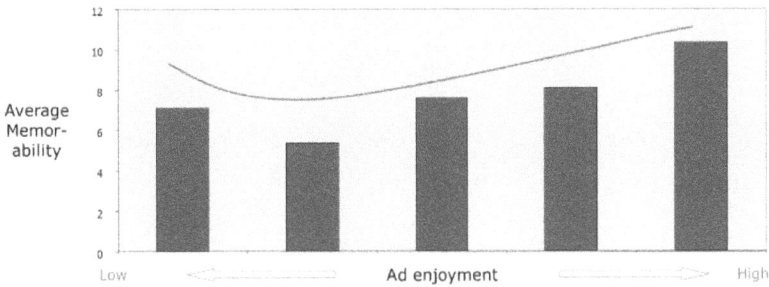

Source: 246 ads from UK Tracking database

KANTAR MILLWARDBROWN

This relationship between enjoyment and memorability was illustrated when an automotive brand introduced a new entrant to the mid-size SUV sector and supported this launch with a TV campaign. Two versions of the ad were produced, with the only difference being the soundtrack. Research showed soundtrack A, which was more enjoyable and involving than soundtrack B, was also likely to be more efficient in cutting through and converting media spend into branded memories. Furthermore, soundtrack A was the most differentiated ad for the brand to date. It also communicated a well–crafted message, and was more likely to create word of mouth and drive traffic to the brand's web site. The launch using Soundtrack A was successful, and web search data showed exceptionally high levels of interest.

The link with sales

Given this three-way relationship between emotionally-charged advertising, engagement, and memorability, you could expect to see stronger sales effects for emotionally-charged advertising when it is more memorable. Kantar Millward Brown's global ad databases support this. Taking 232 ads classified as being focused on emotional appeal, the ads that can generate strong ad awareness are almost twice as likely to see a sales effect, compared to the ads which generate low ad awareness.

Ads with an emotionally based strategy are more likely to generate a sales effect if they generate strong ad awareness

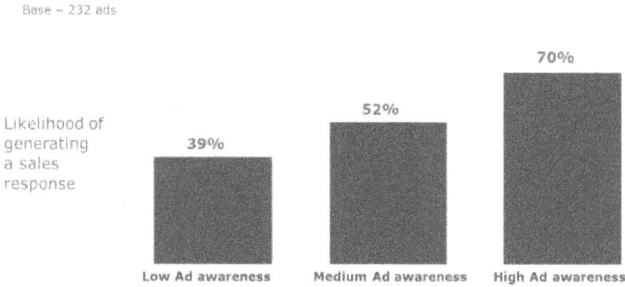

Base – 232 ads

Likelihood of generating a sales response

39% Low Ad awareness

52% Medium Ad awareness

70% High Ad awareness

KANTAR MILLWARDBROWN

Which ads are loved?

Kantar Millward Brown's Link copy test has an affinity question; an 11-point scale from 'hate it' to 'love it.' There is clearly a relationship between enjoyment and positive feelings towards the ad. If you enjoy an ad you are more likely to like it.

However, there is also a strong relationship between ad affinity and measures such as believability, difference, setting trends and meeting needs.

So, to produce likable advertising, you do not need to produce advertising that is enjoyed; advertising which conveys relevant, different information is also liked.

Affinity	Correlation
Enjoyment	0.72
Branding	0.50
Involvement	0.02
Believable	0.71
Brand really different	0.71
Sets trends	0.73
Meets needs	0.72

Base: US online ads   c(5000)

KANTAR MILWARDBROWN

Negative emotions

Sometimes it is necessary to engage consumers in a negative way. Government advertising, for example, often utilizes this strategy to change consumer behaviour (usually to stop it — e.g., smoking, excessive drinking, dangerous driving).

Brand advertising, however, must motivate consumers either to buy the product or to drive a more positive opinion of the brand. Ads that evoke positive emotions tend to have a more positive effect on the brand. So it is important for a brand embarking on a negative strategy to carefully consider the tone, and balance negative engagement with some positive engagement. A more balanced tone of engagement can deliver a better response — encouraging consumers to buy the product and driving a more positive opinion of the brand. Evoking negative emotions may be a key part of such ads, in terms of creating drama and setting up problem scenarios. But given the importance of positive emotional associations in brand success, it is vital to leave consumers with the positive high of the resolution, rather than an abiding negative emotional memory of the problem. Ads which evoke strong positive emotions are more likely to elicit greater brand appeal.

The dangers of generating negative emotions are demonstrated by the following case study for an alcohol brand in the UK. The brand was looking for an impactful ad to help boost awareness after a relatively successful brand re-launch. The ad generated high levels of irritation (the ad was the third most irritating ad in the database). Almost one in three people said that the advert made the brand seem less appealing. There might have been a more positive reaction among some subgroups to help with possible targeting solutions but there were none. The music was a large element of the problem, driving both mild enjoyment and vehement anger. Since the music was integral to the ad, little could be done to resolve the problem at such a late stage. As the ad was likely to damage brand appeal and rile consumers of all types, the recommendation was that it should not be aired. However, the client made the decision to put the ad online via YouTube and the brand's web site. Responses posted on YouTube were numerous and strongly negative. After a week, with no signs of the negative reactions abating, the ad was pulled.

The problem of ads that generate strong negative emotions can often be resolved. An ad for a brand of mouthwash showed someone spitting blood while brushing, before finally a tooth fell out. It was so disturbing and unpleasant that the ad did not generate the desired persuasion and did little to build brand appeal. It even put some people off the brand. It was the most disturbing and unpleasant ad tested online in the UK and was in the top 1% for irritation. A second version of the ad was created which was intended to tone down some of the overtly negative engagement.

The emotional trace (from facial coding) for the ad shows that while negative emotions (largely driven by a sense of being repelled) were off the scale in the first edit, they were far less dramatic in the final edit. This allowed the ad to resolve itself with predominantly positive emotions.

Negative emotions less dramatic in final film

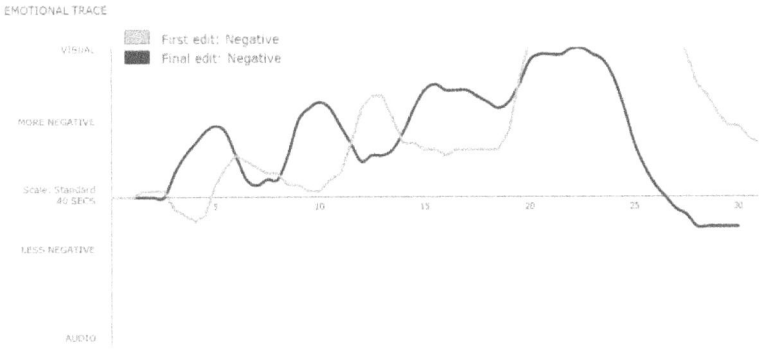

First edit: Negative
Final edit: Negative

Measuring Emotional Responses

Some claim that emotion is 'unconscious' and so not available to conscious introspection, which would mean that individuals are not capable of reporting the emotions they feel. It has been said that Damasio discovered that feelings and emotions are processed automatically and implicitly. The consequence of this would be that the effect advertising has on consumers' emotions and feelings would be largely unknown to them. The reality is that while psychologists often disagree on the exact definition of emotion, there is a wide consensus that a key component of it is subjective feelings — i.e., conscious experience. As Damasio wrote in Descartes' Error: 'I do not see emotions and feelings as the intangible and vaporous qualities that many presume them to be' (Antonio Damasio, Descartes' Error (New York: G. P. Putnam, 1994.), 164); and 'Feelings are neither intangible nor elusive.' (ibid, xxv). There are transient emotions that do not reach consciousness and leave no trace. But the consumer can describe the lasting emotions an ad leaves, and which may influence purchase decisions.

A few years ago, Kantar Millward Brown set up a large-scale investigative study to explore a variety of ways of measuring emotional responses to ads, to make sure they were being measured in the most useful ways.

As one leg of this, the team looked at two matched cells: one cell was asked for their emotional responses to an ad through a simple list of words; the second cell was asked the question in exactly the same way, but with a set of photographs of facial expressions, with the emotions listed underneath. Three markets were covered (UK, US and China) and three ads were covered in each market, specifically chosen to give a range of likely emotional responses.

A database of facial expressions developed by Cambridge University was used; one set for males and one for females. They covered what are generally considered to be Ekman's universal faces of human emotion: sadness, contempt, surprise, fear, disgust, anger, happiness, neutral. The results were extremely similar (R^2 of 0.97), suggesting that the addition of faces does not get a different type of response compared to simply showing a list of words.

Showing faces doesn't affect responses

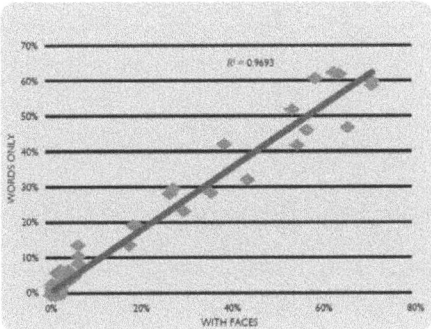

It was clear that you may as well ask a simple list of words. And this is important because one of the great strengths of a direct question is the ability to access a wide range of quite specific emotions.

This can be simply demonstrated. An ad for a European public utility provider featured two cute animated characters, used to represent gas and electricity. The story showed a woman bringing home the 'gas' character to meet the 'electricity' character that she already owned — emphasizing the brand's offer of both gas and electricity services. Some respondents (mostly men) were left unimpressed, but this was evoked at levels only slightly higher than average. For many, the ad prompted feelings of contentment and affection, with the latter in particular being evoked at much higher levels than usual. The ad achieved its aim of prompting warm emotions. In the chart below, the bars represent the ad scores, the lines behind the database norms.

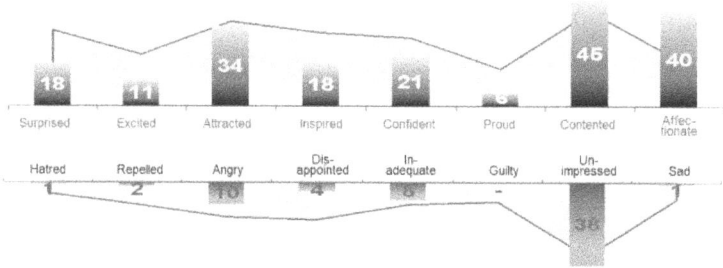

Affectionate, Contented, and for some, Unimpressed come through strongly

Emotional footprint

Surprised	Excited	Attracted	Inspired	Confident	Proud	Contented	Affec-tionate
18	11	34	18	21		46	40

Hatred	Repelled	Angry	Dis-appointed	In-adequate	Guilty	Un-impressed	Sad
1	2	10	4	6	-	38	1

Measuring people's emotional responses during a piece of creative using facial coding adds a crucial view of implicit responses to the ad. This indirect measurement supplements direct metrics in two important regards: people's expressions reflect their overall engagement with the spot, and whether this is emotionally positive or negative; expressions also illustrate the emotional journey through the ad, highlighting key elements that were engaged with, and allowing a judgement of whether responses to key concepts and scenes will be as intended. In particular, it allows an assessment of whether the ad resolves in an emotionally positive way.

Facial coding has proved to be very useful. One Indian ad, for a new launch, had a persuasive message but weak branding. The ad featured an engaging story involving a mother and her son; however, in the middle, a male voice-over explained the product benefits in a demonstration sequence. There was a marked dip in positive valence during the demonstration sequence. The valence curve was explored, splitting the sample by those who gave a high branding score compared to those who did not. The findings were clear: the dip in valence was much stronger for those whose branding scores were weaker. It was clear that the male voice-over interrupted the story. It was argued that if the mother explained the benefits instead, the demonstration sequence would be better integrated. The subsequent ad did this, ensuring the demonstration sequence was seamlessly integrated. The emotional response held steady, and branding was much stronger.

What Makes an Ad Persuasive?

Some advertising works in a very direct way. Sometimes seeing an ad can have an immediate result, increasing likelihood of buying the advertised brand. Most advertising is not immediately persuasive like this. But when your goal is to influence consumers in a way that has this type of immediate impact on their behaviour, there are four key factors which dictate how successful you will be. To achieve a strongly persuasive effect, your ads need to communicate something seen as new, relevant, believable and differentiating. However, an ad which is not enjoyed may hinder the ad's persuasiveness; an ad which is disliked is unlikely to be highly persuasive.

Achieving strong persuasion

A lot of advertising seeks to influence behaviour over a long period of time, but here I'm looking specifically at how ads can bring about an immediate alteration in consumer behaviour — changing their opinion of the brand at the time of viewing.

Historically, this type of persuasion has been measured by looking at pre-post exposure shifts in predisposition towards a brand. But experimental research by Kantar Millward Brown in 1993 ('Persuasion shift testing' published in Admap by Andy Farr) showed that when this sort of shift occurs, people know their opinion of the brand had changed, and this can be assessed directly.

There is a clear relationship between having a persuasive ad and the likelihood of a short-term sales share increase. With new or small brands in particular, weak persuasion seriously reduces the chance of an increase in sales share; whereas ads for new brands which score highly on persuasion result in larger than average short-term increases in share.

Kantar Millward Brown's database shows that four factors contribute to an ad's ability to communicate a motivating message that achieves the desired persuasive effect.

Persuasion correlates strongly with how ads perform in conveying **new information.** If your ad does not contain news, you are unlikely to be persuasive.

Persuasion correlates with news

Link Database : USA

$R^2 = 0.59$

Immediate Persuasion (y-axis)

New Information (x-axis)

An important corollary to this is that once the communication is no longer seen as 'new', it is unlikely to be persuasive; a second burst of the ad is unlikely to be as effective.

Also important is the **relevance** to the consumer of what the ad communicates:

Link Database : USA

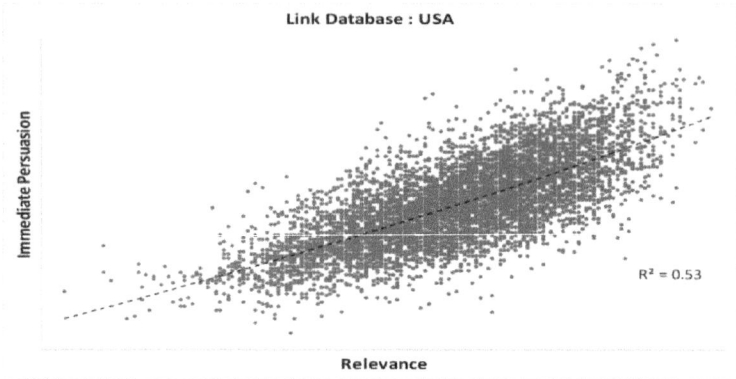

$R^2 = 0.53$

KANTAR MILLWARDBROWN

.... and the extent to which the messages communicated are credible. Actually, the key thing here is that the communication should not be seen as *in*credible; by contrast, a sceptical response such as 'I would have to check it out first before I believed it,' is common, and could actually encourage trial through curiosity.

Persuasion correlates with credibility

Link Database : USA

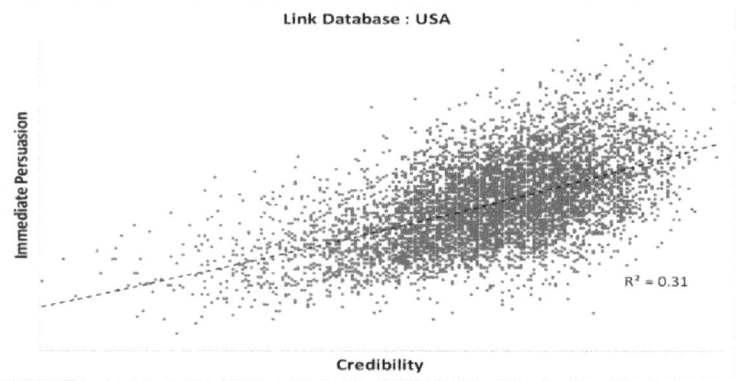

$R^2 = 0.31$

KANTAR MILLWARDBROWN

Finally, ads have a much better chance of achieving a strong persuasive effect if they are **differentiating**; if they are able to communicate news that is perceived as genuinely distinctive — or, better still, unique — that sets them apart from other brands in their category.

Persuasion correlates with difference

Link Database : USA

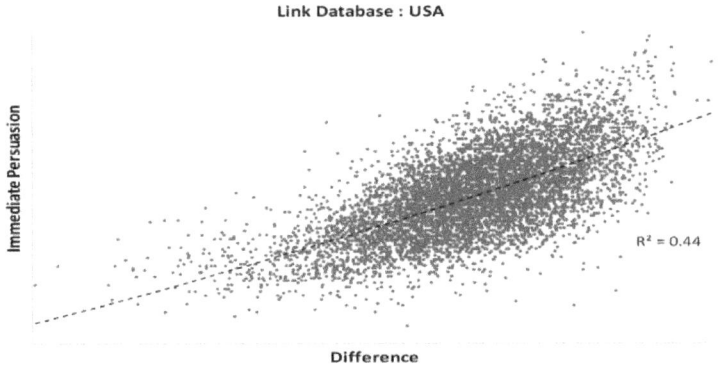

An ad being rated as enjoyable does not have a big positive effect on its ability to persuade; but there is evidence that ads which aren't enjoyed are less likely to achieve strong persuasion. Disliking the messenger can be a barrier to accepting the message:

Immediate persuasion is unlikely if enjoyment is poor

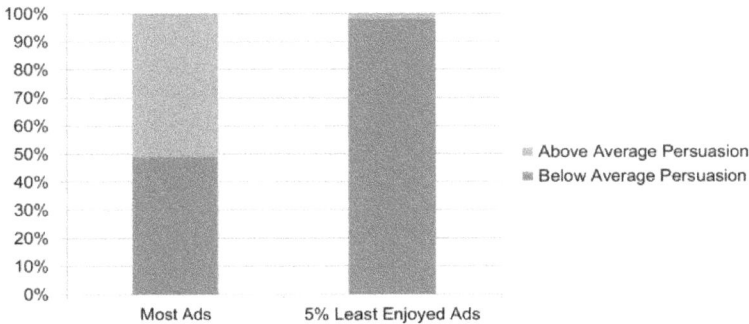

Which factor is most important?

Sadly, there's no simple answer. What's clear is that none of the four factors described above has enough weight by itself to compensate for poor performance by the others. Rather, they are conditions which all need to be met if an ad is to generate the motivation necessary to immediately change consumer behaviour. As my old colleague Dale Smith used to argue, you should think of persuasion like a cake: if just one of the main ingredients is missing, then the final result will not be very appetising. If an ad performs well against most or all of the four key diagnostic factors, its chances of being persuasive are greatly increased.

TV advertising can have many different objectives; but if immediate persuasion is your goal, addressing the issues raised here will help you maximise the effectiveness of your next campaign.

Using Advertising to Deliver Long-Term Growth

In one campaign for a major multinational client, the long-term return per GRP from the brand's advertising was calculated to be almost six times the short-term return. The short-term return (over the first eight weeks) was small; not enough to justify continued investment. But when the extra returns, generated after the first eight weeks, were added in the picture became far more positive.

Most advertising doesn't pay for itself in the short term. So, at a time when marketers are under ever-increasing pressure to justify expenditure, it's useful to understand the potential of advertising to deliver long-term sales growth. Typically, the long-term return per GRP is between two and three times greater than the short-term effect on sales. But the ratio varies a lot by campaign, and even better long-term results can be achieved, usually through a combination of weight of spend coupled with highly impactful and memorable advertising.

The value of taking the longer-term view

In general the ratio of long-term sales to the corresponding short-term impact is very variable. The overall average is between two to three, and this is a ratio often quoted in the industry.

However, across 94 ads analysed by Kantar Millward Brown using econometric modelling, 11 showed no long-term effect; while, for 20% of those that did, the long-term effect was at least five times greater than the short term impact:

% Brands

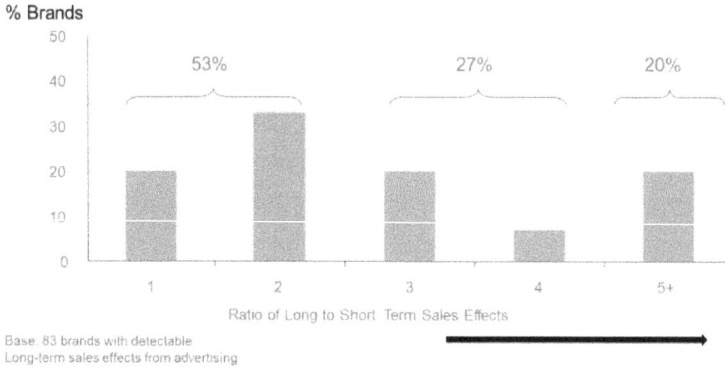

53%   27%   20%

Ratio of Long to Short Term Sales Effects

Base: 83 brands with detectable
Long-term sales effects from advertising

KANTAR MILLWARDBROWN

Spend v share of mind

There is a clear relationship between advertising impact and long-term sales effects. The more impactful the advertising, the stronger the long-term effect. This is true across categories.

The value of impactful advertising is highlighted by looking at changes in market share over time. Raw GRPs explain very little of the change in market share. But Effective GRPs — taking into account the ad awareness generated by the advertising — is around four times as effective at explaining the change.

More useful than raw GRPs is share-of-voice. But 'effective share-of-voice' — again factoring in the ad awareness generated — is even more successful at explaining changes in market share.

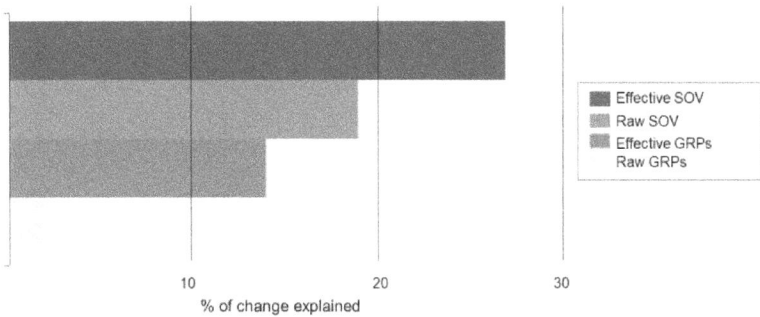

Legend:
- Effective SOV
- Raw SOV
- Effective GRPs
- Raw GRPs

x-axis: 10   20   30
% of change explained

Is increased spend more important than greater impact?

While, ideally, you should aim for both, it is possible to grow a brand with lower budgets providing the copy quality at least compensates for this.

In the following chart, the bottom left quadrant shows brands where both share of voice and share of ad awareness declined. On average 20% more brands lost share than gained. In the top right quadrant, you can see what happens when both share of voice and share of ad awareness increased. Nearly a third more grew than declined. The top left box shows what happened to those brands which increased share of voice — but with weaker copy than their competitors: 19% more declined than grew. The bottom right quadrant shows that when share of ad awareness grows, despite a drop in spend, more brands grow than decline:

115

Share of awareness and share of voice

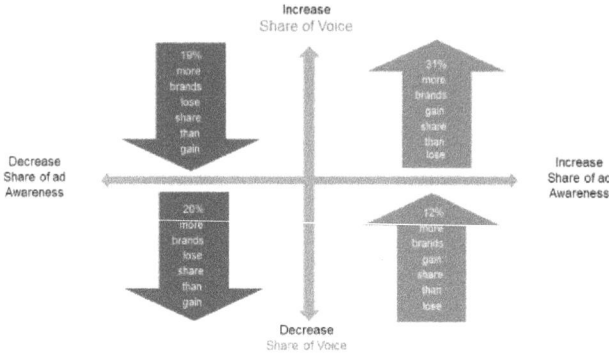

Share of voice v share of market

Having a higher share of voice than your market share is also likely to result in growth. In the chart below, brands were ranked based on the extent to which their share of voice was above or below their market share; then the brands were divided into ten equal groups. Each square represents one of those ten groups.

The bottom two groups, those with a share of voice between 10 and 20% less than their market share — were more likely to lose share over the following 12 months. In contrast, the top 10 percent of brands — spending more than 20% ahead of their market share — were more likely to grow.

For the majority of brands however, there was little or no relationship between relative share of voice and change in market share. This is mainly because there are so many factors which can affect sales that it would be surprising to see a clear relationship with media weight alone; but it's also because the strength of the copy is a crucial variable.

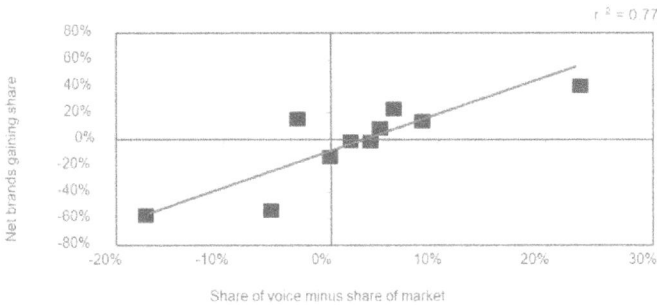

Share of voice versus market share

Increasing your share of communications awareness and having a share of communications awareness higher than your market share are both related to increased market share. These two factors are summarised here:

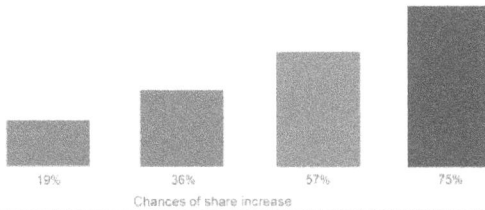

Share of communications awareness relates to probability of share growth/decline

What Happens when Brands go Dark?

A regular and reasonably heavy advertiser, this insurance company came off air with only one subsequent burst two years later. Consideration levels plummeted over the next few years.

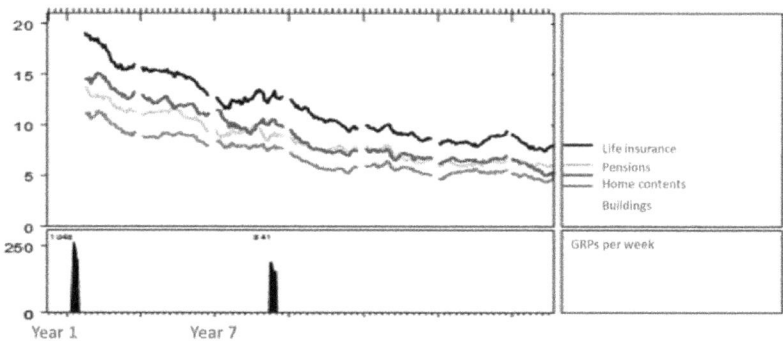

Consideration for types of insurance – Brand X

With marketing budgets always under pressure, it may be tempting for advertisers to consider coming off TV. Brands can 'go dark' for six months or so with little apparent deterioration in their health. But the problems come in the longer term; and once decline sets in, it's hard to reverse. If the brand is well supported in other media, TV advertising may not be badly missed. But overall, the findings are clear: maintaining your spend is the best way to ensure long term brand health. Brand equity is hard won, but easy to lose.

Coming off air: the consequences

When a company's short-term profitability is suffering, the marketing budget is usually the first to be cut. But what are the consequences?

Analysis of the Kantar Millward Brown tracking database shows that brand health is potentially vulnerable when brands stop advertising on TV for six months, with a fall seen in at least one key brand health measure in 60% of cases. And bigger brands are more likely to suffer a decline than smaller brands.

Net Effect on Brand Measures Six Months after TV Advertising Stops

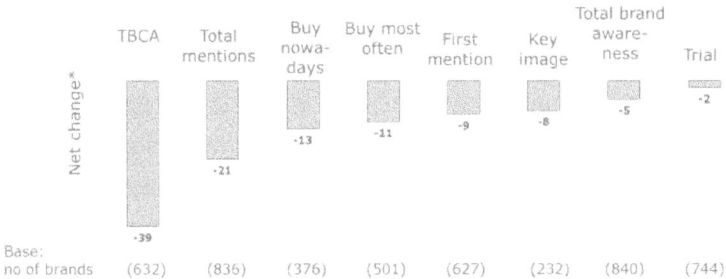

	TBCA	Total mentions	Buy nowa-days	Buy most often	First mention	Key image	Total brand aware-ness	Trial
Net change*	-39	-21	-13	-11	-9	-8	-5	-2
Base: no of brands	(632)	(836)	(376)	(501)	(627)	(232)	(840)	(744)

KANTAR MILLWARDBROWN   *Net Change: Percent of brands increasing – percent of brands decreasing

Maintaining equity through other marketing activity

In contrast, one major retailer came off TV for two years, moving the budget into below-the-line activity. Preference levels held up well.

Supermarket would prefer to shop

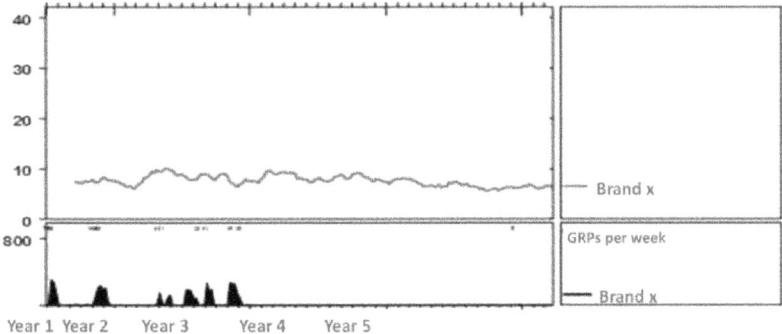

KANTAR MILLWARDBROWN

119

Switching spend to other media can also help maintain the brand. See the chapter on the 'media multiplier effect' to see how advertising in one medium can evoke memories of other advertising for the same brand.

Value brands are also more likely to maintain consideration levels.

Harnessing the 'halo effect'

Another way in which brand health can be maintained without advertising is by taking advantage of other related brand activity.

For example, one brand came off air for a year, but sales actually increased. A variant of the brand had been advertised during this period; and the advertising also benefited the parent. But this approach is by no means guaranteed to be effective. A review of 131 case studies shows that only 23% demonstrated a positive 'halo effect' on short term sales.

I've also seen cases where strong historical advertising memories have helped support the brand.

Returning to air: the challenge of reversing decline

Once equity and sales have declined, it can be hard to get them back up to previous levels. One brand came off air in one region (Region B), but continued advertising in the rest of the country. Within a year, market share had dropped 2% in the region without advertising, while holding steady elsewhere. In the following year, when the advertising was resumed, Region B's market share continued to lag behind the rest of the country.

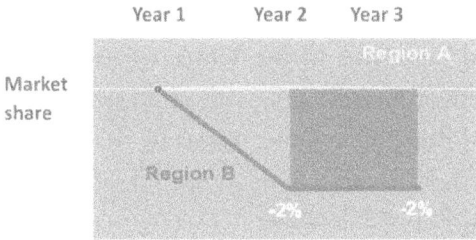

Region B suffers in Year 2 *AND Year 3*

However, it is possible to fully recover. I've seen examples of advertisers returning to air with strong new executions, often using well-recognised historic brand cues and persuasive copy. But if the new advertising continues an existing strategy, it's crucial to ensure that the strategy continues to be relevant and ownable — market conditions can change rapidly.

Overall, the lesson is clear: the best way to ensure long term brand growth is to maintain marketing expenditure.

Laying Down Media

A few years ago, a UK food brand conducted a simple experiment with its TV media laydown. In the North of the country, the brand bought 668 GRPs over nine weeks, with an average weekly weight of 74 GRPs. In the South, using the same ad, it bought fewer GRPs (596) but spread them over a longer period of 16 weeks, with an average weekly weight of 43 GRPs.

Though weight was approximately 12% higher in the North, ad awareness in the South was higher. The 'drip' strategy also generated stronger perceptions that people had recently heard a lot about the brand.

Signs That The Drip Strategy Benefits Perceptions

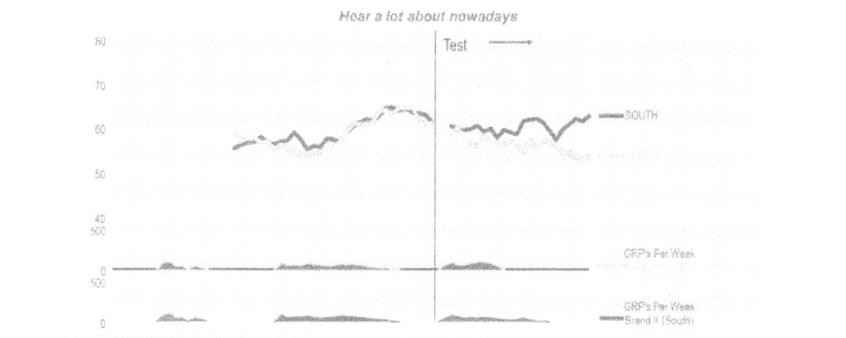

With the increasing complexity of marketing activity, patterns have become harder to understand. However, spreading spend over a longer period—rather than in a shorter burst—is usually an efficient way to avoid 'over-exposure.' But this approach will not suit all brands and is not appropriate for every occasion.

Drip strategy and TV

While most modern major campaigns use multiple media, TV is still the main element for most major campaigns, so it is worth highlighting that the example above is not unique. Kantar Millward Brown's global tracking database identified TV ads that flighted with 400-600 GRPs over a six-to-eight-week period and compared them with ads that flighted with the same number of GRPs over a 16+-week period. The drip strategy tended to be more impactful. When ads aired over the shorter time period 47% generated an increase in unaided awareness of 4% or more. When ads aired over the longer time period, 56% generated an increase of 4% or more.

Drip strategy and other media

The best way to deploy other media will depend on the campaign objectives and the nature of the creative. TV reach can be extended through online video; but media multiplier effects can also be successful.

There are several ways the media multiplier effect can work. Multiple channels can be used to reach the same target audience at about the same time, surrounding the consumer with an integrated set of messages through different vehicles, resulting in a greater effect than what could be achieved through one medium alone. Using different touchpoints and dayparts offers the potential to connect in a more relevant way with consumers. Additionally, because TV can often 'prime' the effectiveness of other media, continuing the campaign using cheaper media after the TV activity has ended can serve as a powerful reminder and extend the life of the campaign.

Drip strategy: use when appropriate

Advertising tends to work on a diminishing returns basis, with the first exposure generating the strongest impact, while subsequent exposures have less effect. Taken to its logical extreme, this would lead to brands being on air throughout the year at relatively low weight, which aligns with the tenets of recency planning theory. However, while spreading spend over a longer period has advantages, there are several occasions when it is not appropriate:

Sometimes making a big 'noise' with a burst for special events (like launches) is effective.

Sales teams often appreciate a heavy burst because it helps them gain shelf space or warms up customers prior to tactical activation such as promotional activity.

In addition, it is generally not efficient to support seasonal brands out of season; although advertising can be employed in the run-up to the season.

Also, in countries where media costs are higher in particular seasons (e.g. Christmas), advertising for brands that do not have substantial sales increases during those seasons may not be cost effective.

Campaigns may be planned with TV at the centre, which can quickly build reach or frequency; this can serve to 'prime' tactical touchpoints, helping them deliver their own objectives.

Pragmatically, demonstrating the effect of a year-round continuous drip strategy can be difficult, which could make it harder for the marketing team to justify their budget down the line.

Used judiciously and appropriately, however, a drip strategy is an effective way for many brands to increase ad awareness and brand perceptions while avoiding over-exposure.

The Value of Advertising a Launch

Even in today's overcrowded markets, it is still possible for launches to be highly successful as demonstrated by this U.S. food brand. The new food brand was launched into an existing category that was crowded and heavily promoted. Yet within five years, the brand had become almost universally known.

Brand A became almost universally known in just a few years

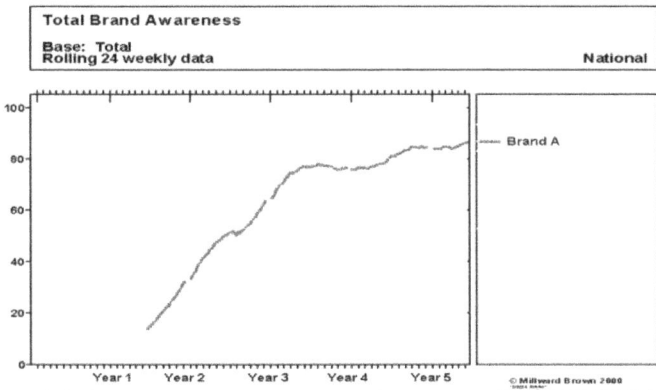

KANTAR MILLWARDBROWN

Consistent advertising with strong brand cues was used to generate both rational and emotional imagery. This helped the brand to achieve a consideration level of almost 60% — the highest level within the market.

Most successful launches are supported by strong advertising. The quality of launch advertising can affect the development of both brand awareness and trial. And, as with all good advertising, it must have motivating communication and focus on branded memorability.

Is advertising necessary?

There are some cases where advertising wasn't required to launch a brand. The Body Shop is one example. Instead of using advertising,

Anita Roddick harnessed the power of the media. She used positive PR about environmentally-friendly cosmetics to build the Body Shop into a powerful, global brand. Starbucks and Google also established strong brands without advertising.

However, most FMCG brands would struggle to generate consumer interest in this way. Because people do not actively seek out new products, FMCG marketing generally needs to build awareness that the new brand exists and generate curiosity in trial. Advertising a new launch can have a significant impact on awareness and trial of the product. This U.S. analysis shows the levels of awareness and trial for 16 FMCG launches in three related categories. Of the 16 ads, 10 were advertised on TV, six were not. The launches that were supported by advertising created higher levels of brand awareness and trial.

The impact of advertising launches (US)

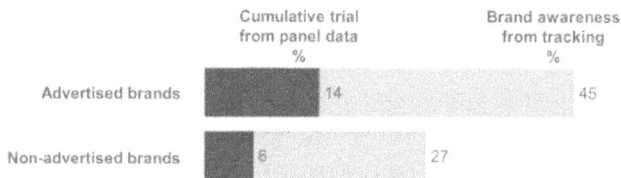

	Cumulative trial from panel data %	Brand awareness from tracking %
Advertised brands	14	45
Non-advertised brands	8	27

KANTAR MILLWARDBROWN

Brands with heavier spend are also more likely to enjoy higher brand awareness.

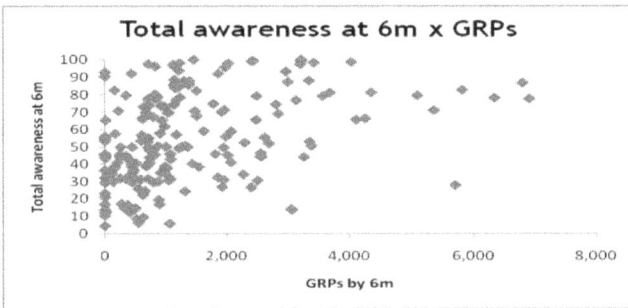

Total awareness at 6m x GRPs

Another major benefit of advertising is that it helps ensure distribution for your product. It demonstrates a commitment to the launch, which is often necessary to persuade retailers to commit shelf space to the brand.

Category spend

One factor that can't be ignored when comparing the success of different advertising campaigns is overall category spend levels in the market. Brands with a greater share of voice will achieve more successful launches and better brand growth. And share of voice is affected by category spend — a product launched into a category with a high spend level will struggle to achieve a high share of voice. The following analysis of a product launched into the U.K. and French personal care brand category illustrates this. The same advertising was used in the U.K. and France, advertising which had performed well in research in both countries. The U.K. launch achieved a 20% share of voice. However, because the French annual category TV spend was 40% higher than in the U.K., the launch achieved only a 9% share of voice. In order for the ad to make an equivalent impact in France as in the U.K., a greater ad spend would have been required. But the spend levels were similar. As a consequent the UK launch was far more successful, as indicated by the trends in a key image below.

Personal care brand

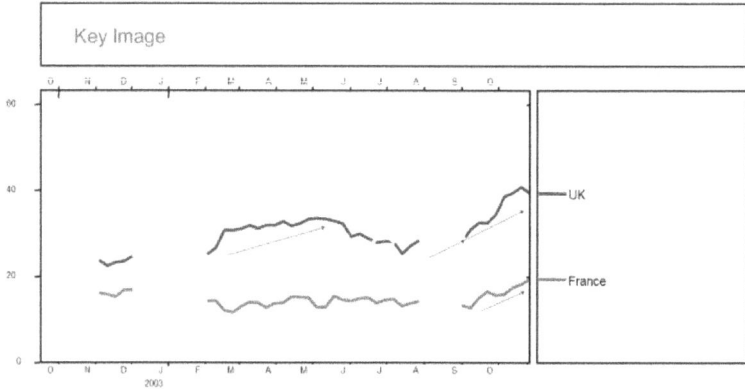

KANTAR MILLWARDBROWN

Timing

The timing of a launch is also important. One instance in which this played an important role was during the U.K. launch of a range of 'healthy' prepared meals. During the launch there were two bursts of ad activity (with only minor re-editing to the ad between the two bursts). Ad diagnostics were virtually identical on both occasions — the ad conveyed the same messages in the same way. The ad awareness generated by each burst was also the same. But impact on brand health measures was much more favorable the second time round. Sales also responded more favorably in January/February versus October/November. These differences can be attributed to the differing timings of the ad bursts. In the run up to Christmas, the advertising world is flooded with images of appetizing treats for the Christmas period. The impact on the consumer of the launch of a healthier food option this time of year lacked relevance. The re-airing post-Christmas when people are feeling guilty about their festive indulgences seems to have given the ad more relevance and meaning.

It is likely that the more sensible timing also facilitated improved distribution.

How to advertise a launch

There are three key areas to all advertising:

- Branded memorability
- Communication
- Response

These are just as important for new product launch advertising.

Branded memorability An ad must engage viewers and communicate the brand name in order for the presence of the brand to be logged. New brands advertised with highly impactful advertising tend to have higher levels of trial than those with weaker impact.

New brands with launch ads with higher impact have higher claimed trial on average

Claimed trial for new products (USA)

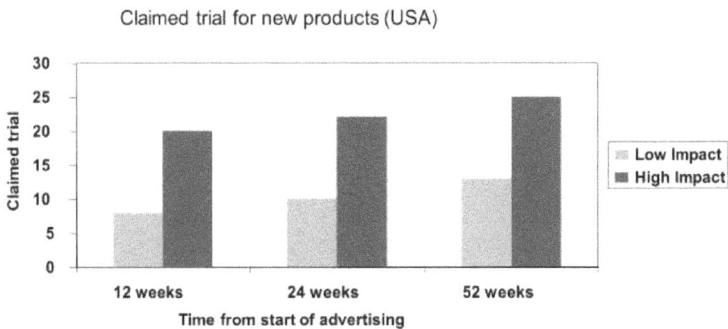

Communication Simplicity of communication is crucial to a successful launch. When Cravendale milk was launched in the U.K., the advertising tried to convey too many messages: the milk was fresh, whole, semi and skimmed; it contained vitamins and minerals; there were no additive or preservatives; it contained fewer bacteria so the milk stayed fresher for longer; and it tasted great. As a result, while sales grew, they were not on track to hit target. Research identified that the taste of the product was the key driver of trial and so a new execution was developed to dramatize this single message in a memorable way. Communication improved, cut-through more than doubled, and trial levels jumped from 13% to 27%.

Response The creative must communicate news to the target audience that is both relevant and credible in order to motivate viewers. However, news is only news if the consumer truly sees it as such. If it is not perceived to be news then you are unlikely to see a strong immediate response.

Ads can motivate viewers both emotionally and rationally. Generally rational advertising is most important in driving trial and sales for a new launch, but this will vary by category. In some categories where mood or tone is a more important driver, emotional affinity can be just as successful.

Kantar Millward Brown database analysis shows that persuasion (driven by news) is particularly important for launches. However, creative quality (as measured by branded impact) also helps to boost sales.

Persuasion is important for smaller brands

Advertising in a Low-Interest Category

A long-running campaign for one UK credit card was exceptionally successful. In each execution, the brand name was the focus of the ad, and the campaign was hugely enjoyable. Ad awareness levels were high, peaking at over 40%. Even a dull category like credit cards can produce wonderful advertising.

From financial services to frozen vegetables, some types of product are undeniably less interesting than others. So it's understandable that advertisers in these categories may feel it's impossible to create impactful advertising.

The reality is that in some media, particularly TV, category interest makes little difference to an ad's ability to cut through. However, in other media — notably print — it's a different story. Here, category interest can play a major role in determining an ad's impact.

On TV, most advertising is 'low interest'

Certainly, there are very significant differences in category interest. Category interest scores range from around 15% for financial services to around 80% for skincare products and perfumes.

A common response to this is for clients and their agencies to try to make their ads look as if they are for something else, on the grounds that this is the only way to hold viewers' attention.

But for TV advertising, such an approach simply isn't justified. The average ability of TV ads to generate ad awareness varies very little by category. The reality is that most people are fairly uninterested in the vast majority of advertising, whatever the product category. Unless the ad is providing news that is immediately relevant to them, they are unlikely to pay much attention. They are certainly not going to make an effort to remember the details of an ad.

Effective TV ads need to earn the viewer's interest

So to be effective, your ad — whatever it's for — needs to earn viewers' attention. And the only way to do this is to ensure that it's engaging; and that the brand message is creatively integrated into the engaging parts of the ad's story.

Sometimes, advertisers point to a succession of ads with weak impact to 'prove' that it's not possible to achieve good cut-through in their category or for their brand.

But, as they say in financial services, past performance provides no guide to future performance. Several years ago after a series of ads with weak cut through, one UK financial institution launched a new campaign which started with advertising cut through which was nearly three times higher than previous executions. In this case, it built on an old established branding device, which had been dropped from the previous campaigns.

How TV differs from print

In summary, for TV ads, product field is of minimal importance in generating impact. This is because people watch ads in an uninvolved way and make little effort to process the information at the time. They don't care whether an ad is for insurance or washing up liquid. It is the job of the creative to engage the viewer, and the brand needs to be creatively highlighted as part of this process.

However, for some other media, different rules apply. In print advertising in particular, product field has a major effect on impact.

With print there is a strong correlation between category interest and impact

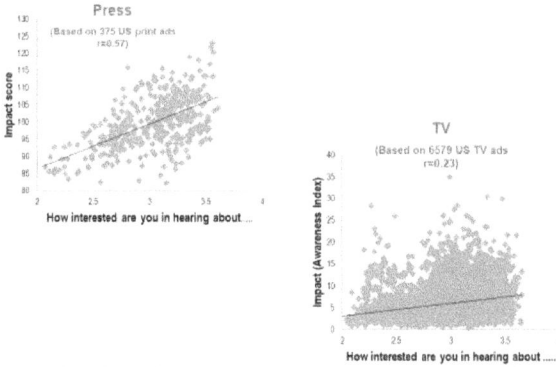

This has huge implications for advertising low interest categories in print. If you are trying to communicate with a broad audience, it's crucially important to use creativity in a way that will prevent readers from turning the page, and then to draw them into the product story.

But there is still a balance to be struck. High impact creativity must never be allowed to obscure an ad's key communication — as might happen, for example, if a print ad highlighting attractive mortgage rates used an amusing cartoon to grab readers' attention, which got in the way of a message with real relevance to those in the market. It might be that simply shouting about the rate will be sufficient to grab the attention of those actively in the market for a mortgage.

What Time Lengths are Best for a TV Campaign?

There is surprisingly little difference in the performance of different ad lengths. The strength of the creative has much more of an impact on how effectively an ad will work than the length of the ad.

In terms of generating ad awareness there is no consistent cost efficiency of using longer or shorter time lengths; and different ad lengths communicate similarly in terms of primary message levels.

In terms of persuasion, there is likely to be some cost-efficiency advantage to using the 15-second, because the same budget will buy more exposures – so you should be able to reach more of your audience with your communication.

On the other hand, longer ads allow more time for engagement and so will be more appropriate for complex impressions.

These last two points highlight the importance of the objective of the campaign in choosing the ad length. When to use different ad lengths depends on a brand's objectives and the individual ad under consideration.

When to use 6 seconds

The use of short-form video has emerged in recent years as a way to deal with the speed with which people skip online ads. Such short ads are more respectful of viewers' attention.

While they cannot communicate complex messages, they can be useful for a number of tasks. These include: teasing before a full campaign starts; building awareness (the format is a good one for building frequency); cut-down reminders of a full-length ad (when the full ad has been already established). They can also be effective as a series of brief episodic stories.

When to use 15 seconds

Ads of this length work best when communicating core advertising ideas, providing a reminder to consumers. Situations where a 15-second ad may be appropriate:

• If it's important for the brand to have a continuity advertising plan, the lower cost of 15-second spots may be an efficient way to stretch advertising spend (if the proposition and branding can be communicated in this time).

• If the brand is a seasonal product, as users may need a reminder.

• A 15-second ad which is a cut-down may be effective as a reminder of the longer ad — but only if the longer ad is fully established first.

In some cases where a brand has a simple compelling offer that needs no explanation, a 15-second ad may be able to stand on its own and deliver good payback.

When to use 30 seconds

Generally, 30-second ads are better than shorter spots at communicating complex messages. This can be particularly helpful:

• When launching a new product or campaign.

• When introducing a new campaign or after a long advertising hiatus.

• If a brand has complex or multiple messages or is seeking to create an engaging impression.

When to use 60 seconds or longer

Though relatively rare, 60-second ads can be useful in specific circumstances, tending, on average, to be more involving.

Additionally, they can generate strong PR and word of mouth for a brand, by offering a sense of being an 'event'. I've seen ads as long as two or three minutes which easily justify their cost by their ability to generate this kind of spin-off activity.

Impact: little to choose between ad lengths

Working on 30-second equivalent GRPs, overall there is no real difference in the average impact of ads across different ad lengths. A 15-second ad is as likely to achieve as strong impact as a 60-second ad.

I've seen a wide range of ad awareness levels for all different ad lengths, so if your key objective is to generate impact, there is no reason to choose a particular ad length to achieve this.

Persuasion: more power through more exposures

On average, all time lengths are comparable in terms of their persuasive power, per exposure. And if a 15-second ad communicates as persuasively as a longer ad, it is likely to be more effective in-market as a result of the higher number of exposures — and greater reach — delivered by the same amount of air-time.

Enjoyment and involvement: harder to achieve in 15 seconds

On average, 15-second ads are slightly less likely to be thought enjoyable or involving than longer ads, reflecting the fact that the ad holds the viewer's attention for less time, or has less time in which to engage the viewer's interest or sympathy.

Communication: it's all about the creative

There is a wide range in how successfully ads communicate their key messages; but this is largely unrelated to length. In general, 15-second ads communicate primary messages as well as longer ads. The key factor here is the strength of the creative treatment.

Given that 30 and 60-second ads have longer in which to communicate, they are generally better able to convey multiple messages.

Longer ads offer slightly more opportunity to
communicate multiple messages

Key message communicated

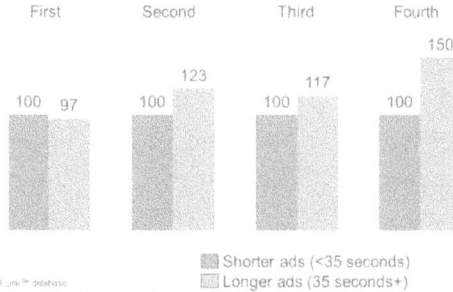

First	Second	Third	Fourth
100 97	100 123	100 117	100 150

■ Shorter ads (<35 seconds)
■ Longer ads (35 seconds+)

Source: MB Link™ database
Scores are indexed on short ad (<35 second) values

KANTAR MILLWARDBROWN

Clarity and focus on a single key message are critical for 15-second ads to communicate effectively.

In addition, longer ads have more opportunity to develop a story. However, they are no better at evoking an emotional response.

Aiming for the perfect mix

In view of these findings, your TV campaign may well benefit from a mix of ad lengths — each being used to achieve slightly different objectives.

In particular, using cut-downs can be highly cost-effective, stimulating memories of the full-length ad, once it has been aired enough to be established in the minds of viewers.

Using Cut-downs to Stretch your Budget Further

In the UK, a 30 second ad for an established brand was completely replaced by a 15 second cut-down, and the ability to generate ad awareness doubled. Significantly, when respondents were asked to describe the 15 second ad, many described elements from the 30 second ad which were not included in the cut-down. The cut-down was triggering memories of the full ad.

Used well, cut-downs can undoubtedly increase the efficiency of your campaign, and aid communication. By stimulating the audience's memories of the full-length version, a cut-down can deliver virtually the same result at a much lower cost. But creating a strong cut-down is not always straightforward. To begin with, the full-length ad must first be sufficiently established in the audience's minds. And choosing the right scenes for inclusion requires an understanding of how cut-downs work.

The benefits of cut-downs

Cut-downs can be a highly effective means of improving the efficiency of a campaign. In one example, a 30 second ad aired in two bursts, generating around average ad awareness. The following season, a 10 second cut-down was introduced into the mix, and the ability of the campaign to generate ad awareness almost doubled, while communication stayed strong.

At their most effective, cut-downs work by stimulating memories of the full-length ad, which effectively means the advertiser gets the benefit of the full ad at a fraction of the cost.

Choosing the right scenes

The most effective cut-downs use the most memorable scenes of the original ad.

For example, a 90 second TV ad made up of a series of vignettes was used to launch a broadband service in the U.K. The ad was highly involving. After an initial burst of the 90 second ad, two cut-downs were used to continue the campaign. These performed less well because they didn't feature the most memorable parts of the original ad — and, as a result, both enjoyment and cut-through were weaker.

In the U.S., the cut-down of a deodorant ad generated only a fifth of the ad awareness of the original; the cut-down did not use the most involving scenes.

But creating a strong cut-down isn't just a matter of using the most involving scenes. An ad for a cleaning product was researched as a 30 second ad, and performed well. But when the brand considered running a 15 second cut-down, research showed that enjoyment and persuasion were both considerably lower.

So what went wrong? In the original, the most involving and memorable scene showed someone knocking over a glass of wine on a tablecloth. This scene was also present in the cut-down. But in the original there was a twist; the first half of the ad featured a wildly gesticulating man almost knocking over the wine glass, building tension. This was resolved entertainingly, when it turned out to be someone else who spilt the wine; and it was this that was missing from the cut-down.

What this demonstrates is that you can't create effective cut-downs mechanically, by simply using the most memorable elements; you need to give careful consideration to the structure of the full-length ad.

What can cut-downs communicate?

Longer ads offer slightly more opportunity to communicate multiple messages. But the difference is not large; and, as we've seen, cut-downs can be effective in reminding the consumer of the full ad, including its communication.

There is also the potential for cut-downs to emphasize slightly different aspects of the intended communication. Here, an otherwise strong ad failed to communicate the intended key benefit. A cut-down, aired with the 30 second ad, and later alone, focused on this benefit. The tracking results showed that the different patterns produced different results.

Unaided Communication

	30 sec ad %	30 sec & 10 sec c/d %	15 sec c/d %
Key benefit	-	14	25
Base: Definite recallers of ad	(142)	(130)	(122)

KANTAR MILWARDBROWN

When to introduce cut-downs?

To maximize the benefits of using cut-downs, it's important to wait until the full-length version is sufficiently in the audience's mind before introducing them. You can best judge this by monitoring recall or recognition of the full ad. But there are no hard and fast rules for the level of recall that needs to be achieved before cut-downs become effective; it will depend on your overall spend and the length of your ad burst.

Do TV ads Work Harder as they 'Wear in'?

When I conducted advertising research for clients, after presenting early, bad results it was not uncommon for someone in the room to express the hope that the ad would wear in over time — after all, it had been on air for only a few weeks. Such wishful thinking is generally misguided.

Repeated exposure to the same ad is likely to result in it becoming better established in consumers' memories. So, in this sense, advertising does 'wear in'. However, it's very unusual for an individual ad to communicate more clearly, or to become more impactful, enjoyable or persuasive, through repeated exposures.

Occasionally, though, case studies show that a 'breakthrough' ad in a campaign, synergistic use of media within the campaign, or a clever marketing concept, may help the creative idea become better established, helping the campaign wear in over time.

Wear-in of advertising memories

There is one way in which individual executions can be said to wear in. One of the key roles of repetition of advertising is to help build advertising memories. This is illustrated by the Andrex example below, where it takes time for memories of the new execution to supersede old advertising memories.

In this sense, the little boy execution has worn in — but not through increased cut-through or improved communication.

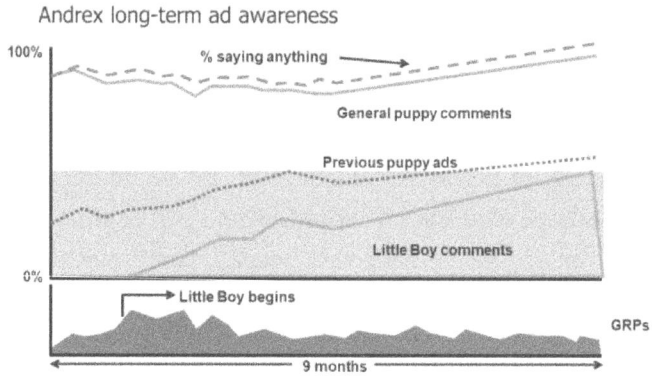

Andrex long-term ad awareness

Will an execution improve with repeated viewings?

It's very unusual for there to be a change in the nature of the response to an ad.

Wear-in in response could be said to have occurred if there is an improvement over time in any of the following areas:

- executional comprehension

- advertising communication/message takeout

- executional visibility

- emotional response to execution

- rational response to execution

- campaign visibility

Wear-in of this kind for individual ads is rare. Key measures for an execution generally don't change with repeated viewings. Consumers watch TV in a passive mode and tend to focus on the same elements of an ad each time they see it; they don't take in more with subsequent exposures. After the first viewing, people tend to home in on the interesting elements of the ad, reinforcing their original impression of the ad.

If the brand and key messages are integrated into these involving elements, then viewers will remember having seen the brand advertised and what the ad was trying to tell them. If the brand and key messages are not integrated in this way, it's unlikely they will be remembered.

The following example represents the norm: an example of an ad showing no signs of wear-in even after 10 months on air and around 700 GRPs.

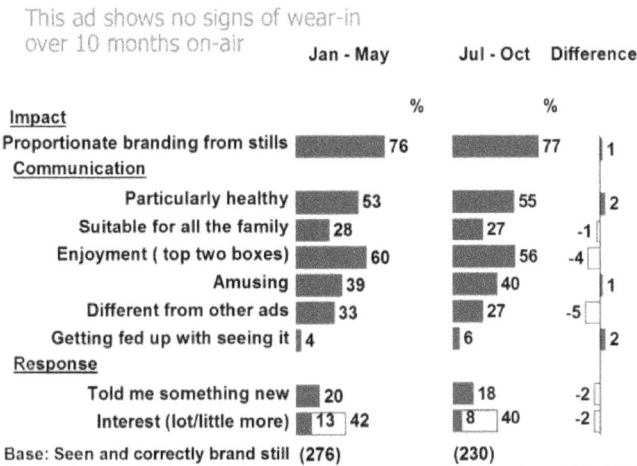

This ad shows no signs of wear-in over 10 months on-air

	Jan - May %	Jul - Oct %	Difference
Impact			
Proportionate branding from stills	76	77	1
Communication			
Particularly healthy	53	55	2
Suitable for all the family	28	27	-1
Enjoyment (top two boxes)	60	56	-4
Amusing	39	40	1
Different from other ads	33	27	-5
Getting fed up with seeing it	4	6	2
Response			
Told me something new	20	18	-2
Interest (lot/little more)	13 42	8 40	-2
Base: Seen and correctly brand still	(276)	(230)	

One thing that can decline is the perception of the amount of 'news' in an ad — and its persuasive ability — declining over time.

So, generally, it is unwise to rely on responses to a specific ad improving over time.

Do responses to specific executions ever improve?

An analysis of 450 ads aired in two or more bursts shows that 94% do not change their ability to build ad awareness. In the few cases where an execution appears to have worn in, further investigation usually demonstrates that factors outside the execution itself are responsible. Things such as:

- Increased interest in a character featured in the ad, through exposure in a popular TV programme

- Change to execution/mix of executions

- New products — through increased distribution/brand awareness

- Seasonality/relevance at time of advertising (e.g. advertising for a brand that sponsors a specific sporting event may achieve a higher awareness when screened at the time of that event)

- Campaign wear-in mistaken for executional wear-in (e.g. second/third bursts of Ad A being screened after other ads in the campaign had better established the link to the brand, resulting in Ad A performing better).

- Other activity for the brand, including promotions, and direct mail.

Campaign wear-in

As opposed to individual executions, campaigns can wear in. Campaign wear-in occurs when subsequent ads in a campaign perform better. Although not seen often, you are more likely to see campaign wear-in than executional wear-in.

When an integrated, distinctive branding device is used, wear-in is possible. In one example, the first ad in a new campaign didn't perform very well and the link with the brand was poor. The second and third ads in the campaign established the link with the brand better. So, as spend continued, the idea became better associated with the brand, resulting in improved cut through.

Campaign wear-in can occur:

- As new executions create the opportunity for more consumers to remember the branding device/campaign idea and make the brand link.

- Through 'campaign breakthrough' — when a new execution more clearly establishes the link between the creative format and the brand. This can happen as creatives learn from the success or otherwise of previous executions.

- Through insight from research.

But it's still more common for a campaign not to wear–in over time.

What enables a campaign to wear in?

Campaigns which do wear in tend to:

- have a strong idea at their core, rather than, say, a one-off joke

- have a distinctive branding device (e.g. music, personality, distinctive creative style, slogan)

- run for a protracted period

- have a high weight of spend

One of the reasons that campaign wear-in is rare is that there is often a lack of willingness to commit — both in terms of time and financial investment — to a genuine, long-term campaign. Often, inherently good campaign ideas may not be sufficiently explored due to poor initial execution of the idea at an early stage of the campaign.

To avoid this, treat the idea itself and the execution of that idea as two clearly separate entities. That helps identify when an idea has merit but the execution has simply not done it justice. The first ad in the Stella Artois Reassuringly Expensive campaign was comparatively weak. But the creatives took the lessons from research on board and subsequent executions improved branding and addressed other weaknesses, resulting is a campaign that won multiple awards and was highly effective.

Identifying opportunities for campaign wear-in

In deciding whether you have a potentially successful, campaignable idea consider the following:

- Is there a strong idea? Can other ads be made within the campaign, with a recognisable common theme?

- Does it have a distinctive branding device?

- Will other activity expose the branding device in connection with the brand?

- Is it a new brand/one with increasing distribution?

- Can a 'breakthrough ad' be made to better establish the link between the campaign and the brand?

Do TV Ads 'Wear out' with Repeated Showings?

Some years ago, I conducted a tracking programme for a major UK household brand. They'd run a hugely successful TV ad; it was very enjoyable and impactful, and tracking showed it was benefitting the brand. They ran it for a second burst. Then they ran into problems. The marketing team decided the ad had run its course and briefed the agency to come up with a new execution. But the agency was unable to come up with an idea as strong as the successful ad. So they ran the it for a third burst. Tracking results showed the ad to be as successful as previously. The agency redoubled their efforts to come up with a replacement. Again they failed. Much to the client's anxiety, they ran the original ad for a fourth burst. It was as successful as ever.

Wear-out of TV ads is rare. Broadly speaking, the response an ad evokes — in terms of impact, memorability and enjoyment — changes very little over time. However, ads that focus on product news may become less immediately persuasive as they rapidly convert all those who are receptive to such a message.

Saturation of media weight over a short space of time can create the impression of ad wear-out; though in such cases it is the media buying strategy, rather than the effectiveness of the specific execution, that may need to be reviewed.

How do TV ads wear out?

With continued showing and/or extremely heavy media spend, there are four key areas in which ads could wear-out:

1. Generating ad awareness

2. Attitudes/empathy

3. Communication

4. Brand response, including sales

But when an ad performs less well over time, it may well be factors outside of the ad itself that are to blame. So when assessing whether an ad may have worn out, it's important to look at the broader picture, considering areas such as the continuing relevance of the strategy and positioning; changes in the target group; and where the brand is in its lifecycle.

Executional wear-out

1. Generating ad awareness

Database analysis suggests that this type of wear-out very rarely occurs in TV ads — in marked contrast to print ads, which tend to wear out after 3-4 exposures. Analysis of 450 ads which aired in two or more bursts showed that 94% did not change their ability to generate ad awareness from burst to burst. In only 3% of cases did it decrease (and in 3% of cases it increased).

TV ads that are impactful tend to remain so over time. However, factors external to the ad itself can be the cause of this type of wear-out — for example, if the personality featured in the ad falls out of favour with the public.

Sometimes apparent wear-out may be due to heavy spending over a short period of time. People see the ad multiple times, but the ad is not reaching new consumers — thus limiting any possible increase in ad awareness. It may be that the media strategy is intended to build heavy frequency, in which case this outcome is to be expected. But if this isn't the intention, the media strategy should be revisited.

2. Attitudes/empathy

It is possible for wear-out to be observed in an ad's ability to generate empathy, although this is only seen occasionally; mostly attitudes hold steady over bursts as in this example:

No sign of wear out

	Sept – Oct %	Jan – Feb %	March - April %
Enjoyment	88	83	85
Interesting	38	47	46
Involving	46	39	46
Boring	7	8	7
Irritating	2	2	1

That was one example; the pattern is seen across these 258 ads, where the same ad was aired in at least two bursts and enjoyment levels held steady.

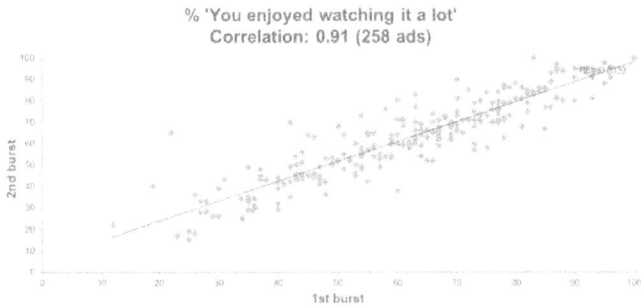

Enjoyment

% 'You enjoyed watching it a lot'
Correlation: 0.91 (258 ads)

Millward Brown Tracking Database. Global data

Similar results are seen for getting fed up with seeing it.

% 'You're getting fed up with seeing it'
Correlation: 0.89 (141 ads)

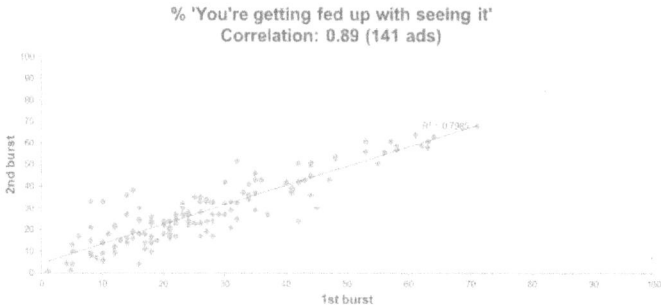

Millward Brown Tracking Database, Global data

KANTAR MILLWARDBROWN

This kind of wear-out tends to occur when an ad which some viewers find irritating is aired with heavy spend; further irritation can then build fairly rapidly.

Alternatively, an ad can become less enjoyable if the music used goes out of fashion. For example, one ad featured a current pop song. The ad was aired in three bursts over a two year period. By the third burst, the 'enjoyment' score was well down, as the song had long since dropped from the charts and had lost its appealing freshness.

3. Communication

Consumers don't tend to notice new things each time they see an ad; rather they focus on the involving parts of the ad, which generally don't change over time. As a result, communication take-out from the ad will also usually remain unchanged.

4. Brand response

Responses to brand measures and immediate impact on sales may weaken with repeated showings of the same ad.

In assessing whether this has occurred, it's important to consider the ad's objectives and whether the message is seen as new. Ads with new communication can generate an immediately persuasive effect, generating a short-term sales uplift. Wear-out in this type of brand response is likely to occur, as such ads rapidly convert all the consumers they are capable of converting. After that, the 'news' is no longer seen as new. This effect can be seen in the example below.

News does wear out

	Sep-Oct	Jan-Feb	Mar-Apr
	%	%	%
Enjoyment	88	83	85
New Information	67	61	55
More likely to buy	66	62	50

Similarly, sales modelling work carried out for a new toilet cleaner in the UK showed that the first burst of the ad generated 1900 sales per GRP, while the second produced just 1100.

But many campaigns are very successful without relying on a constant supply of new news; immediate persuasion is just one route to sales.

Airing the same ad for ever

For most ads which reinforce an existing claim or positioning, the expected response would be an increase in (or maintenance of) brand awareness. It's rare for such ads to wear out over a few bursts. Indeed, repetition can help to build a brand in the long-term, even if a short-term brand response is minimal. So before wear-out is assumed, long term sales effects should be investigated.

But this doesn't necessarily mean that the same execution can be used ad infinitum (apologies for the pun). While it's true that many executions could be used longer than they are currently, there are several reasons for advertisers to move on. One of the most important is that, to ensure long term success, brands need to project a sense of leadership - whether through improved product offerings, or through showing contemporary relevance. Creating this sense of a brand leading the way is likely to involve new ad executions.

In addition, the competitive context needs to be kept under review; if a competitor changes campaign, this could negatively affect your sales, making it necessary to refresh your activity.

Campaign wear-out

Campaigns of ads can wear out in the same ways that individual ads can. In this example, a long-running campaign featured a particular celebrity with the potential to irritate. Irritation grew over the campaign; this was particularly evident in ad L, but even ad P, where strenuous efforts were made to address the irritation issue, was still found considerably more irritating than the early ads in the campaign. The client continued with the celebrity. He was well-established as a branding device, and they recognised that a strong branding device is like gold dust. But each new script was carefully judged in terms of its potential to irritate.

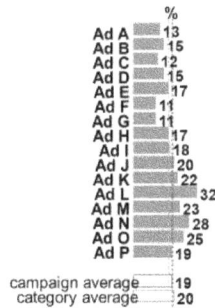

	%
Ad A	13
Ad B	15
Ad C	12
Ad D	15
Ad E	17
Ad F	11
Ad G	11
Ad H	17
Ad I	18
Ad J	20
Ad K	22
Ad L	32
Ad M	23
Ad N	28
Ad O	25
Ad P	19
campaign average	19
category average	20

Another possible cause for campaign wear-out is related to changes in society and attitudes over time. This may impact feelings about your category, your brand, or your creative device. A good example from the UK is the PG Tips 'Chimps' campaign, which was dropped after 40 years, because attitudes to performing animals had changed.

Is the campaign worn out, or is it just a specific execution?

With campaigns, some specific issues need to be taken into consideration when assessing apparent wear-out:

- the problem could be with specific executions, rather than the campaign as a whole. A new ad may be performing less well in terms of brand integration or clarity of message.

- campaigns that seem to be wearing-out can be revived, for example by a new slant to the scripts. One European detergent brand had successfully used a pair of characters over many years, but it was judged that the format was getting tired. Instead of ditching the pair, who were strongly linked with the brand, the creatives played with the relationship between the two. The results were more successful than the original campaign. In another example the ability of the campaign to generate ad awareness seemed to be declining over the campaign. Research found two reasons for this wear-out. The weight of spend was growing, resulting in a degree of media saturation. But also there was a lack of product integration in the later ads; the structure of the individual ads needed to be refocused. When these two issues were addressed, the campaign effectiveness was restored.

Will ads wear out faster in future?

People are far less tolerant of ads on laptops, mobiles or tablets than they are with ads on TV. But still it is rare to see an engaging ad wear out. It's possible that, with the increase in watching recorded programmes, with the ability to fast-forward or skip ads, wear-out of TV ads will increase, as viewers come to feel that ads are not something they need to put up with, but currently there is little evidence of this having a significant effect.

However, when thinking about this topic it is worth bearing in mind that in general, the first place an ad tends to wear out is in the minds of the marketing team.

How Should Voiceovers be Used in Ads?

I once researched an ad for a major European financial institution. It featured an engaging cartoon creature, but had a continuous voiceover which was about as informative as the buzz of a wasp. Even after watching it a few times I was still vague about what it was trying to convey. I urged them to edit it, cutting down the number of words. The agency did so, doing a brilliant job of cutting the words to the minimum essential, and managing to make them tie in with the visuals. This edit maintained its high engagement, but communicated the key message far better.

The voiceover is a very common feature of TV advertising across the world; around 90% of ads include voiceovers. Since they are so common and can be edited relatively easily, voiceovers are a worthy topic for scrutiny. They seem to aid slightly the communication of factual messages. However, the way a voiceover ties in with an ad's visual content is critical. When voiceovers and visuals compete, the voiceover message can get lost.

What voiceovers do well: aid communication of information

Voiceovers are often used to convey information, and they can do this effectively.

Changes made to a voiceover can lead to dramatic improvement in an ad's performance. When a taste message came through only weakly for an ad for a new biscuit in China, adjusting the voiceover made a difference. In the original ad, the intended message registered with just 34% of respondents, well below the norm of 55%. When this new voiceover was added: 'delicious but does not leave the mouth feeling dry,' communication of the taste message shot up to 53%. When the voiceover was modified further, to 'really delicious,' communication reached 61%. The advertising contributed to a successful product launch; trial levels for the new cookie reached 80% within six months.

A change in voiceover also made a huge difference for a personal care brand. Two versions of an ad were tested. Both had the same end frame, but one included a voiceover to support the super of 'developed with experts,' The takeout of the message was more than twice as high for the ad with voiceover, 44% versus 17%.

But voiceovers don't do it all

The fact is, it is not always appropriate to use a voiceover.

While ads with voiceovers can communicate better than ads without voiceovers, not all ads are intended primarily to communicate information or to be persuasive.

If your primary goal is to stimulate an emotional response or remind people of your brand, a voiceover may interfere with the achievement of your objective. Ads without a voiceover are slightly more likely to be enjoyed and slightly more likely to be seen as different to other advertising. However they are also slightly less likely to be understood. So in deciding how and when to use a voiceover, keep your key objectives in mind.

Voiceovers must work with both story and images

Voiceovers don't always aid communication, particularly when they compete with an engaging or compelling story being shown in the ad. An ad for a food product in India was designed to communicate that the brand contained ingredients that helped enhance immunity. The commercial showed a husband feigning sickness and his wife catching him in the lie. A voiceover explained the brand's benefit, but most viewers seemed to be focused on the story being told on the screen, because they did not pick up either the voiceover or the message. The ad was modified so that the wife explained the benefits to her husband as part of the ad's story. The edited version performed substantially better.

Timing with visuals

Voiceovers need to complement the visual content of the ad. If they don't, the message is unlikely to register. This is the most common problem I've seen with voiceovers. One personal care brand tried in several ads to convey that it was now 75% more efficient, but in none of the executions did the visual content support the message, and as a consequence, the message was lost. Television tends to be a far more expensive medium than radio—this is partly due to its wider reach, but it is also because it gets moving images, accompanied by sound, into people's homes. You pay more for those images, which are often the most memorable parts of the ad, so it is sensible that those images should also be conveying the intended communication rather than distracting from it. It is crucial that voiceover works well with the visual content. TV ads tend to communicate far more successfully when they both show *and* tell.

Less can be more

Voiceovers should be used sparingly.

Pauses and silences can help add emphasis They allow time for the message to be absorbed.

On the other hand, as the financial example at the start of this chapter shows, continuous voiceovers can wash over viewers and lull them into inattention.

An ad for a new deodorant scored poorly on all key metrics. Analysis showed the ad had a comprehension problem. The ad was already in a finished film state, so the changes that could be made related mainly to the voiceover. The voiceover in the original ad had a French accent. The revised version featured an English accent. But the voiceover was leaner – only 69 words, v 80 in the original. In addition there was a title card, setting up the story from the opening shot. Comprehension improved dramatically, and the ad's persuasive strength moved from low to high. The subsequent launch was a success.

We tend to see continuous voiceover used more often with dubbed ads. When an ad is translated into another language, sometimes it takes more words to explain certain concepts (especially when the concept is one that has special resonance in the ad's original market). A UK deodorant ad that had performed well in research was subsequently dubbed in Polish and tested again. In the Polish version, viewers did not play back the differentiating message; instead, they took out a generic deodorant message. As a result, the ad did not convey strong news, persuade, or create a sense of differentiation. A comparison of the audio soundtracks of the two ads showed that the Polish version was sonically 'busier.' It provided less aural down time to allow viewers to process the ad's message.

A louder pattern for the Polish ad with no real breathing space

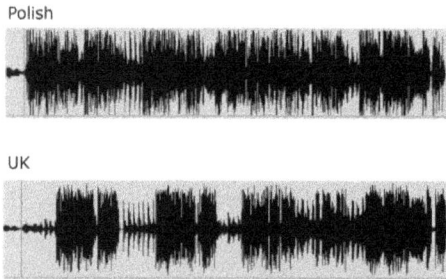

Polish

UK

Sound wavelength from audio soundtrack

KANTAR MILWARDBROWN

158

The voice in the voiceover

The voice in the voiceover can make a big difference. The same ad, dubbed with different voiceovers was tested in UK, France and Italy. In the UK the ad received a high level of dislikes, which was largely due to the voiceover. The voice was regarded as 'silly,' and detracted from the key message. However, in France and Italy, there were almost no mentions of 'silly voices.' This mattered; persuasion was greater among those who did not mention the silly voices compared to those who had mentioned them.

Regional accents can often add to enjoyment, especially when they are used in a playful manner. However, if an accent is too strong, it can be hard to understand, and this can lead to lower comprehension and enjoyment for the ad. Also, since people tend to be proud of their accents, if the accent is over-exaggerated and clearly not genuine, it can annoy people from that region.

Slogans in Advertising

What brands do you associate with the following? 'I'm Lovin' It', 'Finger Lickin' Good', 'Taste the Rainbow', 'Snap! Crackle! Pop!'

They probably gave you little trouble. When well-used and oft-repeated, a slogan can become part of the fabric of a brand. But how do you build a strong connection between slogan and brand? It's not simply a matter of tacking a slogan onto an ad, because an ad with a slogan isn't necessarily more effective than an ad without one. A slogan that is merely an endline or sign-off to an ad is unlikely to make a contribution to the success of either the advertising or the brand; the creative must integrate the brand and slogan in such a way that the slogan can strengthen branding or have some other effect.

Slogans are a familiar feature of advertising; about two-thirds of the ads in Kantar Millward Brown's global database include slogans. However, there is a great deal of variety in the way slogans are used. The brand name may or may not be included. The slogan may be set to music. The slogan may be a new phrase or it may be one that is already familiar. Overall, among all TV ads that include slogans, 44% include the brand name, 36% are slogans that have been used before, and 7% include slogans set to music.

What slogans can do

At an overall level, the presence of a slogan has very little difference on any key measure.

However, a slogan can make a difference. The chart below shows the interest levels for two ads that were tested in Germany. The ads were identical except for the slogans. At the points in the ads where the slogan was spoken and/or written, Slogan 2 generated more interest than Slogan 1. What was the difference between the two slogans? Slogan 2 was more closely related to the product and its key feature.

The difference a slogan can make

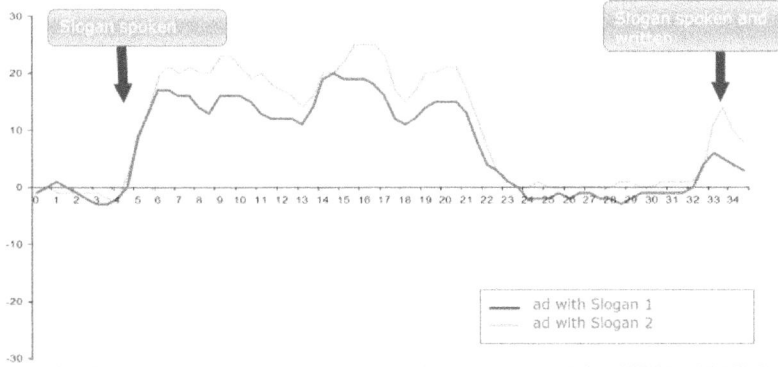

The difference a slogan can make

Slogans and brands

I've seen two ways in which slogans seem to lead to stronger branding. The first is when a slogan is part of a jingle. Gillette's jingle, *'Gillette, the best a man can get'* is a good example. However, of all the ads Kantar Millward Brown has tested that contain slogans, only 7% put them to music. The second factor that seems to allow a slogan to lead to better branding is familiarity — that is, the slogan has been used before. Slogans such as L'Oreal's *'Because I'm worth it'* have developed as strong established branding devices over time.

Once a slogan catches on, it can have a long shelf life. Peugeot's *'The drive of your life'* ran for a total of 13 years. In India, having made heavy use over years of the slogan *'Iron Kahoge To Dimmag Chalega Nahi Daudega'* (*'your brain will run not walk'*) Kellogg's Cornflakes now 'owns' the phrase, which enhances the ad's message 'Eating more iron will help your memory.'

The memorability of slogans

In general, slogans are not well remembered. Across over 3000 ads in the United States, the median percentage that claimed to remember a slogan was 36%; in the United Kingdom, the median across over 6600 ads was 46%.

Playback of the 'correct' slogan is even lower. In the United States, across 2500 ads, the median is less than 25%. In the UK, among over 500 ads, it is less than 15%.

From looking at some characteristics of the most- and least-remembered slogans I found the following: slogans are most likely to be remembered when they are included in a jingle, and slogans that have been used before and that are repeated within ads are better remembered. These findings reinforce the earlier findings on branding. (It is also worth noting that the overall length of the slogan wording seems to make little difference to recall. Although I'd urge common sense.)

Examples of memorable slogans

The best-remembered slogans fall into several categories.

A simple slogan can be effective if it is **relevant** and **meaningful**. In Slovakia, the people from the Šariš region are renowned for their warmth, friendliness, and sense of humour. So the beer brand Šariš succeeded with a slogan that communicates this regional pride: 'Šariš Srdcom vychodniar' ('Šariš, heart of Easterners'). In Hungary, Kinder Chocolate's simple yet assertive slogan 'A csokoládé extra adag tejjel' ('The chocolate with an extra dose of milk') was also very well recalled.

A slogan that acts as a resolution and makes **sense of the whole ad** can also be memorable. For example, in the uniquely styled Guinness campaign, the mysterious narrative of each ad is finally clarified by the slogan *'Good things come to those who wait.'* In the Felty campaign for Anchor butter, the slogan *'Anchor, the free-range butter company'* serves the same purpose. And the slogan *'Kinder Maxi King - Tyèinka s maxi chutí'* (*'Kinder Maxi King – Bar with maxi taste'*) not only resolves the story of the ad (in which a rapper-gangster eats a Kinder Maxi King bar at a party where everything is 'maxi') but also communicates a message for the Kinder brand in the Czech Republic.

Catchy slogans that use rhyme or alliteration to connect the phrase to the brand are also well remembered. Examples include *'Lick the lid of life'* for Muller yogurt and *'Sulit sa Pito Prito,'* a rhyming slogan that summarizes the offer for Golden Fiesta Cooking Oil in the Philippines ('A cooking oil that can be used seven times over').

 Incorporating the brand name in a catchy way can also prove effective. Two examples from the UK are PC World's *'Where in the world? PC World'* and *'Don't search. Just YELL.com.'*

Creative slogans that evoke some memorable image or stimulate a new way of thinking about a brand also have staying power with viewers. The Brazilian ad for Johnson's Pele dos Sonhos, *'Boa Noite para seu Sono, Bom dia para sua Pele'* (*'Good night for your sleep, good morning for your skin'*) cleverly communicates the key message, which is that a relaxing fragrance had been added to the moisturising product to help with sleep. Milky Bar's 'Ungrow up' in the UK also proved to resonate with viewers.

Distinctiveness can also make a slogan memorable. In Bulgaria, Fanta lent distinctiveness to its slogan *'Pij Fanta - budj Bamboocha'* (*'Drink Fanta – be Bamboocha'*) through the use of the made-up word 'Bamboocha,' which suggested parties, fun, and happiness.

Slogan use across touchpoints

Most of the effective slogans quoted here were used across a number of brand touchpoints. Repetition across different media seems to help establish slogans in consumers' minds. Slogans can also support a brand by being used on packaging or at the point of purchase; this can bring key communication to the shopper's mind during the decision process.

Decline in slogan usage

Over the last twenty years there has been a decline in the incidence of slogan use in both the United States and the UK (the countries for which Kantar Millward Brown data goes back the furthest). While slogans overall make little difference to the success of an ad, a good slogan can become a memorable part of a brand's identity. It seems likely that with the increased use of voice in technologies such as Alexa, jingles or 'sonic devices' may be set to grow in popularity again.

Product Demonstrations: How to Make Them Work in TV Ads

I remember as a boy seeing an ad for a skincare brand. It showed a couple going for an autumn walk. One of them scrunched up an autumn leaf which fell to bits. Then the skincare cream was put on a similar leaf. It was scrunched up, but the leaf unfolded intact. I remember that sequence over forty years later. Demonstration sequences can be very powerful.

Around a third of all TV ads include product demonstrations and they can make a strong contribution to advertising effectiveness. But demonstrating product benefits is no guarantee of success. If demonstration sequences are dull or uninvolving — and particularly if they are not fully integrated into the storyline of the ad — they can actually be counter-productive, in terms of audience involvement and enjoyment.

Ads containing product demonstration are most widely used in Asia, accounting for 66% of all advertising in Thailand; and least popular in Northern Europe, making up only 15% of ads in Denmark.

What demonstration?

Sometimes, demonstrations are missed by the audience.

In Sweden, a diaper ad was tested with a demonstration sequence being central to the communication. Yet the demonstration was found to be the least interesting part of the ad. The key absorbency message was taken out by just 22%.

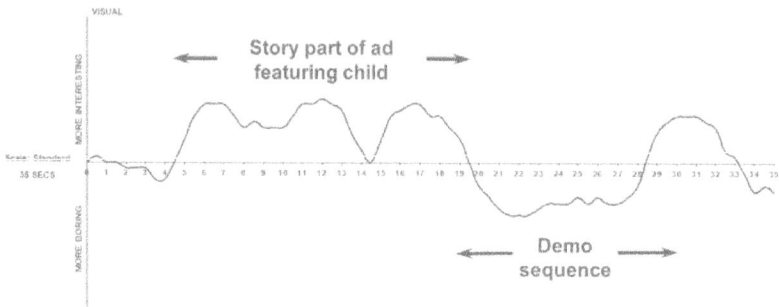

VISUAL

MORE INTERESTING

Story part of ad
featuring child

Scale: Standard
35 SECS

MORE BORING

Demo
sequence

KANTAR MILLWARDBROWN

In Poland another diaper ad was researched in two formats; one with and one without a demonstration sequence. The story related to a father holding a baby — and not getting wet because of the anti-leakage diaper. This scene was twice as well recalled in the version without the demo sequence, while the demonstration sequence itself was only weakly recalled. As a consequence, the version without the demonstration communicated the anti-leakage message better.

Viewers will only remember the parts of an ad that they find involving.

The problem with demonstration sequences is that, too often, they are dull and uninteresting, and not integrated into the main flow of the story. In this example, when respondents were asked what aspects of the ad stood out, the most memorable sequence related to the ad's main character. By contrast, the demonstration sequence was poorly recalled:

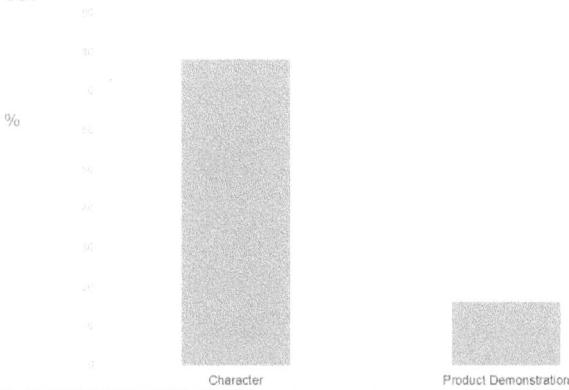

Stand out

%

Character   Product Demonstration

So, unless a way is found of making the demonstration sequence involving in itself, it is likely to be ineffective.

Three ways to make a demonstration effective

Product demonstrations can be made involving by ensuring that they:

Illustrate a highly relevant and different benefit

Form an integrated part of the ad's storyline

Are executed in an involving and distinctive way

To take each in turn . . .

Illustrating a highly relevant and different benefit

A skincare brand in Japan advertised a highly relevant product efficacy message. Interest in the ad revolved around two demonstration sequences:

Interest revolves around the product benefit

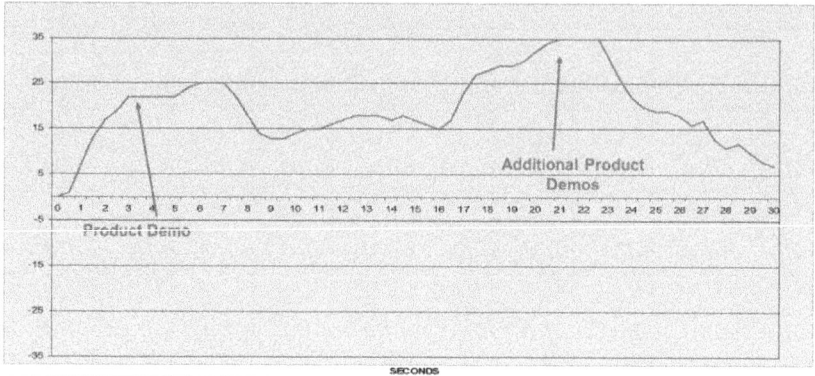

The message was seen to be highly relevant, credible, different, and new. As a result, the ad was highly persuasive and the resulting effect on sales was very strong:

Market share increased dramatically

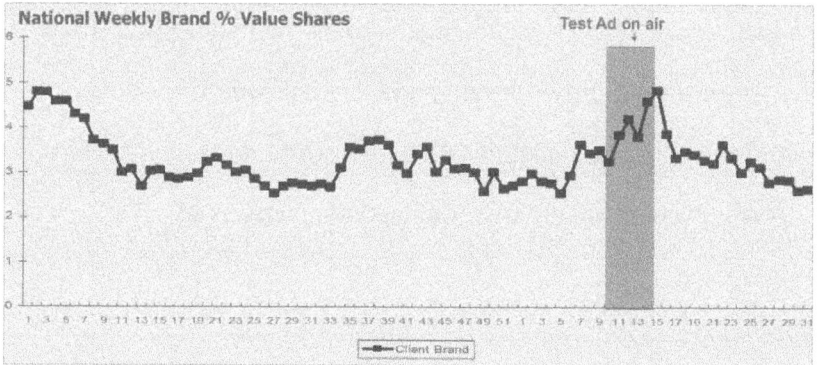

Integrating the demonstration into the story

Often, the most effective demonstration sequences are those that are integrated into the flow of the story. In this example from Australia, interest in the ad peaked during the product demonstration:

Interest trace peaks during product demonstration

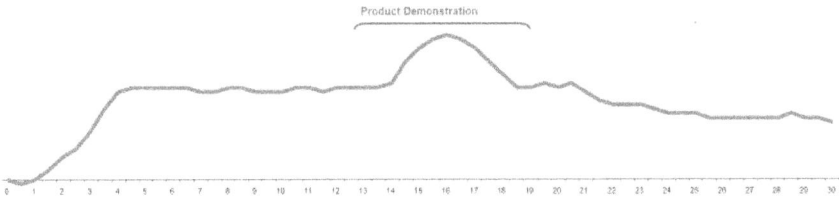

Product Demonstration

KANTAR MilWARDBROWN

The first part of the ad showed the main character experiencing a problem. The middle section showed him using the product, and the third part showed that the problem had been solved. As a result, spontaneous communication of the key benefit was high, at 72%.

How interesting is the demonstration sequence?

The third route is to ensure that the demonstration sequence is executed in an involving and creative way. For example, an Australian ad for panty liners was researched before it went on air. The ad featured a low-interest demonstration sequence, and communication of the intended 'flexible' message was weak (25%).

In the finished film, the demonstration sequence was made more visually interesting, and the voice-over was revised to focus on key points. As a result, the ad became more impactful and recall of the demonstration itself increased markedly from 11% to 44%. Communication of the 'flexible' message increased from 25% to 49%. Persuasion doubled.

So it is worth giving careful consideration the role and creative execution of demonstration sequences in your ads, and developing ways to make them more effective.

Branding in TV Advertising

In 2016 Birds Eye frozen foods brought back their well-established white-bearded Captain for a new advertising campaign, having not used him for ten years. Brand awareness and desire increased, and the campaign reversed a sales decline. As Brand Manager Steve Challouma observed, 'Make sure you mine your historic assets before you look at creating new ones.'

The extent to which consumers will remember that the ad was for a particular brand is a key aspect of effective TV ads. If people don't associate the ad with your brand, it is not likely to do you much benefit; and, worse, might actually benefit a competitor. Strong branding is not achieved through introducing the brand name early and often; instead it relies on creativity to integrate the brand, or a branding cue, into the ad.

In a European mobile phone market, Brand A's advertising was very poorly branded. When shown stills of the ad, over half of the respondents didn't know what brand it was for, and many thought the ad was for the main competitors. During the period this ad aired, consideration for Brand B outstripped consideration for Brand A for the first time; since Brand B had little spend over this period, it seems likely that this was at least in part due to misattribution of Brand A's ad.

So it is crucial that consumers remember what brand is being advertised.

As this range of branding scores given to ads show, the art of branding a TV ad isn't very widely understood:

The range of responses: from very strong to very weak

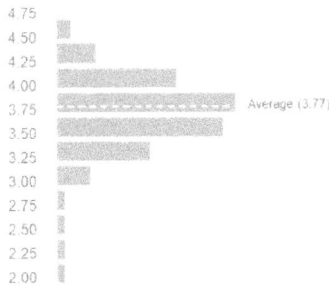

Base: 2494 UK ads

How can strong branding be achieved?

Some believe that the key thing is to show the brand name early and often. This is not the case.

Brand linkage is *not* related to the time at which the brand appears in the ad:

Brand linkage is *not* related to the time at which the brand appears in the ad

A: You couldn't help but remember the commercial was for brand

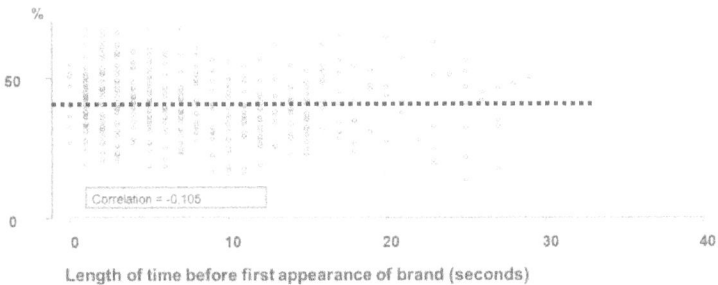

There is also little relationship between the number of brand appearances and the branding of the ad.

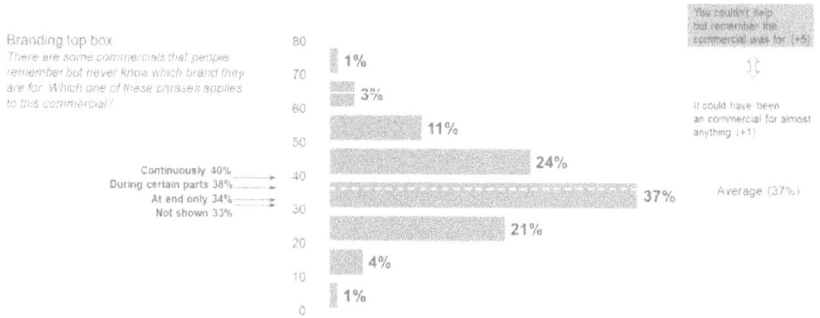

Little relationship between number of brand appearances and the branding score

Good branding is clearly not achieved by following a formula or by creating an entertaining ad in which the brand simply makes frequent appearances.

But, in that case, how do you create a strongly branded ad? The reality is more complex, and far more interesting.

The role of creativity

Neuroscience shows that we have a 'mental workspace' which holds information to be used in making decisions. However, only three or four items can be in this workspace at any time, so access is highly competitive — and many TV ads fail to get over the threshold.

Why? Because attention and emotion are the gatekeepers to access, and since most people aren't interested in ads per se, these need to be generated by the intelligent application of creativity.

But this in itself is not enough. The role of creativity is to ensure that the communication is associated with your brand in a way that is effortless for the consumer. And the key to achieving this is to ensure that the brand is integrated into the more memorable parts of the creative. The ad needs to highlight the brand in a distinctive, enjoyable and involving way.

There are many ways to do this.

One route involves characters using the product in an interesting way. If the characters find the brand — or the effects of the brand — enjoyable or involving, the viewers are more likely to become involved too. But the focus should be the brand, not the category as a whole, otherwise misattribution may result.

Branding cues (visual or aural devices that provide viewers with a shortcut to the brand) are another route. Such devices can take many forms, but the most common include the use of a celebrity, characters, music, or an animated brand icon. It is no coincidence that some of the best branded ads use established branding devices.

What's more, the use of established branding devices can be effective when incorporated in an ad for a variant, by efficiently delivering the parent brand cues, evoking warmth, and communicating core brand values.

But there are potential drawbacks to using a branding device: if the memories associated with it are too specific, it may be difficult to extend this device to new messages, or to product variants with different characteristics, under the same parent brand.

In addition, while the message of the advertising may be understood, the parent name, rather than that of the variant, may be recalled - because the branding device is associated in consumers' minds with the original brand name. It's also possible for branding devices to be overpowering, to swamp the overall communication of the ad; although with careful structuring this can usually be overcome.

Questions to ask if branding is an issue

If branding is a problem, there are a few aspects that can be explored:

- **Is the problem structural?** Is the brand not properly integrated into the story? It can often help to ask: 'can I describe this ad in a sentence without mentioning the brand (or an established branding cue)'. If you can, branding may be a problem.

- **Is the advertising idea at odds with the brand's essence?** Particularly if you are trying to reposition the brand, it may be that you need to make the brand connection absolutely explicit.

- **Is there enough signposting through the ad?** Perhaps the advertising idea is clear enough to you, having lived with it for the past few months, but do consumers need more help to understand the story?

Humour in Advertising

Several years ago the UK supermarket Sainsbury's used John Cleese shouting through a megaphone in a series of ads. Cleese was highly respected as a funny man, and the ads were intended to make the country laugh. But the ads were voted the most irritating of the year in a Marketing magazine poll. Sainsbury's admitted the campaign had failed to hit sales targets.

Humour can undoubtedly be used very effectively in advertising. Funny ads are more likely to be enjoyable and involving, and hence memorable, than others. But, as with all creativity, humour needs to be used with care. To be successful, it must help focus on the brand and the intended communication; otherwise, it can detract from the ad's effectiveness. In addition, humour works differently around the world and across different audiences — which may limit the ability of a funny ad to be used in several markets.

Do funny ads work better?

Broadly speaking, funny ads are more likely to be memorable than others. Almost half of the world's most impactful ads are humorous; whereas just 1% of the least impactful ads are humorous. Furthermore, humour is an emotional response, and much has been written on the importance of emotional responses to advertising.

But the effect of humour on communication is not so straightforward.

Certainly, humour can aid effective communication. For example, one ad was criticised for being boring and irritating, with a joke that was just not funny. Enjoyment was below average. While there was much in the ad that did work well, the ad needed more original humour. A new version was produced which included a more original joke at the beginning of the ad. The enjoyment rating improved, and so did the communication levels. The improved humour was resulting in more attention being paid to the ad overall.

But it is also possible for humour to hinder communication. When the humour is unrelated to the key message, it may 'swamp' the ad, resulting in the message being lost.

There are no rules here; each case needs to be judged on its merits, with a careful consideration of the focus of the ad. So, overall, there is no direct relationship between using humour in an ad and the ad's ability to communicate a message.

How well does humour travel?

For advertisers considering the use of humour, there are some important differences between countries.

Consumers in Spain, the Netherlands and Chile are far more likely to be exposed to funny ads than those in other countries, whereas humour is far less likely to be used in China. And in countries used to a lot of humour in their advertising, humour fares particularly well; the most successful ads are even more likely to be funny.

However, humour is subjective and often culturally specific. There are very few sources of humour that are found funny universally.

Several types of humour find it difficult to travel, including mockery, humour dependent on subtleties, parodies, kitsch, slapstick, off-the-wall and dark humour.

In addition, there are some specific country issues. For example: in China sarcasm is not widely appreciated; the English have a particular love of irony; in Singapore humour based on sexuality is taboo; and images found sexy in most of Europe may be considered sexist by British women.

So, in view of all this, is it possible for humour to work across markets? It can, providing:

- The subject matter is universal

- The references used are universally understood (e.g. young romance, new baby)

- The subject is not offensive or taboo

- The humour is visually based, rather than relying on anything that may be lost in translation

Humour among men and women

While advertising can be seen as equally funny by both sexes, there may also be marked differences, particularly with scatological, violent or sexist humour.

In the example below, where the humour focused on body parts being pulled off, men found it distinctive, involving and interesting, whereas women considered it disturbing, unpleasant and irritating:

Huge difference in response between men and women

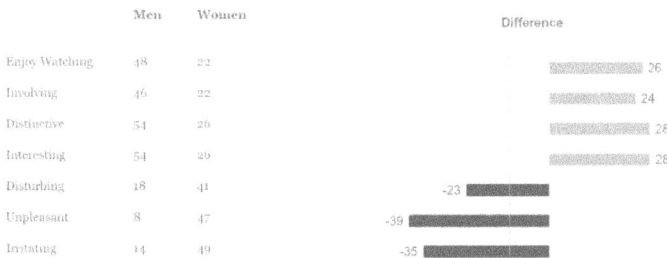

	Men	Women	Difference
Enjoy Watching	48	22	26
Involving	46	22	24
Distinctive	54	26	28
Interesting	54	26	28
Disturbing	18	41	-23
Unpleasant	8	47	-39
Irritating	14	49	-35

One form of humour that women can find particularly enjoyable is jokes at the expense of men. As an example, in Brazil, buyers of fabric conditioners tend to be traditional housewives, and humour is rarely used in the category. One ad, showing a man doing the washing while the woman relaxed watching TV, was greatly appreciated, being seen as involving, distinctive and interesting by housewives.

The right media for humour

With online advertising, when many consumers skip an ad as soon as they can, humour can be a great device to overcome this tendency. In a Kantar Millward Brown AdReaction global study, humour was given as the top reason for not skipping ads.

While humour can work across all media, some are more private and some more public — so consideration needs to be given to how your humour will be best received.

A Nestle condensed milk ad in Australia featuring a semi-naked good-looking man making a cake was appreciated better when people could watch on the privacy of their mobile phone screens, rather than on a TV screen.

In the UK, one ad based upon a crude joke, was aired in two adjoining regions; but in one it aired on TV, while in the other it appeared only in the cinema. The demographic profile of respondents was similar, but those who saw it in the cinema enjoyed the ad more than those who viewed it on TV. Choice of media can have a substantial influence on the effect of the humour.

Humour can be very effective when used well. But as the Sainsbury's example at the start of this chapter illustrates, the first step is to ensure that your target audience finds the humour funny.

What are the Pitfalls of Using Sexual Imagery in Advertising?

One of the most successful ads I researched was one for Magnum ice cream. The ad featured a young couple kissing. The man goes off to buy a condom, but sees a machine selling Magnums, and buys one instead of the condoms. The ad brilliantly conveyed the sensual nature of the ice cream. 'It's better than sex,' as one respondent said.

Using sexual imagery in an ad campaign, especially one aimed at the mainstream audience, is a risk that should be carefully considered and measured. While it can grab attention and help position a brand, there are significant drawbacks to be considered; the acceptability of sexually charged images varies considerably across cultures. Women can find ads that portray them in subservient roles offensive. Additionally, the sexual content may overshadow the intended message.

The benefits of sexual imagery

The use of (typically female) nudity and sexuality in advertising copy dates back to the 1870s. Today, the images may look a little different, and are often somewhat more explicit — but the role that sex plays in marketing communications remains unchanged.

Sexual imagery can grab attention and, depending on how it is represented, imbue a promoted brand with qualities of desirability, sensuality, youth, vitality and indulgence. This is more typically utilized by high fashion and luxury brands, as well as indulgence foods such as ice cream and chocolate. The use of sexual imagery in advertising can also convey the effect (direct or otherwise) that a product or service will have on the users' attractiveness to the opposite sex.

A good example is the Lynx brand in the U.K. (Axe elsewhere). After years of conveying sexual imagery in its advertising, the brand has a sexy, fun and playful personality.

What is positive about the brand?

2007 - UK - Deodorant (Male) - Lynx

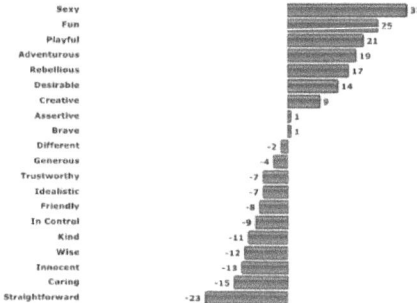

Sexy	33
Fun	25
Playful	21
Adventurous	19
Rebellious	17
Desirable	14
Creative	9
Assertive	1
Brave	1
Different	-2
Generous	-4
Trustworthy	-7
Idealistic	-7
Friendly	-8
In Control	-9
Kind	-11
Wise	-12
Innocent	-13
Caring	-15
Straightforward	-23

(Base 365)

KANTAR MILLWARDBROWN

The risks of sexual imagery

While viewer reaction may be strong, it is not always positive. In the same way that consumers react to humor, the reaction to sexual themes is individual and personal. As a result, a scenario which can surprise and interest some viewers, can irritate and offend others. An offensive ad can be banned from air and worse, it can leave an unintended negative sentiment even among the brand's users.

In an ad for an indulgence food targeting young adults, the sexual imagery used in the ad was moody, edgy and dark. The ad was found involving, but, for a significant proportion of respondents the involvement was negative. For them, the tone and images were disturbing, unpleasant and irritating. Even among the under-35 age group, one in three viewers described the style as too provocative.

Sexual imagery can be a distraction

Because of the attraction that sexual content wields, it can easily overshadow the intended brand and communications. An example of this is an ad aired in Germany to launch a variant of a food brand. The ad was provocative, featuring three nude people. Understandably, it caused quite a stir. Its performance was tracked to show that while the creative was well recognized, the message was missed. Despite the attention it commanded, the execution was unsuccessful at supporting the launch.

Cultural differences

The acceptance of sexual content in advertising varies greatly across cultures. A review of ads across the globe shows that use of sexuality in advertising should be carefully considered to fit cultural norms, target market and brand values. Without a sound understanding of how the consumer will react to the creative, the use of sexuality can be a risky strategy. Cultures differ markedly in their attitudes to sex and nudity in general and to its use in media and advertising.

One personal care brand used a campaign featuring sexual imagery globally, to great success; enjoyment, appeal and branding were all above average — except in Asia, where the campaign's performance was weaker than the previous ads.

In China, strong sexual imagery does not work and could turn people off. This culture views sex as something that is alluring, but only when it supports wider views on love, marriage, career and success. The brand provenance plays a role; foreign brands can (in the eyes of consumers) have greater license to explore their sexual side, but not Chinese brands. Another issue is that advertising content is strongly controlled by the state so advertisers need to understand local censorship laws.

An ad for an indulgence food targeted at Malaysian women failed because it did not resonate with how the target market related to sexual imagery. Indulgence was depicted within a sexualized intimacy between a woman and a man where the women showed preference for the food. Young Malay women rejected the ad because they found the sexualized behavior unrealistic and outside their moral code.

This is not just an issue in the conservative cultures of the Middle East and Asia, it can also be observed across seemingly homogenous Western markets. Lycra (stretch fabric) was promoted across Europe as 'adding comfort to clothes.' The textile is most recognized for its use in underwear, hence fittingly, the creative featured beautiful women being active in various states of undress. The ad was hugely enjoyable to the female Italian viewers but failed to impress U.K. women who disliked it because it was too sexy — and even sexist.

Similarly, a TV advertisement for a skincare product was researched in Germany and the U.K. The ad featured a naked woman dancing in the shower while using the product. Whilst the scenario was liked by women in Germany, the English scored the ad significantly below average, largely because they disliked the woman.

It is worth noting that in the U.K. 20–25% of the ads that the Independent Television Commission (the official body) receives complaints about feature sexuality that was deemed inappropriate for a general audience or demeaning to a particular gender — typically women.

One ad for a shower gel in Germany featured a nude female. To illustrate her pleasure at using the product, a voice-over moaning with pleasure was added. As this approach had not been attempted by the brand before, the same copy but without the moaning soundtrack was tested at the same time. The difference in results was clear. While the version of the ad with moaning was significantly more engaging some found it unpleasant and irritating; 20% specifically said they disliked the girl moaning. More importantly, a quarter of viewers exposed to this version said the brand was less appealing to them after viewing the ad.

An ad aimed at German teens featured nudity within a context of a beach scene. This was criticized by a number of viewers, but otherwise the ad performed well. The execution was re-cut with a less explicit beach scene and researched again. The dislikes of the ad were minimized, and the positive aspects relating to the humour and communication were unchanged. The ad's impact improved.

The gender divide

Men respond very actively to images of female nudity. An ad for Nivea deodorant is a good example. The ad showed a woman rushing to get dressed in time to greet her date who is making his way up to her apartment. It's an entertaining ad which performed well overall, but what is interesting here is that for the male sample, interest peaked each time the visuals shifted to the semi-dressed woman, and dipped as soon as the scene changed to the man. This pattern was repeated throughout the entire sequence. In contrast, female interest was related to the story line.

When used in ads targeted at men, sexual imagery commonly references 'conquest'. Quite often this is accompanied by visuals of attractive and sexualized women. While this can appeal to the male audience, it can alienate the female consumer. An ad for a confectionary product was found offensive by a high proportion of women. The source of the offence was not nudity or implied sexual behaviour per se, rather it was the portrayal of the female characters as sexually subservient to a group of males.

Avoid upsetting the mainstream audience through media choice

If your target market can be reached during a particular TV programme, or via an online site, then ads featuring sexual content could be delivered this way. Additionally, as covered in the previous chapter, people can respond more positively when they can view an ad with sexual content in the relative privacy of a mobile device.

In the U.K., an ad for IKEA was found to be polarizing in terms of humor. The ad featured a near-naked couple caught playing 'farmyard' by their children. The kids' embarrassment at catching their parents in a sexual romp was not comfortable for everyone, and many found the ad disturbing, shocking or repelling; but, in a study covering 29 ads, the IKEA as was the second most likely to be passed on.

Making the Best use of Music in an Ad

A few years ago, I was involved in a project where we asked UK consumers what memories and associations they had with Cornetto ice cream (we didn't reference advertising). A quarter of the respondents mentioned music from the advertising, a variant of *O Sole Mio*. What made this result particularly remarkable is that when we conducted the research the music had not been used by the brand for 12 years.

Music can be a powerful enhancement for an ad, when it is used well. Although the use of music does not automatically confer benefits, the inspired use of the right music can affect every aspect of an ad's performance.

Music is a regular component of TV advertising. About seven in ten ads in the Kantar Millward Brown database have some form of music, but it varies enormously across the world, ranging from around 95% in Romania and the Ukraine, to under 40% in Denmark, Serbia and Montenegro, India and Egypt.

While most ads have some music, at an overall level its presence or absence has very little impact on the commercial's performance.

However, the use of music which has been specifically adapted for the brand can boost levels of enjoyment. So too can the use of well-known music. For one client, two versions of an ad for a mobile phone network were tested. The ads were identical, except for the choice of music. One used a well-known song, *Teenage Kicks*, the other used a song that had not been a hit. The differences were clear: the *Teenage Kicks* soundtrack positively benefitted both rational and emotional responses.

Positive reaction to music track helped generate a stronger response

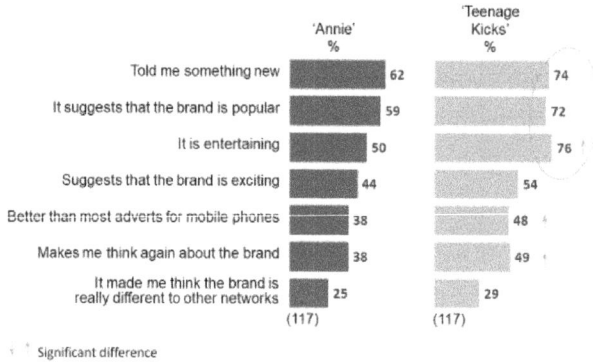

	'Annie' %	'Teenage Kicks' %
Told me something new	62	74
It suggests that the brand is popular	59	72
It is entertaining	50	76
Suggests that the brand is exciting	44	54
Better than most adverts for mobile phones	38	48
Makes me think again about the brand	38	49
It made me think the brand is really different to other networks	25	29
	(117)	(117)

Significant difference

KANTAR MILLWARDBROWN

However, this result is not guaranteed. An ad for a skincare brand featured the well-known music *Bittersweet Symphony* by The Verve. It performed well. Two alternative versions were also tested with unknown music. One performed significantly worse, but the other performed as well as the Bittersweet Symphony edit.

The way the music is used can have a powerful effect on the levels of interest in the ad. In Australia an ad for a non-alcoholic beverage featured a well-known piece of music. While the visual pace of the ad remained fairly level throughout, the music began after the first six seconds of the execution and built in intensity. The music then stopped for about five seconds, before continuing quietly in the background for the remainder of the ad. The chart below, showing levels of interest throughout the ad, clearly demonstrates the impact the music had on interest in the ad.

Interest closely reflects the changing use of music

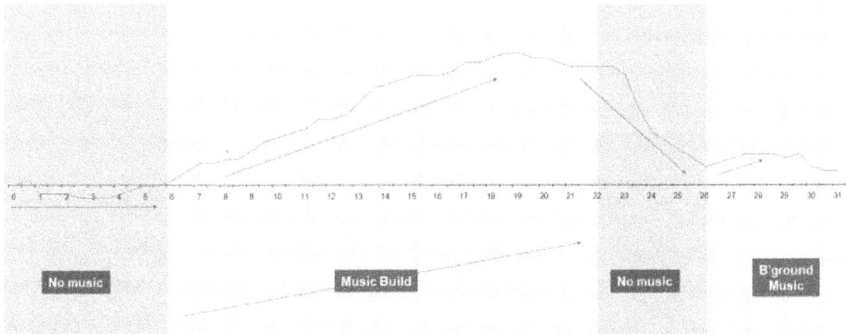

Branding

When the music has been used previously in ads for the brand, branding scores tend to be slightly higher. Also, incorporating the brand name into the music can have a beneficial effect on branding. The use of jingles also aids branding. It's interesting to note that despite this there has been a decline in the use of jingles.

Music can provide a powerful influence on branding. An ad for Soft and Gentle deodorant featured the song *Move Closer*. The song was well liked and was a focus of recall from the ad, but branding of the ad was weak. The ad was re-edited, with the words 'soft and gentle' being included prominently in the song. The ad's branding greatly improved.

Understanding

Overall, music has little effect on levels of understanding of an ad. However, music can hinder understanding. An ad for a brand of beer was tested in two edits; one featured mellow music, the other featured upbeat music. The version with mellow music was enjoyed more and was considered easier to understand. Analysis showed this was because the upbeat music drowned out some of the key parts of the conversation in the ad; respondents were unable to follow the story.

Communication

Overall, there is little evidence that the use of music aids communication, even when it is connected to the message.

Nonetheless, on an individual basis, there are exceptions to this pattern. Two ads were tested in the U.K. for a car launch. The ads were identical except for the music. One used the well-known song *Anything You Can Do*, the other a song less well-known. Responses to the ad were markedly different. Communication from the *Anything You Can Do* edit focused far more on an argument between the characters in the ad, whereas the alternative version was less confrontational. Consequently, the ad with the less well-known music produced far stronger results and was the version that was successfully aired.

Persuasion

Overall, the use of music has no effect on persuasion; however, in specific instances, if the right choice of music enhances communication, it can improve persuasion. In one ad researched for a brand of ice cream a change in music highlighted a change in atmosphere in the ad, which helped clarify the story and enhance the communication, which contained a strong new message. Persuasion was already strong, but grew much stronger.

Enjoyment of the music

Choosing music that is liked can boost an ad. Looking at U.K. and U.S. ads, when the music is enjoyed, the ads are enjoyed more and are more memorable.

The edit

The way the music is used can also have a major effect. In the U.S., ads in a campaign for a food brand all featured the same song, but in different edits, with some being more upbeat than others. While the ads with the most upbeat music were enjoyed the most and were found to be the most involving, branding and communication were strongest when the mid-paced music was used.

It isn't just the song that counts, the part of the song you use can make a difference. One brand made two edits of an ad, both featuring the Monty Python song *Always Look on the Bright Side of Life*. One focused on the upbeat chorus, while the other included the downbeat verse 'If life seems jolly rotten...'. Since the ad was structured around a problem/solution scenario, this latter approach was more suitable. Enjoyment of the ad grew from 42% to 59%.

Wear-out

One issue facing ads which are reliant on music is the possibility of wear-out. Wear-out is rarely seen in TV ads; however, when the ad is reliant on a fashionable song, an eye needs to be kept on that fashion. An ad for a confectionery brand was focused around a hit song. It was aired in three bursts over two years and targeted teenagers. By the third burst, endorsement of *It's amusing* had dropped from 81% to 63%, enjoyment from 71% to 56%, and a quarter found the ad irritating.

Music can be hugely beneficial for advertising, but only when its role has been carefully thought through.

Celebrity-Based Ad Campaigns: what are the Pros and Cons?

For many years, the supermarket Sainsbury's used the celebrity chef Jamie Oliver to front its campaign. The fit was good, and Oliver had strong appeal. Sales modelling showed the campaign delivered £1.12 billion in incremental revenue.

Celebrities are used in advertising around the world. The right celebrity, used in the right way, can undoubtedly be a powerful brand asset. But using a celebrity does not guarantee effective advertising; overall, there's very little difference between the performance of ads with celebrities versus those without. However, celebrities can make *campaigns* more effective. There are pitfalls to using celebrities. To gauge whether a celebrity is right for your brand, you need to establish whether they are known, whether they are liked, and what they stand for, among your target audience.

Where are celebrities used in advertising?

The use of celebrities in advertising varies enormously around the world. It continues to be highest in Asia Pacific. In terms of individual countries, use is highest in Japan and Korea, where around 40% of TV ads feature celebrities; and lowest in Norway, Austria, Croatia, Kazakhstan, El Salvador and Costa Rica, where the proportion is under 3%. It is 31% in China, 23% in India, 11% in the U.S., and 11% in the UK.

While celebrities are less likely to be used for medical ads, there is little other pattern of celebrity use by category.

The type of celebrity used varies a lot by region. Movie stars are particularly popular in Asia, notably Japan. TV presenters are particularly popular in the UK; while sports stars are more common in the US.

Are they effective?

Celebrity-based campaigns can be very effective. The Snickers 'You're not you when you're hungry' campaign won a Cannes Lion Creative Effectiveness award; as did Virgin Mobile Australia for their 'Fair Go Bro' campaign featuring Doug Pitt, the brother of Brad Pitt. In the US, one client had used a celebrity in some of its ads over a ten year period and wanted to know if they should continue the relationship. The ads featuring the celebrity performed better on key measures than those without the celebrity, and the celebrity had become a strong branding cue. It was estimated that the celebrity was worth over $5 million per year to the client. After an ROI calculation, the client continued the relationship.

An in-depth analysis of Twitter volumes and sentiment for 16 brands across 5 countries found that celebrities are one of the drivers of short-term buzz; celebrity associations and endorsements are likely to increase positive sentiment for the brand in the short term.

Whilst most of these effects are largely short term, a successful celebrity-brand partnership can also strengthen social buzz in the long term. In February 2014, Mila Kunis was announced as the new face of Jim Beam and featured in a number of ads and videos for the brand. Kantar Millward Brown was able to quantify that this was an efficient use of the brand's marketing budget, and delivered a greater return on investment in both the short term and the long term.

While individual celebrity campaigns can be highly effective, there is very little difference overall between the performance on most key measures of ads with celebrities versus those without. Some regions, notably the US and Central and Eastern Europe, find celebrity ads slightly more involving; but in other regions, particularly where celebrity ads are more common, this is not the case. Overall, branding levels tend to be similar.

However, Kantar Millward Brown's CrossMedia database suggests that *campaigns* with celebrities tend to be more effective than campaigns without. Why should this be? It seems the presence of a celebrity can provide an instant link to other elements of the campaign, promoting synergy. But other audio and visual elements can also provide that 'instant link'.

For some long-running campaigns, particular celebrities can have, over time, become synonymous with the brand: for example, William Shatner and Priceline in the US, Gary Lineker and Walkers in the UK, Carina Lau and the cosmetic brand SK-II in China.

In Japan, however, branding scores tend to be slightly lower for ads with celebrities — possibly due to the celebrities endorsing too many brands.

Ads featuring celebrities are no more likely to be seen as conveying new, relevant, credible news than others; so, unsurprisingly, they are no more persuasive than other ads.

Three key questions for the effective use of celebrities

Given that using a celebrity does not guarantee a successful ad, what are the guidelines for getting it right? I'd say there are three key questions you need to answer.

Who is the celebrity?

Where the celebrity is central to the core idea, it's important to establish how well known they are among your target audience. In the US, a lipstick brand was launched using a British model. Among those who recognized her, communication, enjoyment and purchase intent were much stronger. However, less than a quarter of the audience recognized the model, severely limiting the effectiveness of the campaign. Overall, the effect of the fame of the celebrities differs by country: for instance, in the US and UK, well known celebrities can help slightly with branding. However, in China (Shanghai) there is little difference in key measures whether the celebrity is well recognised or not.

Is the celebrity well-liked?

While it isn't essential for a celebrity to be liked, this can have a significant impact on the emotional response to an ad. A snack food brand in Turkey wanted to explore whether to use celebrities in their campaign. They researched two ads, both with and without celebrities. The presence of a (much liked) celebrity made a slight difference to the first ad, improving its enjoyment and impact; but the celebrity in the second ad was perceived to be pretentious and arrogant, and had almost no effect on the ad's performance; both versions performed poorly.

The effectiveness of likeable celebrities is more similar across countries: enjoyment is higher when the celebrity is liked, in all countries. In the US, UK, China and India salience is also higher. Branding is higher in India, Russia and the UK when the celebrity is liked, and understanding in the US and India. All countries tend to see higher scores across persuasive measures when the celebrity is liked.

In particular the likability of the celebrity needs to be assessed among the target audience. In one project for a cereal brand in the UK, Kantar Millward Brown asked about celebrities who were considered positive role models. One particular male TV and radio presenter was rated highly; but this ranking was driven by the 40+ age group. When an animatic version of an ad for the brand featuring him was researched, he was dismissed by the younger target respondents as being too old and old fashioned. In the ad he played with a younger woman's hair; a scene which respondents found disturbing and uncomfortable. The ad was not produced.

What does the celebrity represent?

It's important to understand how well the celebrity fits with the brand, or with where you want to take the brand. When the celebrity is perceived to be appropriate, communication can be enhanced.

One automotive brand in India was looking for the most suitable celebrity to use to represent its brand values and aspirations. Kantar Millward Brown explored which celebrities were best known across India, which were most popular on Twitter and Facebook, and how many brands they each already endorsed. But their personalities were also explored, to establish which was the best fit with the brand. The client followed the recommendation, and saw an almost immediate improvement on brand health and sales.

Potential pitfalls

Unlike an animated character, celebrities are human, and subject to human failings. So there are a number of ways in which a celebrity could become a liability to the brand.

The Chinese athlete Liu Xiang was in the London Olympics, but had apparently disguised an injury; the injury flared up and he had to pull out. Chinese public opinion turned against him for his perceived dishonestly, and a year later was still far from recovering.

Other examples of celebrity activities potentially damaging a brand include: OJ Simpson, the face of Hertz, being charged with murdering his ex-wife, Nicole Brown Simpson; Whoopi Goldberg, failing to lose weight while endorsing Slim-Fast; Tiger Woods' adulterous affairs and a public divorce from his wife. Brands are quick to distance themselves from such issues. In early 2016, when Maria Sharapova failed a drugs test, brands she had promoted such as Nike, Tag Heuer and Porsche all distanced themselves from her within 24 hours.

In addition, there is always the risk of a celebrity becoming the hero of an ad, rather than the brand. A new campaign was developed for a tea brand in India, featuring popular movie actors. Kantar Millward Brown researched two versions of the ads in animatic forms; one with the celebrities, and one without. The research showed that, in the versions with the celebrities, the message takeout was weaker; the celebrities were 'drowning out' the communication. And while the celebrities were intended to help gain attention, the versions without celebrities were just as impactful. The client went ahead and filmed and aired versions without celebrities.

But experience suggests that this tends to be more an issue of ad structure than the fame of the celebrity. Testimonial ads, for example, with their clear focus on the brand, rarely suffer this problem. But the celebrity needs to come across as likeable and genuine, or the endorsement may lack credibility.

Alternatively, the celebrity may just be a poor choice. In the UK, two ads were tested for a brand. They had identical scripts, but one featured a genuine former pop star, while the other featured an actor playing the part of an old pop star. The version with the actor was preferred. The celebrity was considered inappropriate and weakened the credibility of the ad.

However, the right celebrity, used in the right way, can be a powerful brand asset; in any country, in any category.

Is there Value in Comparative Advertising?

A pet supply company in the United States developed two ads with very different creative elements and storylines, but both mentioned why a specific competitive product was inferior. Both ads were extremely persuasive. The competitive comparison message resonated with consumers and came through at levels well above average, helping drive the motivating power of the ads. The fact that the ads had different creatives yet were both very persuasive underscored the value of the competitive comparison.

Comparative advertising (comparing the advertised brand with a named or unnamed competitor to make it look superior or more appealing) can be effective even when it does not disclose the name of the specific competitor. However, caution should be taken before employing a comparative ad strategy. There are some common pitfalls that can introduce risk to the advertised brand.

Many countries outside the United States have banned advertising that makes a comparison with a specific competitor (although advertisers can still reference undisclosed competitors). In the United States, advertising that mentions named competitors is tightly regulated and must be 'substantiated, truthful and not misleading'.

From Kantar Millward Brown's Link™ copy testing database, I estimate 4% of ads can be classified as comparative advertising. The United States, India and the Philippines have a higher proportion of comparative ads (7%). The European figure is slightly below average.

Do comparative ads work?

Comparative ads can be effective. Overall they are slightly better than others in conveying the key benefit of a brand, even when the competitor's name is not disclosed; probably because the format encourages a focus on the key benefit.

What to watch out for

The acceptability of comparative ads will vary from country to country depending on culture. In some countries comparisons are seen as arrogant and inappropriate, and so should be avoided. Even in accepting cultures, employing competitive comparisons can be a risky strategy, particularly when you are naming a specific competitor.

Misattribution should be a concern. We know that people watch ads passively, and there is a danger that the positive points you want to communicate about your brand could be attributed to your competitor.

Comparative advertising generally works best in categories where benefits are very rational and there is very little emotional benefit. A well-remembered claim for efficacy could be enough to influence brand choice at the point of purchase. However, this type of ad almost inevitably provides fewer opportunities to build the emotional values of brands.

Here are a few 'rules of thumb' based on qualitative findings:

> The big guy should not be seen to be picking on the little guy.

> The advertising should not be mean-spirited.

> It is best to use symbols for competitor brands rather than the actual products or brand names. This limits the potential for misattribution and liability for defamation of character, since you are not directly attacking a competitor.

Comparative advertising gone too far

Some comparative advertising crosses a line and makes an unsubstantiated negative claim about a competitor. Commonly referred to as a 'smear campaign', this represents an intentional attempt to undermine a competitor's reputation, credibility or image.

This was seen in Mexico when a new yogurt brand claimed that the leading brand in the category caused weight gain. While the category leader's name was not mentioned, and its package was not shown in the advertising, there were some obvious brand cues which made it clear which brand it was. The negative message about the category leader got through to consumers (although the new brand's own message did not) and sales decreased for the category leader and the category as a whole, while the new brand enjoyed a steady increase.

The category leader fought back with advertising which convinced consumers that it would not cause weight gain and did so without counter-attacking the new brand. At the same time, the category leader took legal action against the new brand to have the negative spot removed from air.

The category leader's sales recovered, while the new brand could not sustain its sales increase.

Lessons learned from smear campaigns

Attack claims can be considered morally wrong in some cultures and may backfire. Additionally, communicating negative messages about a competitor may overshadow the brand's own message. It can even have a negative impact on the category as a whole.

If attacked, a brand should defend its reputation but do so without counter-attacking the other brand.

Successful International Advertising

One French brand developed a very successful ad featuring a divining rod. They decided to use the ad elsewhere; but it bombed in Thailand. It took only a little research to discover that divining rods were not understood in Thailand. The ad needed to be adapted to use locally understood symbols.

For global businesses, the financial benefits of producing ads that can be aired internationally are obvious. But several key factors — ranging from differences in brand status to cultural issues — may prevent an ad which works well at home from achieving success abroad. However, there are a number of models and routes that can be used to produce great international advertising.

Transferring is hard

Analysis of Kantar Millward Brown's Link database shows that an ad strong in one country has only around a 1 in 3 chance of being strong in a second country. These are not good odds to invest against, especially when the pay-back for effective adaptation is high.

To take the US as an example; the ability of ads to transfer to or from the US varies enormously; from 30% in Shanghai to 72% in Australia (incidentally, it is worth noting that US ads tend to transfer better to many European countries than they do to US Hispanics).

Why might an ad not transfer?

For any global business aiming to create great international advertising, the starting point must be to understand the factors known to affect ad transferability:

1. The status of a brand is one of the major influences on the kind of communications that are effective for it. Ads with only an implicit message tend to work best in countries where the brand is very highly regarded and familiar; where the brand can assume the consumer will fill in the gaps based on what they already know and feel about the

brand. In countries where the brand is new or less well known, consumers tend to respond less well to this kind of advertising. This is one reason why advertising for an established brand in one country is unlikely to work effectively to launch the brand in another country.

2. Socio-economic factors, such as differences in disposable income, can have a major effect on how people respond to messages for discretionary products.

3. The marketing and advertising experience of consumers in a country can have a major influence on how they respond to ads. The kinds of advertising consumers see every day varies enormously between countries and this often shapes both what they expect from ads and how they interpret them. For example, advertising in Honduras, Mexico, Poland, Hungary, El Salvador and Slovakia is over three times more likely to be intended to be funny than in many Asian countries. Additionally, ads where the message is not overtly expressed and requires a degree of 'advertising literacy' on the part of the viewer tend to work better in countries where advertising with implicit messages is commonplace — and less well in those where consumers are accustomed to more 'direct' ads.

4. Category experience may vary in different parts of the world. For example, in some countries, owning a washing machine is not the norm, so an ad showing one in use in a domestic setting won't be appropriate. One food brand developed an ad in the UK which focussed on dipping the product in a sauce. It performed well, so they tested it in the French market. Consumers were baffled – they didn't have the same tradition of dipping food in sauces.

5. Consumer identification — particularly in relation to ethnic type — is an issue in some countries, where ads featuring indigenous actors are more acceptable to consumers (particularly for personal care products, where people want to be reassured about the brand's suitability for their hair or skin type). Additionally, brands which market themselves as American may not be well received in some

parts of the world; while, similarly, Muslim colas will not be universally appreciated.

6. The degree of clutter in the market may have a bearing on the success of international ads in getting noticed. Ads in countries with high levels of clutter, like Japan and the USA, have weaker cut through than countries where clutter is low, such as Denmark and Belgium. In other words, advertising has less impact per GRP because it has to fight for attention. This has implications for the level of media investment required to have an effect and for the type of advertising that will cut through.

7. Cultural differences are another factor that influence how international ads perform outside their home territory. One obvious difference is in attitudes to sex; for instance, just within Europe, I have seen strongly sexual ads perform well in Germany and Italy, but not in Finland or the U.K.. Many parts of Africa are very community minded; public mockery (even just the mildest joke) are not acceptable. Brazil is seen as a sensual country; but it is also religious, and it is still taboo to use sexuality in ads.

Organising for success

In tackling the challenges of international advertising, I have seen four internal structure models working well.

Controlled

Here a highly centralized team is responsible for brand positioning, advertising ideas, and creative executions. The role of local markets is pretty much limited to translation. It could be that the brand has two centralised teams; one for developed and one for emerging markets.

Adaptive

Here there is a centrally developed brand positioning, and centrally developed advertising idea; but executions are developed locally, taking into account brand or market cultural differences.

Contageous

Again, there is a centrally developed brand positioning, but successful locally developed advertising ideas and executions are shared and adapted, crucially, encouraged by the central team.

Local

Here, advertising ideas and even aspects of positioning are locally developed, and all executions are local. The central team shares learning and facilitates knowledge exchange

Which model?

All four models can be effective; but the organisation needs to be clear about which model is being used, to help avoid friction.

In deciding which model is most appropriate for your brand, there are two main questions to ask.

Is the category equally developed everywhere? In some markets, such as Turkey, waxing and root hair removal are well known and accepted. While in others, including Russia, the use of razors is more common. So messaging for root removal needs to be adapted to account for the different environments.

Does the brand have a consistent status everywhere? Some brands, such as Coca-Cola, Pampers, and the iPhone, have a consistent positioning around the world; but many brands do not have this status. In that case, is it possible to cluster countries by the task to be done? Brand status has been found to have a considerable influence on the kind of communications that are effective for a brand. The example below illustrates this approach, showing the world segmented into three regions according to the status of a particular brand; note these clusters do not represent traditional geographic divisions:

Cluster one — USA, Mexico, Brazil, Poland, South Africa; consumers know what the brand stands for (high efficacy), but this is not enough — it is seen as a category entry-point only. The brand needs to finds additional benefits or find more differentiating ways to talk about efficacy.

Cluster two — Argentina, U.K., Germany, Turkey, Australia; consumers know what the brand stands for, but don't feel close to it. The brand needs to become more emotionally appealing.

Cluster three — Chile, France, Italy, Japan, Thailand; the brand is relatively unknown, there is a need to establish what the brand stands for.

In each cluster of countries, the advertising task is clearly different — although it is possible that, in cases like this, the same advertising idea could work well for more than one cluster (e.g. advertising that differentiates the brand in an emotionally appealing way could work well for clusters one and two).

Clusters by brand status

- The first 'cluster'
- The second 'cluster'
- The third 'cluster'

Source: Kantar Millward Brown case study

KANTAR MILLWARDBROWN

Successful routes

There are several routes we've seen for developing successful global advertising.

Functional benefits

It is extremely difficult to discover/leverage customer insights at a global level. Differentiating functional benefits can be the start point – when they exist. In which case, advertising should clearly demonstrate the unique product benefit. Brands like Gillette, L'Oreal and Head and Shoulders have successfully adopted this approach. This can be an effective and successful strategy when there is a genuine product-based advantage.

Global Culture

Aspects of global culture can be used successfully in international advertising. **Movies,** especially big Hollywood productions, are seen all over the world. Many brands, like Pepsi, have successfully exploited the global obsession with sport, particularly football. In an age when **Celebrities** can be known globally, their use in advertising is widespread. **Youth culture and music** represent another way of uniting audiences across the globe. Coke was one of the first brands to use this approach with their 'I want to teach the world to sing' campaign.

But it's also worth noting that some advertisers have created effective global advertising by celebrating the cultural diversity that exists in the world (like HSBC) or the ethnic diversity of its customers around the world (like Benetton).

Universal truths

Universal truths and motivations can act as the platform for creative ideas that can span countries and cultures. These include: the drive shared by many people across the globe to find a partner; enjoying spending time with the family; children expressing themselves in order to develop; the older generation still getting a lot out of life; the desire for wealth.

There are two key challenges: Will the campaign idea be understood and emotionally relevant in each market? And can that universal truth be 'owned' by the brand? Can the brand be relevant to that truth?

Brand Space

Some successful campaigns have created their own unique 'Brand Space' which isn't tied to any particular place or time but is owned by the brand.

Creating this kind of Brand Space isn't easy. It's essential to avoid any reference points, iconography or use of language which are not shared across cultures. But once found, a Brand Space can form the basis of an advertising campaign that is distinctive and travels well.

Coke created a fantastic Brand Space with their famous Christmas ads 'Caravan' and 'Convoy'. With these ads, they created a highly appealing magical world which evoked the childhood excitement of Christmas, and are now seen by many viewers as a welcome signal that the Christmas season is approaching.

How to make the idea come alive in local markets?

The challenge all international advertisers face is how to bring alive a global advertising idea in all the local markets across the whole communications mix.

With their relatively low production costs, print, digital and poster advertising lend themselves to local adaptation, to optimize the campaign's effectiveness in local markets, by accommodating cultural differences and tactical needs.

But what about TV advertising? It's certainly true that many successful TV campaigns have travelled well without any changes to the execution. But there is sometimes an opportunity to optimize the power of the advertising idea in local markets through adaptation. Sometimes just rerecording the voiceover in a local accent can be enough.

Making an Ad go Viral

As I write this, Christmas is approaching, with its plethora of seasonal advertising. One ad for the UK supermarket brand Iceland, which focused on the effects of palm oil on the rainforests, has been banned for being too political. Yet I've been exposed to this ad more than any other Christmas ad – people are keen for its message to be seen.

Though the proportion of ads that 'go viral' in any meaningful way is small, it is possible to increase your odds of success. Several factors influence the success rate: promotion, support in other media, and creative elements including the use of humour, celebrities and edginess. Before implementing a viral strategy, however, you should consider carefully whether such an approach is right for your brand.

Viral potential is very limited for most ads

The reality is, the chances of achieving a major viral success are pretty low. Very few ads achieve high enough viewing levels to make substantial marketing impact. The average number of total YouTube views for typical ads is just 150,000 in the United States and 34,000 in the UK.

To help assess the criteria for viral success Kantar Millward Brown conducted a research project. They identified 102 ads (31 from the UK and 71 from the United States) that had been researched using the Link copy test, and that were available on YouTube. YouTube's publicly available viewing info were used as the measure of viral success. The number of views (aggregated across all posted versions of the ad) was divided by the number of weeks the ad had been posted to create a 'views per week' measure; this measure of viral spread ensured a fair comparison regardless of how long the ads had been on YouTube.

Only 5 of the 31 UK ads (16%) achieved over 1,000 views per week, and only 9 out of the 71 U.S. ads (13%) achieved over 5,000 views per week.

What determines whether an ad will go viral?

There are many factors that will determine an ad's viral impact.

Celebrities Celebrity presence can help drive viewings, especially in the United States.

Promotion Videos that are advertised on YouTube have very different viewing patterns to those that only get 'natural' viral viewing. They get more views overall, but they also get more unpaid viral views - typically around double the number of views that would have occurred naturally without promotion. YouTube home page ads are directly or indirectly responsible for 86% of all views; they increase expected views by over 600%.

Executions Executions that are linked by a common theme or device seem to benefit from being part of a campaign.

Paid Media Support Often campaigns will be supported by paid media. The video ad itself may have appeared on TV, at cinemas or in paid online video slots. Other media such as posters or print can play a supporting role. PR can have a major impact, first in seeding the ad appropriately among opinion formers, and later in 'fanning the flames' to ensure wider awareness. Dove's 'Campaign for Real Beauty' benefited from all of these elements; viral viewing was driven by a major campaign that used TV, outdoor, online and PR.

Campaign Placement Ads that are easy to forward are more likely to go viral. Forwarding can be facilitated by investing in a prominent home for the videos (such as a dedicated campaign microsite, a Facebook page or a branded YouTube channel).

Ad Name The name attached to the ad can contribute to it being easy or difficult to find. Advertisers can only control the name of the 'official' versions of their videos but they should consider the implications of how they do this. Among random surfers, an intriguing name may help drive viewing, but among searchers, a more obvious name may help increase viewings.

Creative factors

Aside from the factors listed above, the main factor that will influence whether an ad will go viral is the strength of the creative. To help predict in-market viral viewing, measures from Link were used to build a measure of Creative Viral Potential. The relationship, with an r of 0.63, helps isolate and understand some of the major creative factors underlying viral success.

So what creative factors drive viral viewing? Four measures relate to views per week.

Brand-linked Memorability Ad memorabilty had a strong correlation with viewings on its own.

Presence of a Celebrity Twenty-three of the ads within the dataset contained a celebrity (or celebrity grouping). For each of those ads, the status and popularity of those celebrities was estimated using online search volume as captured via the publicly available Google Insights for Search interface. Using this, the popularity of all the celebrities in the dataset was benchmarked against the popularity of Angelina Jolie, a celebrity who consistently achieves a very high search volume. (This benchmarking was necessary because the Google Insights tool provides a search volume index score, rather than an absolute search volume figure.) In general, the more popular the celebrity, the higher the ad views.

Distinctiveness Being distinctive is very important. To succeed virally, ads need to stand out from all other ads, not just those from direct competitors. Distinctiveness has been critical to the success of some of the most notable virals, including Old Spice's 'The man your man could smell like', and Coca-Cola's 'Happiness Machine.'

Buzz The other factor is summarised as Buzz – the quality that makes someone want to send an ad on to someone else. To understand this area of buzz, a quantitative research project was specifically designed to examine this phenomenon. The study, conducted in the UK, involved over 3000 consumers and 29 different films. The films ranged in their origin and style; some were well-known virals, some were lesser-known virals, and some were regular TV adverts.

The act of sending an ad on contains a consequential element – personal endorsement. In sending a viral on, the sender is saying that he or she think it's good. Sending a bad viral is rather like telling a joke that falls flat – embarrassing for all involved.

The research indentified four factors which can be summarized in the acronym LEGS. Strong viral ads are:

Laugh out loud funny

The sender of the viral often needs to be sure that the recipient is going to laugh when they see it. The likelihood of this outcome will be gauged against their own reaction to the film. A wry smile won't usually motivate sufficiently for the viral to be sent on. Four of the top five films researched over-indexed in terms of being funny.

Edgy

Best described as the sort of film most people wouldn't show to their mother, edgy films operate on the edge of social acceptability. They might be viewed by some as being offensive, shocking, sick, or unpleasant. Importantly however, they combine this edginess with humour. The shock element contained within the film is felt, on the whole, to be funny as opposed to gratuitous.

Gripping

Finding a film gripping, engaging or involving isn't the same as enjoying the film. Few people would claim to 'enjoy' looking at a car crash, but the majority of us rubber-neck as we pass an accident site.

Very gripping films are not necessarily particularly enjoyable; importantly, both positive and negative emotions can drive a consumer to be gripped by a film. This research shows that, while a film that is gripping is not guaranteed to be forwarded on, a film that isn't gripping is unlikely to be. The Iceland palm oil ad would fit into this category.

Sexual content

No sexually focused films were included in the research due to common decency and industry codes of conduct. That is not to say, however, that you should underestimate the importance of sexual content as a motivator for the forwarding of a film – particularly among younger males.

Dangers of viral ads

The pursuit of an edgy or sexually focused viral should not be to the detriment of the brand character or proposition. An ill-advised film could be harmful to brand equity if it goes viral, because the brand will have no control over its longevity in the public eye. A semi-pornographic film for many brands would detract, rather than enhance, the brand promise and position.

There seems to be a growing trend for brand managers to suggest or request a viral campaign because 'everyone else is doing it.' Before embarking on a viral project, marketers need to consider the question: Would the brand air a particularly Funny, Edgy, Gripping or Sexy film on TV or in the cinema? If the film wouldn't fit with the brand on TV or in the cinema, it won't fit any better when it's watched on a computer. Media choice should be driven by the communication objective, and not the other way around.

Just as an off-strategy TV or cinema ad can harm a brand's equity, so can an ill-advised viral. The goal, then, should be appropriate distinctiveness, rather than the reckless pursuit of buzz.

Luck

Finally it should be acknowledged that, despite the analysis presented above, there is still an element of luck involved. Some campaigns will inspire mash-ups, spoof responses, re-edits and other online chatter. At this point, the marketer starts to lose control of their campaign, and things may take unexpected twists and turns, but with luck, they could be benefiting from a massive viral surge in brand interest.

Making the Most of Multimedia Advertising

One client launched a range of soups, sealed in foil packaging. The range, featuring traditional favourite flavours with a twist, represented a significant technological innovation, and was intended to reinvigorate interest in packaged soup. The campaign launch included heavyweight TV, Point of Sale, OOH and Digital activity. Aided Awareness, Consideration, Trust and Top of Mind Awareness all experienced significant shifts during the campaign. TV was the key driver of awareness and trust, but OOH was more effective at driving image and purchase consideration.

All media are capable of delivering any campaign objective, whether it is delivering brand engagement, building associations or driving motivation. However, there can be real benefits in re-allocating some budget between channels, subject to reach and frequency considerations, the quality of creative content and the quality of media channel engagement (the degree to which consumers pay attention to ads delivered in that channel at that moment). All of these factors are important and should be considered when planning the campaign.

Reach

TV is acknowledged as the high reach medium. Because of this reach, TV can be great at generating awareness. And while the reach of individual TV channels may have declined in recent years in many parts of the world, TV fragmentation does have the benefit of allowing greater targeting of minority audiences. However, for short- to medium-term sales effects, TV tends to be less cost-efficient than other media; TV punches below its weight with share of investment outweighing share of impact. One of the main reasons behind this lack of efficiency is overspend — TV being delivered at frequency levels beyond the optimum in the short term. However, when your goal is long term brand building, this overspend effect is not obvious, and TV remains powerful for long-term brand building.

If the TV ad is strong, it is worth considering reallocating spend over a longer period, effectively lowering the weekly TV weight. This can mitigate the short-term 'wastage' while maintaining the long term SOV. But this strategy is not relevant for highly seasonal brands.

One of the main roles for using additional media is to cost-efficiently extend reach. While all channels claim to offer incremental reach over TV, non-TV video and press perform particularly well in this role, despite being typically low reach. Print and some elements of the internet in particular are also good at reaching highly targeted audiences segmented by interest.

One soft drink brand ran a campaign with heavyweight TV achieving 73% reach; however despite a relatively low reach of 6%, YouTube delivered an incremental net reach of 2.3% over TV, and was a cost efficient way of reaching the core audience. But other media can also help; in a campaign for a Russian mobile telecom brand, out of home (OOH) advertising helped compensate for relatively weak engagement with the TV ad, achieving greater incremental reach than online video.

But additional reach is not guaranteed; one toilet tissue brand introduced an engaging TV campaign with OOH in support. However, the digital formats used resulted in very low reach for the OOH activity.

When the goal is extending reach, it is essential that the ads in other media perform in their own right; you cannot expect them to build on a response to the TV activity. In assessing the potential of other media, acknowledgment of levels of channel engagement is important; clutter, distraction, daypart, and spot placement may all affect attention levels – as can levels of category involvement. For some static media, print in particular, impact can be hampered by low category involvement. If channel engagement is high then it is more likely that the channels will deliver against their objectives. Under circumstances of low channel engagement, it is far less likely that the channels will deliver their full potential. So, in considering the role of other media to extend reach, understand the level of category involvement, along with other elements influencing channel engagement.

Delivering against objectives

In considering the use of multiple media, another key factor is that different media perform better against some measures. For some communications objectives such as persuasion, low-reach media tend to be more effective than high reach media. This is most likely driven by stronger receptivity/channel engagement (also the more 'niche' the audience, highly targetable media become more effective). However, these low reach media also have greater variation in performance; most likely due to the range of creative quality.

Media multiplier

Another benefit of using multiple media is that it can generate media synergies; the media multiplier effect. In particular, TV can provide context for ads in other channels so that they work harder.

Priming

For some media (particularly print and outdoor) attention is generally paid only to ads that interest the consumer. But TV can add warmth and interest to a brand, which can encourage consumers to want to find out more. Consequently, they are more likely to notice and read a print ad for it.

Additionally, viewing another ad, whether it is print, online or OOH, may awaken associations formed by the TV ad — particularly if the same creative approach is taken. The strength of 'TV priming' through the combination of these two effects can cause a powerful 'media-multiplier' effect.

In one European FMCG product launch, OOH activity preceded TV activity. Research showed that despite having almost half the campaign spend OOH contributed only 5% to the image uplift. In the second wave of activity, following advice, the OOH activity was phased in line with the TV activity. This time OOH accounted for only 35% of the spend, but was responsible for 35% of the uplift.

Magnify

Where multiple channels are used to reach the same target audience at about the same time, surrounding the consumer with an integrated set of messages through different vehicles, the overall effect can be greater than what could be achieved through one medium alone. Specific messages can accumulate into broader ideas.

For a complex and multifaceted message with the objective of changing established perceptions, this approach is the likely strategic choice.

One client introduced a small, portable, single-use toothbrush to clean teeth and freshen breath for on-the-go occasions. The launch campaign was supported by TV, magazine, and online activity. The TV worked in its own right to generate response, however the best results were achieved with exposure to all three media – a compelling demonstration of the Magnifier effect.

Purchase Intent

Q: If you were looking to purchase a toothbrush, how likely would you be to purchase the following brand(s)?

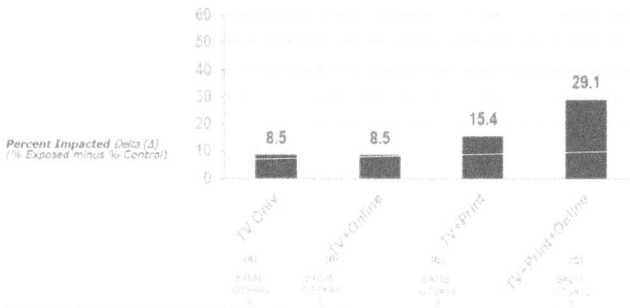

One financial client used relatively low weight TV activity in one region but not another, and poster activity in both regions with a similar creative to the TV campaign. The poster recognition levels were similar in both regions. However, understanding of the posters was stronger in the TV advertised region, and there was also greater message take out.

However the media multiplier effect does not always happen. In a campaign for a UK men's personal care brand, while the TV ad worked well, the OOH ad had high incremental exposure, which meant that expected synergies were not achieved. Since the OOH ad was not intended to work in isolation, the additional reach had little effect. This highlights that when looking for the multiplier effect, not only does the creative theme need to be deployed in such a way that consumers can make the link between ads delivered in different channels, but the phasing of the ads needs to be right. This is in contrast with campaigns where reach is the primary goal, where phasing of the activity across media is not critical; delivery can be spread over time.

Resonate

Campaigns can Resonate when a cheaper medium is used to prolong the effect of a more expensive one. For example, a campaign might run on TV for a period of time, then a radio ad is developed, featuring a notable audio cue from the TV ad. When the radio ads are heard, that cue stimulates associations from the TV advertising. This effectively prolongs the impact of TV and makes the TV budget go further than it otherwise would.

A toothpaste brand used this approach for one of their campaigns. A national burst of TV advertising was used to support the brand. Straight after the TV burst, a burst of radio advertising was deployed in one TV region, using sound cues from the TV activity. At the end of the TV campaign, but prior to the radio ad, awareness and consideration of the brand were the same in the radio advertised region as the rest of the country. The radio advertising successfully extended the brand's media presence, with the extra awareness being misattributed to TV.

Clear indications that radio has strengthened total media presence

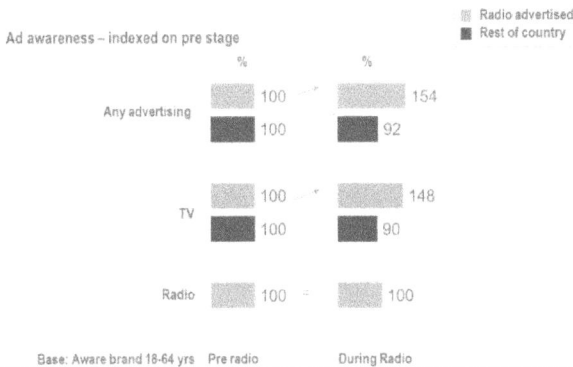

Ad awareness – indexed on pre stage

Radio advertised
Rest of country

	Pre radio	During Radio
Any advertising	100 / 100	154 / 92
TV	100 / 100	148 / 90
Radio	100	100

Base: Aware brand 18-64 yrs   Pre radio   During Radio

The indexed growth in any media ad awareness from 100–154, assuming general media costs, was achieved for the equivalent investment of 30 TV GRPs. The real strength of the radio activity was its ability to cost-effectively generate further presence and purchase intent for the brand.

Radio ad also contributed to a strengthening of the brand

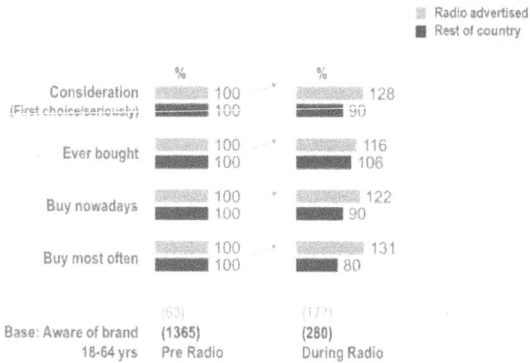

■ Radio advertised
■ Rest of country

	%	%
Consideration (First choice/seriously)	100 / 100	128 / 90
Ever bought	100 / 100	116 / 106
Buy nowadays	100 / 100	122 / 90
Buy most often	100 / 100	131 / 80
Base: Aware of brand 18-64 yrs	(1365) Pre Radio	(280) During Radio

Retail

One area where the media multiplier effect can be used advantageously is in the retail environment. Some advertising is better at setting up demand for a product, demand which can then be activated at Point of Sale. Carefully planned multimedia campaigns can capitalize on this effect. This may include discount coupons, posters outside stores, in-store sampling, or displays; but at the other extreme are the brands (such as Apple, Nike and Hershey) who now have their own retail outlets, where they can control the retail experience and ensure it builds on other marketing activity. All this activity can trigger activation. This effect will be strongest when the same creative approach is used across the media, with the activation advertising awakening associations.

Creativity

An OOH advert announcing a new product for a UK credit card failed badly. The advert was poor quality and reach was under 20%; highlighting that multimedia planning can be high risk if all the contributing factors are not well understood. For the media multiplier effect to work well, creative elements need to be shared across media and these should be the elements that stand out. This may be a distinctive visual, such as a celebrity or character; music, such as a jingle; or a slogan. The nature of the distinctive element is naturally important – is it audio or visual? Can it be expressed in a static medium? Such considerations will influence the other media that the idea can be extended to.

In planning a multimedia campaign, a portfolio approach where each channel has its own discrete role has two clear benefits: assigning roles to each channel based on an understanding of engagement and synergy should help maximise media choices; but it should also lead to a more focused consideration of the creative content delivered by each medium.

Using Static Online Display Advertising

Static online advertising can improve awareness and brand perceptions. For a medium where frequency levels can be capped, it is worth noting that the first exposure is the most effective, so aiming for reach among your target is a useful objective to set. There are many factors which affect an ad's ability to perform well online. Placing the ad on a relevant site can make a big difference for some categories, and the amount of clutter on the site can affect performance measures.

Beyond these aspects, the creative itself has a huge influence on the ad's ability to perform, with the best ads sharing some key characteristics.

How the medium works

Online advertising achieves more than just driving behaviour via click-through. In thousands of research studies comparing exposed to non-exposed respondents of various campaigns, static online advertising has demonstrated its ability to drive key brand metrics – brand and advertising awareness, message association, brand favourability and purchase intent.

Brand status

Online advertising works regardless of how well known the brand is. Average ad performance is similar for well-known and lesser known brands for most key brand metrics, although the indications are that it is easier to generate brand awareness and purchase intent for less well-known brands.

This is consistent with Kantar Millward Brown's offline learning.

High awareness >70   middle awareness 30-70   Low awareness <30

Average base across measures static campaigns only:

High awareness: 255
Medium awareness: 137
Low awareness: 37

4.0 4.7 4.7   5.1 5.5   1.9 1.8 2.1
1.8

(static image)

Online Ad Awareness   Aided Awareness   Purchase Intent

Source: Millward Brown Digital
Marketnorm, Database

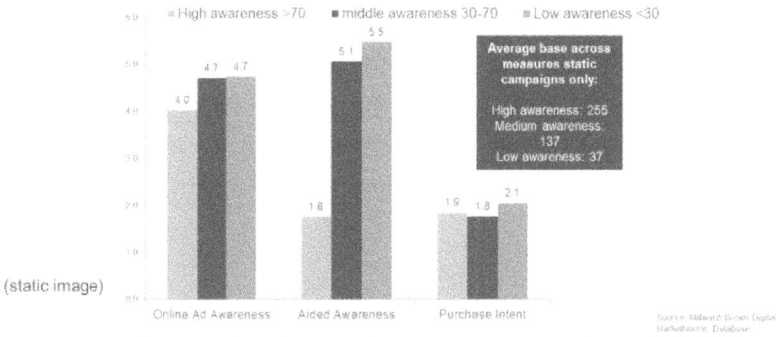

KANTAR MILLWARDBROWN

How popular is the format?

Research has consistently shown that attitudes towards online advertising still lag attitudes towards more traditional advertising, among all age groups. Attitudes towards online display ads are only slightly less favourable than towards direct mail.

Fraud

One major aspect that needs to be acknowledged with this medium is the issue of fraud. There has been a rise in Sophisticated Invalid Traffic. Non-Human Traffic (NHT), activity generated by bots, can hugely influence measurement issues, making it harder to assess reach. However, analysis by comScore has shown that there are many high-quality publishers who deliver inventory that is virtually free of NHT; the Top 50% of websites ranked by lowest incidence of NHT have less than one percent NHT. It is only in the lowest-performing 15% of observed publishers where NHT is a sizeable problem.

Coverage

From a cost-effectiveness standpoint, the first impression is the most effective; the most cost-effective exposure frequency is one. While this is true for many media, this is particularly relevant in the online world, where frequency caps can be set. However, the ability of online advertising to generate purchase intent varies considerably. Notably, there are no signs of 'average' ads 'wearing in'.

Purchase intent by frequency of exposure

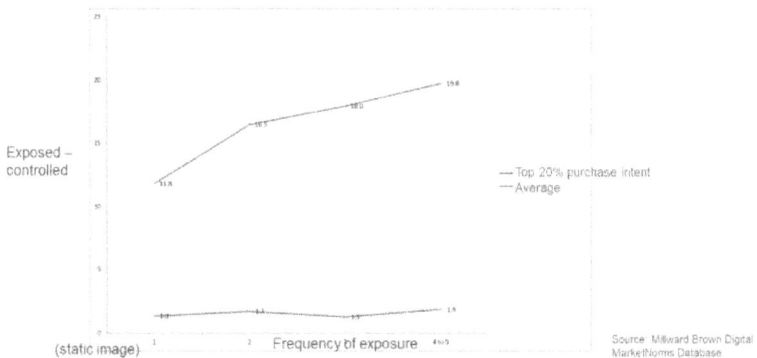

Context

Overall, brands tend not to generate more impact when they advertise on category-related sites.

Ads shown on category websites versus those shown on non category websites

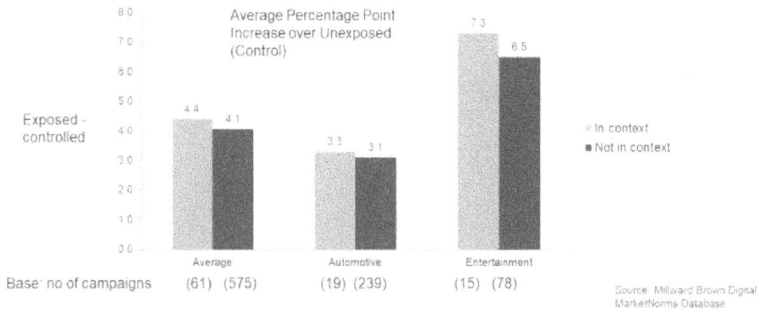

Source: Millward Brown Digital
MarketNorms Database

KANTAR MILLWARDBROWN

However, for some categories, notably Automotive, context is hugely important in driving purchase intent, where being in-context may simply be a surrogate for reaching those in the market. This is not true for all categories, however. Entertainment ads for TV shows and movies tend to appeal to a wide audience and, thus, the in-context argument does not apply.

Clutter affects ad performance. In a study conducted jointly by Dynamic Logic, NielsenNetratings, and Double Click, clutter was shown to negatively affect brand favorability, message association and click through rates.

Length of exposure can also have a big effect. In one study, Kantar Millward Brown found that ads in view over longer periods had dramatically higher uplifts on both awareness and purchase intent metrics compared to those in view for less time.

Percent impacted by in-time view

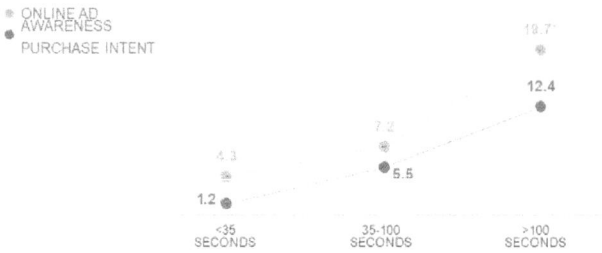

KANTAR MILLWARDBROWN

Additionally some impressions never have the opportunity to be seen by humans, often because inventory exists on parts of a web page that users do not reach by scrolling. Research by comScore has shown that almost half of US display ads are not seen at all by consumers (although it should be noted that some of this is due to user activity rather than any error on the publishers' part).

Ad shape

There are many types of ad shapes used online, but most can be separated into three groups: banners, which appear horizontally (typically at the top of the page); skyscrapers, which appear vertically (typically along the right-hand margin of the page); rectangles, which are much more square shaped than the more classically rectangular banners and skyscrapers.

Both banners and skyscrapers are more effective at generating ad awareness.

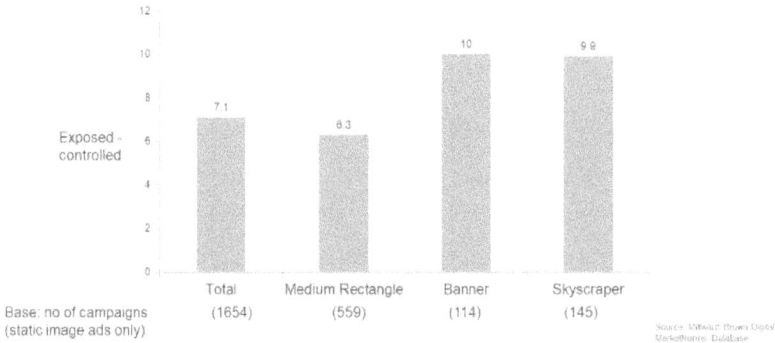

Effect of format on online ad awareness

Average Percentage Point Increase over Unexposed (Control)

	Total (1654)	Medium Rectangle (559)	Banner (114)	Skyscraper (145)
	7.1	6.3	10	9.8

Base: no of campaigns (static image ads only)

Source: Millward Brown Digital MarketNorms Database

Creative

In assessing effectiveness, the creative itself is more important than other variables such as frequency of exposure and category. An analysis of over 2,500 online campaigns showed that the quality of the creative was the biggest explanatory factor distinguishing between strong and weak ads.

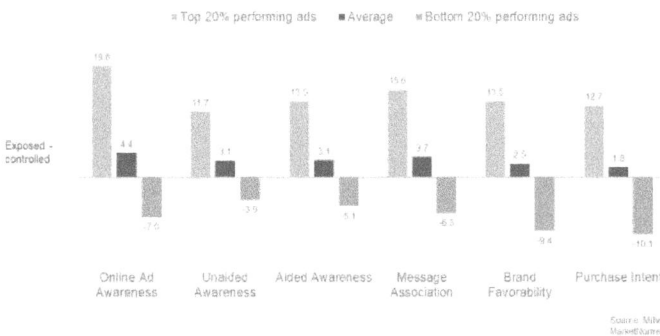

Best/worst performing ads

Average Percentage Point Increase over Unexposed (Control)

Top 20% performing ads · Average · Bottom 20% performing ads

Source: Millward Brown Digital MarketNorms Database

Ads that show adults or children or which use humour are more likely to generate ad awareness.

The best performing static ads both attract and engage. Tips, generated from qualitative insights, include:

Engage the viewer. If your brand or category are not intrinsically interesting, you will need to entertain, or offer interactive experience (such as linking to recipes or downloading a coupon). However, viewers should never have to interact with your ad in order to see your brand or message — click through rates are simply too low. High engagement serves a second purpose; the growth in the use of ad blocking software can at least in part be mitigated over the long term by advertisers airing ads that people want to see.

Avoid heavy text.

When appropriate, exploit recognition – using images or colours from an existing campaign.

Keep communication simple.

In addition, if your campaign is likely to be viewed on mobile devices, legibility is vital; if the ad is likely to be seen on a mobile device, keep screen size in mind; small details may be lost. Also consider the interaction of text and background. Text will almost always be more difficult to read against a dark background.

With these factors in mind, online display advertising can be a useful component of your campaign.

Using Online Video

One campaign used online video and TV. It generated a reach of 74.1% for €1.91m. To achieve that level using TV alone would have cost an extra €200k; the combination of online video and TV delivered reach more cost effectively.

Paid online video has grown rapidly as an effective marketing tool. One of its key strengths is in generating reach among light TV viewers. But in planning the online video component of a campaign, it's important to realize that the online setting is very different than the TV setting, and there are specific considerations. Whether to use repurposed TV ads or original material will depend on your objectives: while successful online video ads share some characteristics with successful TV ads, in other respects they are very different.

Online video works

The case for paid online video is strong: Kantar Millward Brown's database shows that, compared to standard online display formats, online video delivers greater uplifts on measures such as brand favourability and purchase intent.

Online Video Works

Base sizes: Online video (163) Rich media (630) Simple flash (85)

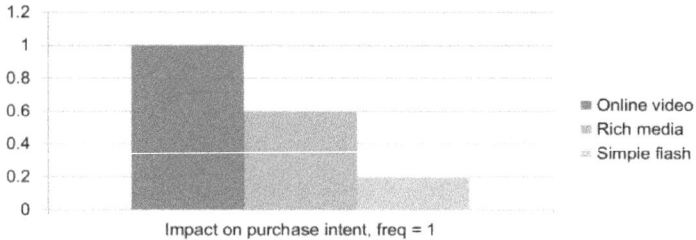

Impact on purchase intent, freq = 1

- Online video
- Rich media
- Simple flash

KANTAR MILWARDBROWN

However, while online video still generates increases in awareness, these lifts are not as large as they were when the medium was new. The novelty has worn off. Consumers now expect to see video ads online. If an ad doesn't engage viewers, they will just click away. So it becomes more important to understand how to use this medium to best effect: there is huge variation in performance between the best and the worst online campaigns.

Online Video Effectiveness Varies Greatly

Top 20% of campaigns, middle 60%, bottom 20%

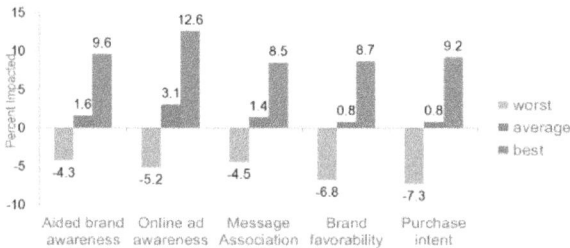

- worst
- average
- best

KANTAR MILWARDBROWN

228

So to harness this potentially powerful format, the content of that video is crucial, along with how and where consumers view or interact with it. It is also worth noting that the least successful campaigns can actually have a damaging effect on brand measures; take care not to alienate your audience.

The advantage of additional reach

In terms of reach, currently no other media is in the position to replace TV. Online video campaigns that have been recorded in Kantar Millward Brown's databases deliver an average reach of 13%, much lower than the reach of TV, which is typically 70% or more. However, online video is especially effective at delivering additional reach among light TV viewers.

Format: In stream or in banner?

The term 'online video' describes all ad formats utilizing some form of video; these include videos delivered both in-banner and in-stream. In-banner video may play automatically when it appears on a page, or it may require the viewer to click on it. The auto-play version is more arresting but also causes more disturbance; the viewer-controlled version tends to generate longer viewing, but this has to be balanced against the decrease in the number of viewers who will choose to watch the ad.

In-stream video plays automatically; web users are not able to skip it (although this is changing on some sites). In-stream is typically used as pre-roll before TV episodes and can be more effective than in-banner video because the audience is captive and more highly engaged. However, some viewers may watch several episodes in a row, and if they are bombarded with the same ad repeatedly, they are likely to be irritated. It's helpful to think about frequency capping or delivering different creative messages each time to avoid driving down favourability and purchase intent.

In-stream video delivers stronger uplifts in awareness and favour-ability, but both in-stream and in-banner have a similar impact on purchase intent.

In-Stream tends to be more effective

Base sizes: in-stream (33-48) not in-stream (316-450)

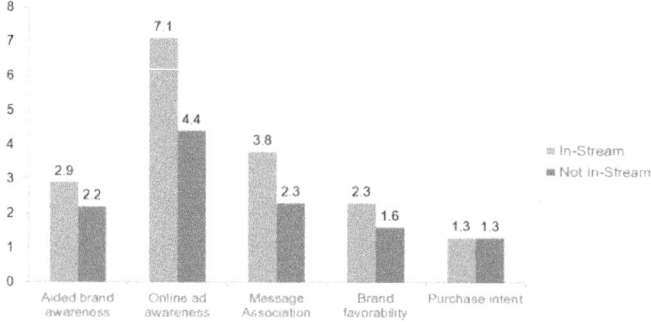

Ad length

In general, the longer the ad, the bigger the effect. While longer ads will cost more, they are also more likely to generate awareness and persuasion.

However, there are relatively few media placements online where consumers will tolerate long video ads, so brands should mostly seek to condense messaging into formats shorter than 30 seconds to enable maximum online portability and reach – hence the growing popularity of short-form video.

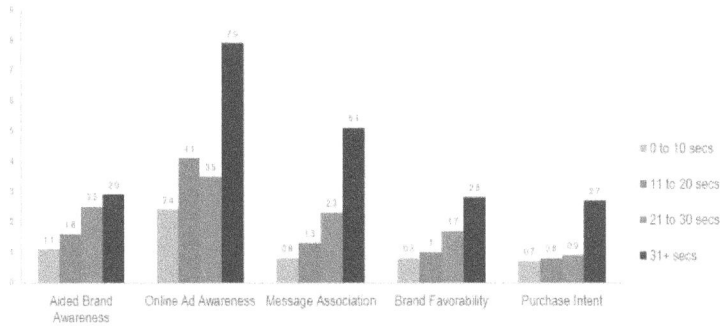

Companion banners

One common issue is whether to support the video with companion banners. Analysis shows that campaigns that combine online video and display deliver the strongest brand impact.

Companion banners can boost the effectiveness of video ads
* However, similar impact seen on persuasion metrics

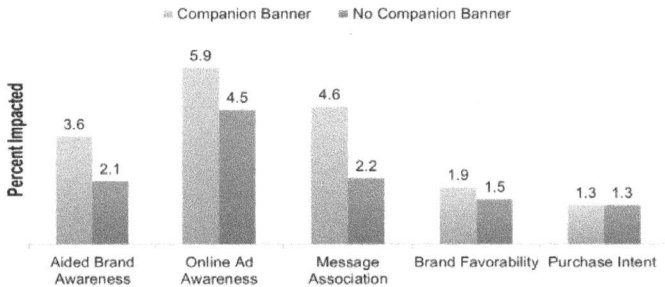

Content: to repurpose or not?

One of the fundamental decisions in implementing online video is whether to create original material or to repurpose TV ads.

Repurposed ads can have synergistic impact on ad awareness; a form of the media-multiplier effect. But a successful TV ad may not always work well in an online environment. Online audiences tend to be more engaged in the activity than TV viewers; advertising which is not relevant to the task at hand is likely to be seen as an annoying interruption. So a successful TV ad may not work as well in the online environment. Besides, video content made for the web can be more relevant and useful to the viewer. As an example, if you know the audience has been looking at specific goods, then you can provide them with more information on that product and convey a key benefit to them.

Repurposed TV is more likely to impact online ad awareness: made-for-web delivers well on brand awareness, favourability and persuasion

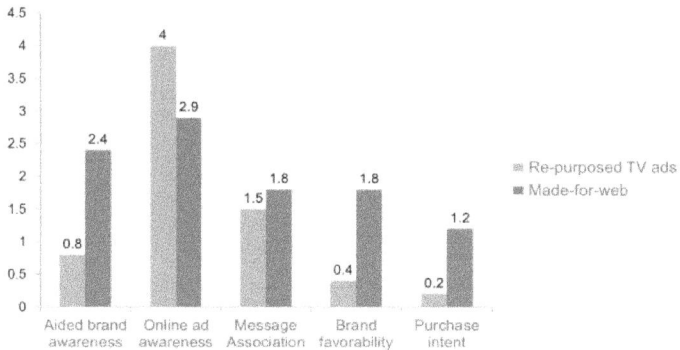

Mobile devices

Many people check up on their social networks daily, if not hourly, and smartphones make this process even more personal and immediate. This represents a huge opportunity for mobile advertisers. Mobile advertising, in its infancy, was more effective than other forms of online advertising. However, the edge enjoyed by mobile ads is diminishing. As seen with other digital technologies, as the novelty wears off, the effectiveness of the advertising declines.

A key benefit of mobile advertising is the ability to tailor a message to the specific time and location of the consumer. Advertisers can capitalize on this in several ways, depending on the product category and circumstances. Time and location are often crucial when people are searching for restaurants. Or if you are marketing for a credit card company, knowing that customers are in a shopping mall could give you the opportunity to tailor your message.

Another way brands can drive relevance is via contextual targeting. One notable example comes from the mobile site of a fashion magazine, where viewers were greeted with a full-page ad for a quality fashion brand.

Other creative issues

Qualitative insights from researching a wide variety of online video ads suggest that successful online video ads have several aspects in common with successful TV ads. Most campaigns appear to benefit from consistent and simple messaging. When conveying brand propositions online, aim to keep the communication simple, direct, and consistent. Focus on one or two messages. Funny ads are more likely to be enjoyable and involving than others, and be more memorable. But, as with all creativity, humour needs to be used with care. To be successful, it must help focus on the brand and the intended communication; otherwise, it can actually detract from the ad's effectiveness.

But successful online video is dissimilar to successful TV ads in other ways. First, for all online video formats, many of the top-performing ads reinforced the message of the voiceover with text or imagery. This ensures that messages can still be absorbed even if the user doesn't have the audio turned on. The presence of humans (adults or children) can boost the effectiveness of online video ads. Other recommendations relate to the reduced patience for online ads. Online video ads need to engage within the first few seconds. And since many digital video ads are not watched through to the end, early branding is also recommended. In order to convey a more complete brand 'story,' two techniques may be useful: sequencing and telescoping. Sequencing conveys a storyline in short instalments over a number of exposures. Telescoping uses one short segment to pique the interest of users and then offers them the chance to continue viewing a longer video on the brand's web site.

Using Web Sites as Part of the Marketing Mix

Web sites can be a valuable part of a brand's marketing plan. You can add considerably to a site's effectiveness if you consider not just the quality of content, but also aspects of site design such as distinctiveness, ease of use, personalization and innovation.

The value of web sites

A corporate web site is often the product of a separate development team, and not the responsibility of the marketing team, but it can be an important element in an overall brand communication. It offers unique opportunities to build a relationship with customers, but also poses specific challenges.

Web sites can be a very successful part of the mix. As part of an online campaign in France, Eurostar leveraged video adverts to drive traffic to a unique microsite intended to raise perceptions of the brand and increase usage intent among business travellers, particularly men. To measure the effects of this microsite, a group of control respondents were recruited from a jump-page that intercepted respondents after they had clicked to access the microsite, but before they had actually visited it. Exposed respondents were recruited upon leaving the microsite. Unaided brand awareness among men increased significantly (+4 points) following exposure to the microsite (exposure to the video adverts alone was not enough to shift top-of-mind awareness). Microsite exposure also generated exceptionally large increases among men in both online ad awareness (+29 points) and brand favourability (+22 points).

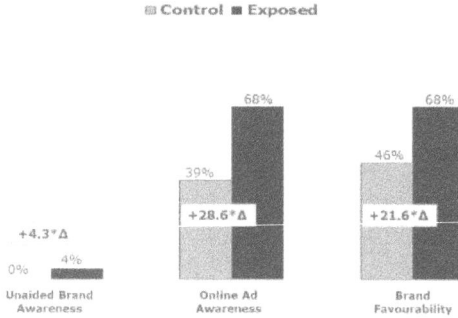

Microsite Impacts Top-of-Mind Awareness Among Male Respondents

⊠ Control ■ Exposed

* Statistically significant at a 90% confidence level. Delta (Δ) = Exposed-control

KANTAR MILLWARDBROWN

Ease of use

Ease of use causes dramatic differences to a web site's impact; site visitors need to be able to navigate effortlessly through the site. An evaluation of over 110 web sites showed the ones that were considered easy to use were most likely to have a beneficial effect on brand health measures.

Site Ease of use Benefits Brand Perceptions

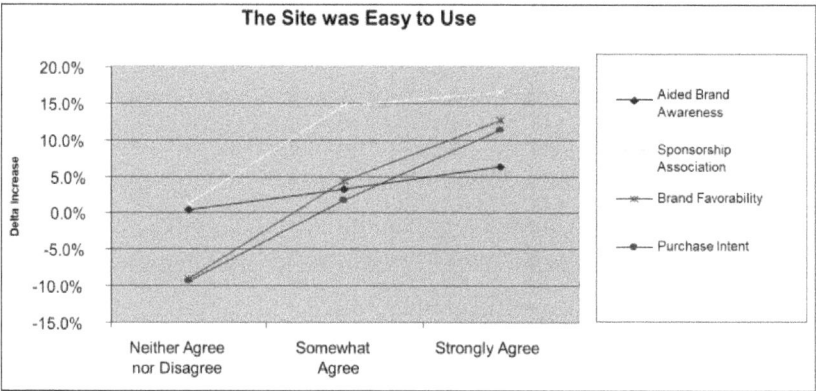

KANTAR MILLWARDBROWN

Ease of use encompasses factors such as the relevance of the information provided, the extent to which the site icons communicate their functionality, clear labelling, and speed of page load.

Personalization

Personalization can also add considerably to a site's convenience, usefulness and speed. At its most basic, personalization will involve remembering a user's details (if the user allows). More complex personalization targets content to customers based on their demographics and their browsing and purchasing history.

However, there are downsides to personalization. Some users feel it is an invasion of privacy. Users must be given the option to specify whether they are willing for the company to retain and use information about them. There tends to be a contradiction in the way people feel about personalisation; for some it is great that they are being shown material that they feel is relevant to them; others find it an intrusion and feel that their online behaviour has been 'stalked'. In most countries there are legal issues around data retention. Personalization also has cost implications for web design.

Distinctiveness

Successful sites need to be distinctive. They need to offer an experience that is useful or enjoyable, which cannot be gained elsewhere.

One leading baby care brand in Australia developed a local site with information and solutions on baby-related issues. It aimed to add value to the brand by being recognized as a valuable, credible and entertaining resource. Research showed the site was liked; it was considered easy to navigate, uncluttered and attractive. Overall, it was seen as a professional site, as people expected from the brand. However, the research showed that the site fell somewhere between a one-stop baby care shop and a fun and games site with some interesting information. There were many other baby care sites on the Internet, and there were no strong reasons to visit the site, apart from gathering information about special offers for the brand, and taking part in competitions. These two reasons became even stronger factors with repeat visitors.

Consumers mainly visit the site for competitions and offers

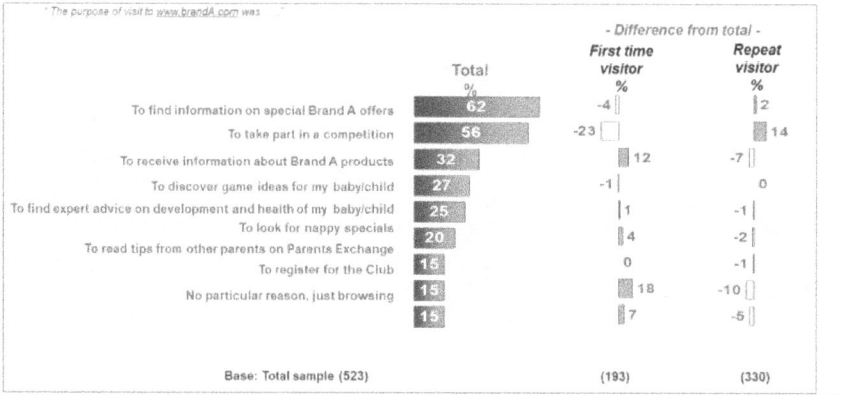

' The purpose of visit to www.brandA.com was

	Total %	- Difference from total - First time visitor %	Repeat visitor %
To find information on special Brand A offers	62	-4	2
To take part in a competition	56	-23	14
To receive information about Brand A products	32	12	-7
To discover game ideas for my baby/child	27	-1	0
To find expert advice on development and health of my baby/child	25	1	-1
To look for nappy specials	20	4	-2
To read tips from other parents on Parents Exchange	15	0	-1
To register for the Club	15	18	-10
No particular reason, just browsing	15	7	-5
Base: Total sample (523)		(193)	(330)

There were several indications, derived from both qualitative and quantitative work, that improvements could be made. Many other baby care sites had a more international emphasis. However, a locally based site was viewed favourably, as there were perceived to be regulatory, cultural and language differences between countries. The recommendation was that the brand positioned its site as 'Australia's premier baby care portal.' It was suggested the site should provide an overall layer of basic information with a good supply of links to reliable outside agencies such as hospitals and health departments, as well as more personal and emotive content to help bond consumers to the site. Another improvement suggested was targeting content to specific groups of parents, for example the first-time pregnant, or those with toddlers. It was stressed that the site should not lose sight of the main reason for an initial visit: the ability to buy direct, with discounts.

The recommendations were acted on and site visits increased.

Innovation

A team running a successful website cannot afford to sit back. New technologies and features are being developed all the time. In the past few years, for example, there has been an explosion in websites making use of chatbots and website notifications.

Websites can benefit from using AI to integrate consumer demographic data with previous browsing behaviour to help ensure people see the most relevant products. More advanced search engines can deal with misspellings and misattribution (to ensure that when someone searches your site for a competitor product, it is your equivalent that they see). And search results can be ordered so that the higher-margin products are shown first.

A new and innovative web site can help build links between the brand and the intended message or sponsorship. The chart below shows respondents who agreed with each site attribute, and the improvement (against a control cell) on linkage between the brand and the intended message or sponsorship. In general, when respondents agree that the experience with the site is positive, brand metrics are elevated. The overall metric norm is indicated by the dotted line.

A new and innovative feel can help build linkage between the brand and the intended message or sponsorship

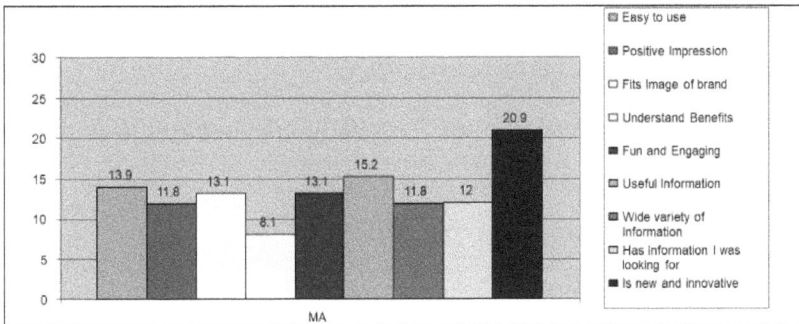

Research shows it is often beneficial if sites convey a sense of dynamism. Regular updates on the site, indicated by a 'What's New' section and links to current news items, are generally appreciated. Additionally, a monthly newsletter with links to the site can help encourage return visits.

Challenges with e-commerce

When the web site is intended to sell products, there are some additional challenges.

It isn't easy for users to fully to assess all the physical characteristics of the product — such as colour, texture, size and shape — when shopping online. People may have concerns about the trustworthiness of a site, particularly if they have not used it before. Customers may worry about their personal details being passed on. They may also question whether the goods they order will actually arrive. The availability of well-known branded products on the site helps give assurance, but customers need to be confident that they are genuine and not counterfeit. Shopping online also raises issues around returns policies; for instance, will postage be refunded?

Kantar Millward Brown was asked by a client to help optimize a new web site selling beauty products in China. Young women in Shanghai were shown other online beauty sites and asked what they liked and disliked about them. Such sites could offer four distinct advantages:

A wide range of brands and products

No pushy salespeople, as frequently encountered in department stores

The convenience of buying online

Lower prices

The research highlighted the importance of using harmonious colours, a clear layout and a fresh style to create an attractive site. Functional aspects were also found to be important, such as an effective search function and categorizing products by brand, price and product type so the right products could be found quickly. Those surveyed liked sites which included a hotline and a help section for inexperienced users, and welcomed additional detailed product information. They also liked sites which offered a choice of payment methods and had a clear refund policy.

The research also highlighted the need to promote the site, not just to bring it to the attention of Chinese consumers, but also to provide it with some credibility and help overcome any suspicion. As well as traditional media, the value of word of mouth was singled out. Enhancements included an online forum, an area for consumer endorsements in the online catalogue, a membership club, and incentive schemes for successful referrals. The site was successfully launched.

Site content is crucial

While promoting site upgrades is important, advertising is no replacement for a lack of site functionality.

Kantar Millward Brown research into an internet portal in the Czech Republic showed that its strongest feature was its e-mail, which was evaluated as the best for both quality and appearance. The site also had a good news service. The site's biggest weakness was its home page, which had both rational and emotional deficiencies.

Qualitative feedback revealed that, to offer a real competitive advantage, the site should become more distinctive. The site needed to be modernized. Suggestions focussed on its structure, functionality and colour. Particular elements included enabling music to be downloaded, providing individual settings for beginners and advanced users, and improving the search engine. The e-mail, while already strong, could benefit from simple improvements such as the ability to add smileys and change the colour scheme. Additionally, an improved chat capability could appeal to the young.

It was highlighted that it was important to publicize the site re-launch, to encourage potential users to visit the portal. A strong campaign was developed which researched well. It generated high levels of ad awareness, strengthened brand awareness, and there was a lift in the number of visitors to the portal. However, these improvements were only short term. The changes made to the site had been largely cosmetic; the other recommendations had been ignored. As a consequence, site visitors were disappointed with what they found, and did not return.

Apps

While not web sites, many use apps interchangeably with websites, and many of the same issues are relevant.

Good apps are quick, free, and easy to download. They work for all software versions without crashing, they have clear descriptions in the app store, and they are more fun than desktop sites (perhaps through location-based functionality).

Apps should offer something of value. However, what constitutes 'value' covers a range of options. One app for a drink brand offered rewards for succeeding at a simple racing game. This branded app was appreciated as being a fun way to pass the time. By contrast, a toilet tissue brand launched the app, 'Where are the toilets?' The app was considered humorous, appropriate to the brand, and helpful.

It can also be appropriate to capitalize on existing apps: some ads encouraging viewers to use the popular music-identifying app Shazam. As well as identifying the music, the app launches a sponsored page.

Using Print Ads

A hair styler brand ran a campaign in the UK that used TV, newspapers, and magazines. While 35% of the campaign spend went toward newspapers, newspaper advertising accounted for over 40% of the uplift in brand measures, and it produced those uplifts as cost effectively as TV.

Print advertising can be very effective. It can work more efficiently than TV, and incorporating print into the media mix can contribute to media-multiplier effects. But there are several key differences between print and TV advertising. Print ads need to actively grab attention, so it is essential for ads in low-interest categories to use creativity to draw the reader in.

Unlike TV, print advertising wears out rapidly, so long-running campaigns need multiple executions to minimize this effect. And, because of the way magazines are read over time and sometimes passed on, magazine ad exposure builds over time. This is an important issue for both media planning and evaluation.

Magazine advertising can be cost effective

On average, magazine executions generate visibility as efficiently as TV. And because print exposures cost considerably less than TV, magazine advertising can be much more cost effective on an exposure-for-exposure basis.

Research conducted by Kantar Millward Brown for the Magazine Publishers of America (MPA) across 113 brands confirmed that, on a dollar-for-dollar basis, magazines deliver higher advertising awareness than television.

Contribution to Total
Advertising Awareness
(500,000 + Respondents)

Percent of Total
Advertising Budgets
($9 Billion)

Television 36%	Television 77%
Mags/TV 35%	
Magazines 29%	**Magazines 23%**

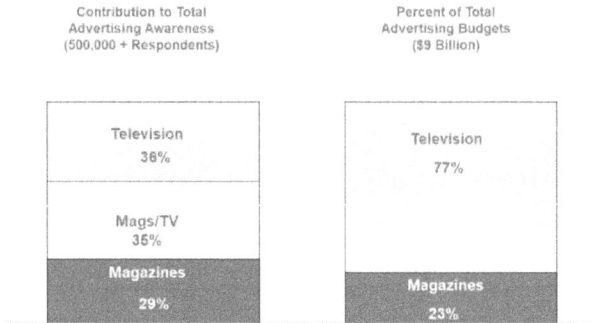

KANTAR MILLWARDBROWN

The research ('Documenting the Role of Magazines in Generating Advertising Awareness') also provided evidence of the media-multiplier effect that can be achieved by using television and print. The analysis looked over a three-year time frame and correlated purchase intent with media awareness. 61% of brands showed a statistically significant relationship between a change in advertising awareness and a corresponding change in purchase intent. Among those cases, a large majority (65%) used the combination of television and magazines (vs 19% for magazines only, and 16% for TV only).

Print in the media landscape

Two key aspects contribute to the way people interact with and respond to different media:

• Control: The extent to which people can control their exposure to advertising. Unless they fast-forward through a pre-recorded program, people have little control over TV advertising. The ad will take over the screen no matter what. By contrast, there is no 'programming' that dictates that people will spend any time at all with a print ad. Readers are in complete control over the rate at which they turn pages.

• Mood: The mindset of people when they engage with different media. When using online or print media, people are usually active and goal-seeking, while with television, they are more passive.

So, print is an actively consumed media and people have complete control over whether they stop and look at ads. To create strong print advertising, it is important to keep that in mind.

What does a good print ad do?

Engage readers

All advertising must engage viewers, readers, or listeners, but print advertising is especially challenged in this respect because there is a product category effect that isn't seen in TV.

With print there is a strong correlation between category interest and impact

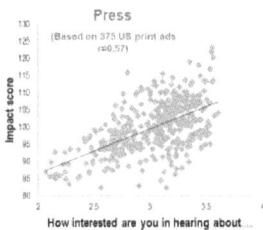

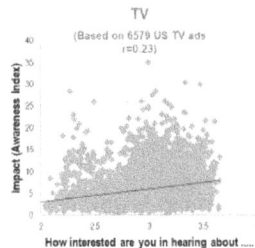

Because print is consumed actively, an ad must immediately give a reader a reason to look at it before they turn the page. Some categories are inherently interesting, and some are not. If you have a relevant message in a high-interest category, excessive creativity can be counter-productive; a very direct image or statement may be sufficient to draw in the interested reader. But it is still possible to have a successful print ad in a low-interest category; ads just must find a way around the 'interest filter.'

As a start point, an ad needs to pull readers into the ad. So it must be eye-catching (to stop them from moving on) and/or intriguing (to make them want to find out more). I've have seen several successful ways this can be done:

• Use of a persuasive message.

• A strong creative hook, such as an arresting or intriguing visual or headline.

• Synergy with other advertising—for example, using a key frame or line from a TV ad as a hook.

• Borrowing interest from something else, such as using a recipe which features the product.

Use the creative hook effectively

However, even when an ad captures attention, consumers may not scan the ad as expected. Consumers spend an average of two or three seconds looking at a print ad; the creativity needs to quickly lead the reader into both the message and the brand. Within the ad, their attention will be drawn to what is most interesting; so key messages can be missed if they are not creatively highlighted. It is also essential that the route through the ad takes in the brand.

Avoiding execution wear out

As discussed earlier in the book, TV executions do not generally wear out in terms of their ability to have branded impact. However, the ability for a single print execution to deliver branded advertising memories does decay with further exposure to the same execution. Wear-out usually occurs after about three opportunities to see the ad.

Readers are in an active mode when reading magazines. When they see something that interests them, they will stop and process the information. But this will usually happen only once. Once the ad is processed and absorbed, the readers know what it says. They don't need to look at it again.

In a similar way, if the reader does not stop at a particular execution, they are not likely to stop with repeated exposures. If they weren't interested in it the first time, they are unlikely to be interested in it upon subsequent encounters (unless their circumstances change, making the communication relevant).

This finding has implications in relation to frequency and copy rotation, as it is vital to address the issue of wear-out when planning a long-running print campaign. Such campaigns benefit from including several different executions in order to maintain interest. Research in the United States has shown that a campaign with eight executions in the mix will only lose 1% advertising awareness week over week, whereas a campaign with three executions in the pool will lose 22% of advertising awareness week over week. In just two weeks, the campaign with fewer executions will have already lost 50% of the initial impact.

Decay in Advertising Effectiveness is Smaller With More Ads in the Pool

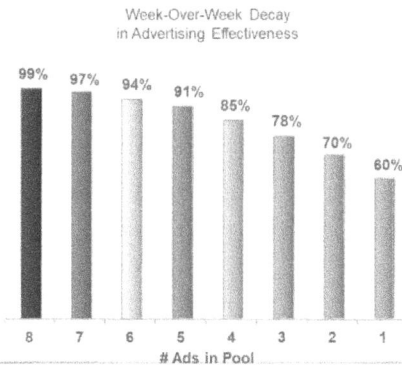

Week-Over-Week Decay
in Advertising Effectiveness

KANTAR MILLWARDBROWN

Patterns of readership

Readership of magazines does not occur immediately after issues go into circulation. Rather, it lags over time. So magazine ad awareness builds very differently than TV ad awareness (most TV exposures occur when the ad is transmitted or soon after). This happens for two reasons. First, purchasers are not likely to read all of an issue the first time they open it. They will often start reading it, set it aside, and return to it later. And second, magazines are frequently passed on, to friends, colleagues, doctor's waiting rooms, etc. Some magazines, such as fat quality monthlies like Vogue, are particularly prone to this lagged readership. Media planning and assessment must take account of the fact that the full reach of the campaign may not be achieved until several months after placement.

TV and Print exposures build differently

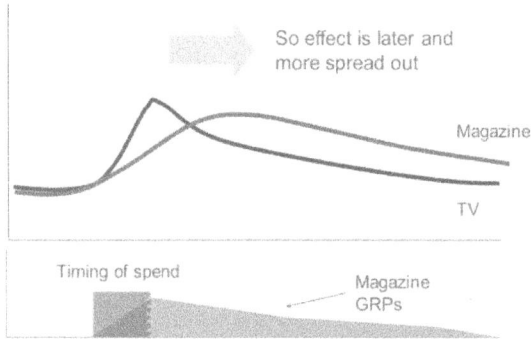

So effect is later and more spread out

Magazine

TV

Timing of spend

Magazine GRPs

KANTAR MILLWARDBROWN

I remember asking a client how his latest print campaign had affected sales. He said it had been disappointing. 'Mind you, there was this odd sales uplift after the campaign ended.' When we looked at the print schedule, we quickly realised that the campaign had been more effective than he had realised.

What does Cinema Advertising Add to a Campaign?

A while ago I had an interesting experience in a cinema. I'd arrived early and was watching the ads while I munched on popcorn. The film was a popular one and the cinema was full. Around me, people were talking and laughing, waiting for the film to start. Then another ad started. This one featured two serious-looking children, a boy and a girl, sitting side by side and facing the camera. A lively electropop tune began to play, and the children, still unsmiling, began moving their eyebrows in rhythm to the music. Within seconds, a hush fell over the cinema as the children's eyebrow gyrations got faster and more complex. Conversations stopped as everyone turned their focus to the facial gymnastics being performed on the screen in the ad for Cadbury's Dairy Milk.

The cinema offers a good opportunity to reach a younger audience across the globe. The 'cinema experience', with its shared nature, can lead to greater attention being paid to advertising, making it more memorable, so cinema ads can boost the impact of a TV campaign. However, not all advertising works well in the cinema, and the best ads tend to reflect the cinema-goer's desire for escapism, fantasy and entertainment.

An opportunity to reach consumers

While the reach of a cinema ad is unlikely to match that of a TV ad, its potential should not be underestimated. Globally, cinema represents a good opportunity to reach consumers. According to TGI, the United States is home to the largest proportion of movie-goers, with around a third of people having been to the movies at least once in the last month. Elsewhere in the world, India, Sweden and Mexico also boast high numbers of movie-goers, with at least a quarter of people in each market having been to see a film in the last month.

The lowest levels of movie attendance are in the Eastern European markets. Just a few percent of respondents in Romania and Poland had been to the movies in the last month.

Despite the variations, some coherent global trends emerge. Movies are particularly important to teens and young adults, who go in larger numbers and more often than older age groups. This is most pronounced in the Asia-Pacific region. In Singapore over half of people aged 18–24 have been to the movies in the last month compared with just a few percent of people aged over 55.

Research conducted in Australia by Kantar Millward Brown showed that more than half of movie-goers always arrived in time to see the pre-show program and agreed that the pre-show program was a good or acceptable part of the movie experience. Additionally, 57% felt that they took more notice of the ads shown at the cinema than those seen on television or in a magazine, or heard on the radio; they found these ads captivating, engaging, unique and having an appealing 'movie' quality about them. 80% felt that cinema ads were more entertaining. 'Everything seems a little more special in a cinema, it's dark and it's on the big screen. Everyone seems to get into the ads more, laughing more than they would at home.'

What can cinema advertising deliver?

This heightened level of attention can deliver greater memorability. A brand of crisps was advertised in London only in the cinema. The cinema spend would have bought around 180 London GRPs. This advertising produced the same peak in ad awareness as an earlier TV burst of the same ad using over 640 GRPs, making it over three times more efficient at generating ad awareness. It is of interest that many re-spondents recalled the cinema ad as a TV ad – a common occurrence.

This finding is reinforced by work by Kantar Millward Brown in South Africa. It compared in-market recall of ads flighted on televi-sion only (6,459 ads) with those that launched simultaneously on television and in the cinema (72 ads). The recall of ads that appeared in both media was significantly higher than ads that appeared on television only. For example, for ads launched with 201–300 TV GRPs, the TV-only recall was 22%, compared with 28% for ads with TV and cinema, an improvement of 23%. It was estimated that to achieve that level of recall using television only would have needed an additional 220 TV GRPs — substantially more than the typical cinema spend.

What stands out for all cinema advertising is its heightened ability to deliver brand appeal. In Australia, Kantar Millward Brown researched a range of ads that were representative of all cinema ads. On average, 52% of respondents reported that cinema ads increased the appeal of the brand — significantly higher than the average of all the TV ads in the database (44%).

The same ad can be experienced differently in the cinema than on television. In the UK, one humorous ad was aired in two different regions. In one, it aired only on television. In the other, it aired only in the cinema. The ad was the same, but it was enjoyed more in the cinema.

Advertising in the cinema can also affect consumers' perceptions of who the brand is targeting. In one example, two samples were recruited: one of respondents who had seen the ad in the cinema, and a separate matched sample who had seen the ad on television. Those who had seen the ad in the cinema were more likely to feel the brand was trying to increase its appeal among a younger audience (82%) than those who had seen it on television (66%).

What type of advertising works best in the cinema?

Qualitative research shows that cinema-goers visit the cinema for escapism, entertainment and an evening out. Ads that focus on escapism or immersive fantasy are likely to be appreciated. The cinema is valued leisure time which has been paid for, so viewers expect the advertising to be entertaining. Advertising that is considered very enjoyable tends to be rated highly as being 'suitable for the cinema'.

One word of caution, though: given that cinema-goers arrive at the cinema with the expectation of being entertained, advertising that falls below their expectations is unlikely to be well received. Unwelcome advertising may make the brand seem insensitive and out of touch. One ad that emphasized news for a brand conveyed the news effectively, but respondents felt the ad was not suitable for the cinema. Additionally, the shared environment can enhance negative responses as well as positive ones; it has been known for audiences to boo advertising in the cinema when the ad was one they already knew from TV.

Making the Most of Radio Advertising

Radio has a lot to offer advertisers. Particularly when used as part of a campaign, it can be a cost-effective means of extending reach, and adding depth to a message. As the number of channels continues to proliferate, radio offers even greater opportunities for reaching specific audiences. But, to get the most out of radio, it's important to understand the strengths of this medium, and how creativity can serve to generate listeners' involvement in an ad.

According to GroupM, the WPP media investment management operation, radio's share of media is strongest in Latin America and weakest in North Asia. Radio has been growing worldwide over the past few years, most notably in Latin America, Eastern Europe, and Africa. The availability of digital stations on the internet has been a factor in the growth.

A highly effective part of a multimedia campaign

Radio is often associated with small, local brands, but it can also serve a useful role for established brands. A study conducted for the Radio Advertising Effectiveness Lab in the U.S. (in which Kantar Millward Brown was a partner) showed that, when used in conjunction with a TV campaign, the ROI per dollar can be stronger for radio than TV.

Radio as lead medium

Radio can also work as a lead medium. Signature Vacations, the first national packaged tour operator in Canada, used radio advertising to give the brand a dominant presence on the airwaves, and to promote vacation giveaways. Brand awareness built quickly over a three-year period, from 16% shortly after launch to over 80%, at which time the brand had a 34% share of the market.

What radio is good at

Radio can be used to extend reach, which shows in increased ad awareness. Work for the Radio Lab in the U.K. demonstrated that if 10% of a TV budget was re-deployed to radio, the efficiency of the campaign in building awareness increased on average by 15%.

Radio can also help achieve a multimedia effect, usually by supporting a TV campaign. This is most likely to happen when radio ads use creative elements from TV ads, prompting listeners to re-experience the television imagery while listening to the radio.

The value of this effect is illustrated in the example below, where the radio campaign echoed the creativity of the preceding TV campaign. The lower line shows the increase in radio ad awareness in response to radio GRPs. What's interesting is that claimed TV ad awareness also increased, even though no TV was then running.

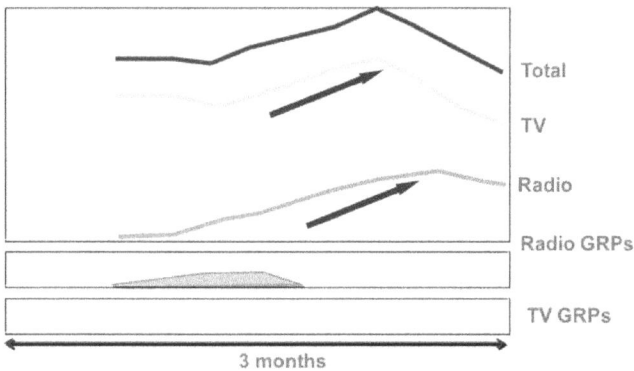

Radio often boosts memories of TV

KANTAR MILLWARDBROWN

Enhancing or expanding upon a TV campaign

Another effective way of using radio can be to enhance or expand the communication from a TV ad — through repetition in a different medium, through alternative examples of the same message, or through complementary messages.

In the example below, radio advertising was used to support the TV communication with a set of specific examples. In line with the rational content of the radio messages, rational brand images responded more favourably than with TV alone.

Pre-Post Changes in Brand Image

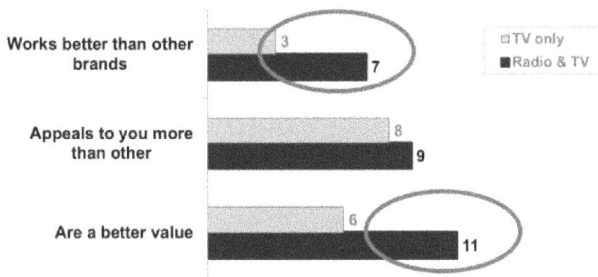

KANTAR MILLWARDBROWN

How radio differs from other media

• Exposure time: As with TV, a radio ad is of fixed and limited duration, leaving the listener no time for reflection: impressions are retained in the memory, but are not likely to be integrated with prior knowledge or experience. Messages need to be kept simple.

• Attention: Listeners are often engaged in another activity when listening to the radio, such as doing repetitive work, driving the car, or household chores such as ironing. This means they are likely to be in a bored/relaxed state of mind, under-stimulated and seeking emotional gratification. So there is a need (and an opportunity) for radio advertising to hold listeners' attention.

• Creative magnifier: As with TV, listeners are unlikely to recall all details of radio ads, but will selectively remember the most enjoyable and involving elements. So ads need to be structured so that these elements will convey the brand name and the key communication.

• Targeting: Radio is particularly good for targeting specific demographic groups as different types of people listen to different types of station and at different times of day.

• Wear-out/in: There is very little evidence that radio ads either wear in or out. So early testing can reveal whether you have a strong ad; and if you have, it may be worth running for some time.

• Irritation: Nonetheless, some advertising is so intrusive that it may become irritating. Such ads need to be treated with care. While they can be hugely impactful, levels of irritation can quickly grow, particularly with the high frequency plans not uncommon for radio. These ads should be identified at a pre-test stage.

Maximizing the effectiveness of your radio ads

As with all other media, brand linkage is critical to the ability of a radio execution to generate advertising awareness. As we've observed, this means ensuring that the key brand communication is integrated into the most interesting and involving parts of the ad. Other ways in which you can maximize radio effectiveness include:

• *Using non-visual brand cues*: While radio can't capitalize on visual brand cues, there is still the opportunity to benefit from the use of other brand cues already established through TV advertising, such as theme music, sonic brand triggers (e.g. Intel), jingles, slogans/ catchphrases or recognized voices. But be sure the brand cue in question is well enough established to work without the associated visuals

• *Creating involvement*: Enjoyment and the ability to involve are also key to successful radio advertising, since listeners are often engaged in another activity. In the U.S. a campaign of three ads was developed for a major beverage company, all using the same format of a narrator telling a story from his past. Two of the stories referred to activities such as fishing, which were not particularly relevant to the target audience, but the third related to a timeless romantic embarrassment. It was rated as twice as enjoyable as the other two, despite the similarity in formats.

• *Making it memorable*: It's important that radio ads communicate in a way that sticks in the listener's memory. This may be achieved through an engaging and memorable storyline. Alternatively, more direct executions can be good at communicating a basic message — such as a phone number — through repetition.

• *Choosing the right stations*: Radio can build advertising awareness as a solus medium; but, since it is often used as a cheaper alternative to TV, it's important to be realistic about what can be achieved with the lower spend involved. The problem can be how to best spend the money; in many countries, fragmentation and highly targeted radio stations means that many reach only a limited audience. If one station's target coincides with your own, maximize the opportunity! In most cases, though, the budget will need to be spread among several stations.

What makes a Great Outdoor Ad?

A bank launched a campaign consisting of four outdoor ads. They were similar in format and style, each relying on a pun to get its point across. Three of them fared well, but the fourth didn't. Checking the ads showed me that for the fourth ad there was a 'short-cut' to understanding it. People were taking out a very basic, banal message, and missing the pun.

Outdoor advertising can be used to reach a broad audience very quickly, but it can also be used very successfully to communicate with tightly targeted audiences, in specific locations.

As with all advertising, creativity is the key: striking, eye-catching ads are far more likely to be successful. But several other factors can also contribute to the success of an outdoor campaign, notably synergy with ads in other media, TV and print in particular.

A medium where speed is of the essence

Outdoor is a catch-all term used to refer to all media seen outside the home. As such, it's a very diverse sector, which includes street furniture, retail, transport, ambient, and roadside.

Outdoor is a low attention medium with generally limited exposure time. So, in most cases, outdoor ads must communicate fast — though, given the relatively low cost, there is the potential for repetition to create a cumulative effect over time.

Generally, ads with a clear and single-minded message perform well, but the message doesn't necessarily have to be simple, particularly once a style has been established.

Different types of outdoor advertising have different exposure times, which alter the creative challenge. While many outdoor ads have a 'dwell time' of only a few seconds, some — for example, ads where people are waiting in transit — can have much longer exposure. In such cases, more detailed communication is possible.

What are the strengths of outdoor?

Outdoor is a particularly good medium for communicating with people on the move; messages can be targeted at particular groups, like travellers in airport lounges. Targeted audiences can also be reached, such as fitness enthusiasts in gym changing rooms.

But, as TV audiences fragment, in many countries outdoor remains a valuable tool for reaching a mass audience quickly — and in a very public way. However, outdoor reach in many developed countries is restricted to urban audiences.

Often outdoor is the closest medium to the point of sale. Many supermarket car parks contain several billboards, which offer advertisers a last-minute opportunity to influence buying decisions, akin to in-store activity. This can be effective: research by ClearChannel and Sainsbury in the UK for a pet food brand tracked sales in matched stores, half carrying ads in the car park. In these stores, sales showed an uplift compared with stores with no ads.

How to make the most of outdoor

Spend is an important factor, but not the most important one.

This analysis from China shows that while there is a relationship between spend and ad recognition, it's only a weak one; there are other factors at play here.

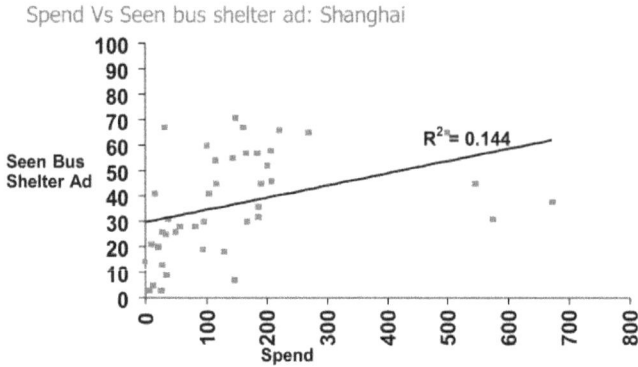

Spend Vs Seen bus shelter ad: Shanghai

$R^2 = 0.144$

The quality of site makes a difference

Analysis shows there are benefits to buying 'premium' sites. Criteria for judging site quality include visibility, and number of passers-by. In one experiment, the average level of shift in prompted awareness for a standard schedule was +2.6% while a premium schedule lifted awareness +3.7% on average.

Outdoor has to grab attention

Creativity is the key to success. 'Want to look again', 'striking' and 'eye-catching' all correlate with impact. Communicating news also aids impact.

The best ads have a 'hook' that remains with people for some time after exposure. We've found that the most striking outdoor ads often feature sex, humour and celebrities.

The best ads communicate strongly in their own right. But it can help if they are linked creatively to other activity — such as events, or advertising in other media.

Synergy with other media

The most impactful outdoor ads tend to be those where the creative is matched across media, particularly TV.

But I've also seen examples of outdoor and print working together well, particularly when the creative is similar.

Integrating the brand

The strongest outdoor campaigns have indelible branding, not just a big logo. Given that people will usually only spend a few seconds with any ad, it's important to consider their likely eye-flow through the ad: will it take in the brand?

Can it communicate?

While there are exceptions, outdoor is generally best for simple announcements, rather than complicated or multi-layered messages. But good outdoor ads can communicate many facets of a brand position, from a money-off message to a subtle aspect of brand personality.

Avoiding wear-out

Finally, like print ads, outdoor ads can wear out; after a few opportunities to see, they can quickly fade into the background. So if your campaign is intended to have longevity, it may be worth planning a number of different executions.

Can Sponsorship be Effective?

One European bank regularly sponsored an annual theatre event. The sponsorship was moderately successful. But the year I took over the account, the effectiveness of the sponsorship almost doubled. Not, sadly, due to my involvement, but the team had gained the budget to spend as much on marketing the sponsorship as on the sponsorship itself.

In recent years, sponsorship has become an increasingly significant part of the marketing mix. This can include sponsorship of existing TV or radio programs, original programming, event sponsorship, and team or stadium sponsorship.

Sponsorship has developed into a universal medium, particularly in the sporting world, and sponsors will pay large sums of money to be associated with properties that have worldwide coverage.

Sponsorship can undoubtedly be a powerful brand communications tool, not just in terms of building awareness but also improving perceptions. But, to be successful, sponsorship must be seen as appropriate, and even then it can take time to establish itself. So it's worth putting effort into promoting the sponsorship (through PR, for example), to ensure consumers are aware of the reason for it. Since it's unlikely to deliver detailed product information, sponsorship isn't generally well suited to promoting little known brands.

A powerful part of the marketing mix

Sponsorship can be an effective way of communicating brand values to consumers. It can also be a highly targeted means of communicating with groups of consumers that other media might find difficult to reach, to reinforce brand values and messages. For example, association with extreme sports could be a very efficient way of communicating with adventurous young males, traditionally very hard to reach with conventional TV advertising.

But sponsorship doesn't work in isolation. Attempts to launch a brand using sponsorship alone might gain some awareness but would be unlikely to communicate a detailed brand message.

As with many other media, consumers are not actively looking out for brands at the time they are exposed to the sponsorship. The potential for the brand to be missed or ignored is high. So, integrating sponsorship into the rest of the marketing mix is key. It needs to be supported and leveraged through other media.

Sports sponsorship

Gillette has been involved in sports sponsorship for many years. The brand has taken a long-term approach to building a relationship with sports fans through sports broadcast sponsorship, association with major global sports events, and commercial tie-ups with high profile sports stars — leveraging the associations across a variety of media.

The Kantar Millward Brown BrandZ study shows that, demographic differences aside, the equity for Gillette among those interested in sports is far stronger than among those not interested. Sports lovers are more likely to see the brand as relevant, and offering good performance with advantages over competing brands.

However, there can be drawbacks to this kind of sponsorship: the degree of control that can be exercised over a sponsored event/team/person is less than for most other media, and the performance of teams or the behaviour of individuals cannot be anticipated with any certainty.

Web site sponsorship

This example below shows the effects of a fashion brand sponsoring a fashion web site. With a control cell visiting an unsponsored version of the site, it was possible to see the effect the sponsorship was having on brand perceptions — and how those perceptions were still stronger among regular visitors to the site.

Brand perceptions improve as the 'exposure' becomes greater...

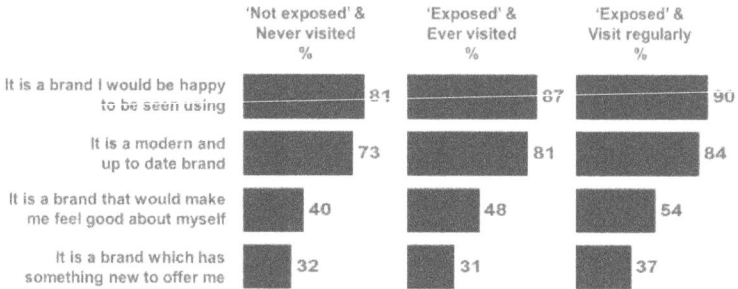

	'Not exposed' & Never visited %	'Exposed' & Ever visited %	'Exposed' & Visit regularly %
It is a brand I would be happy to be seen using	81	87	90
It is a modern and up to date brand	73	81	84
It is a brand that would make me feel good about myself	40	48	54
It is a brand which has something new to offer me	32	31	37

TV program sponsorship

Program sponsorship can also be highly effective. Consumers with an attachment to a particular programme may feel the brand must have some credibility, or the programme which they enjoy and trust would not permit the sponsorship. This can help confer big brand status and build confidence. If the brand can tap into the empathy and programme imagery in a relevant way, a beneficial 'halo effect' can also be achieved.

The following example shows sponsorship of a TV programme that had a particularly good fit with the brand. Because the programme sponsorship was only regional, it was possible to identify those exposed to the sponsorship versus those not exposed (outside the relevant TV regions). While there were no demographic differences between the groups, there were significant differences in terms of their attitudes toward the sponsoring brand.

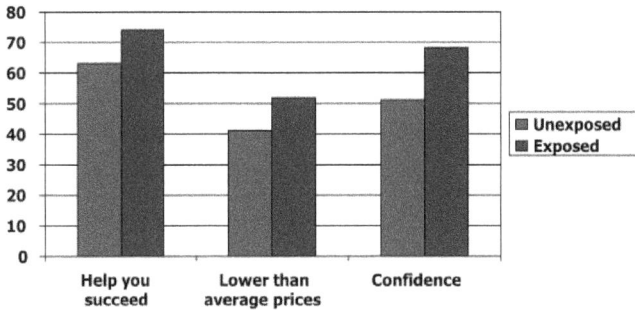

Optimizing the sponsorship: a perfect fit

Making the sponsorship appear appropriate is vital. The appropriateness of the fit between the brand and the property is important in generating awareness and the desired brand impressions.

The most *appropriate* sponsorships are the most *effective*

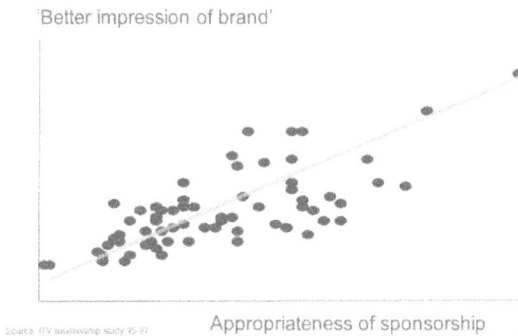

This appropriateness may take the form of a natural fit between brand and property (e.g. Red Bull and Formula 1), or it may be primarily 'tonal' — the connection being established through the creativity of support executions. If there is no natural fit between the sponsored property and the brand, it's essential to create one — in a memorable and relevant way. Without this fit, the value of the sponsorship should be questioned.

Remember, effective sponsorship may take time . . .

Finally, it's important to remember that sponsorship associations can take time to build, particularly when taking over from an existing sponsorship. In the following example, Brand 2 took over the sponsorship of this sporting event two years prior to the start of the chart, but still more people associated the event with the original sponsor. It took a concentrated effort over the following year, using PR and creative 'break-bumpers', to reverse this position.

Awareness of sports event sponsorship

KANTAR MillWARDBROWN

Using Direct Marketing to Build Brand Values

Persuasive leaflets can motivate trial. One brand distributed coupons that entitled the recipient to a free bottle of a new drink. 45% of respondents claimed to have received the coupon, and 80% of these claimed to have used them.

While the primary purpose of direct marketing is the achievement of an immediate and specific response (such as trial, purchase, or inquiry), large-scale direct marketing can have other positive effects as well. It can boost awareness and interest and enhance a brand's image. But direct mail can be ignored, and, worse, have negative effects by annoying recipients. So, if the benefits of direct marketing are to be maximized, several issues need consideration.

Direct mail is still relevant

Given the rise of the internet as well as email marketing, one might expect that the importance of physically delivered direct mail (including leaflets, coupons, postcards, letters and samples) would be limited. However, research suggests otherwise.

In collaboration with the Centre for Experimental Consumer Psychology at Bangor University in Wales, Kantar Millward Brown conducted an experiment that used functional Magnetic Resonance Imaging (fMRI) to understand how the brain reacts to physical and virtual stimuli. fMRI allows us to look directly at brain activity and so see the brain regions most involved in processing advertising. There was more emotional involvement when participants handled material printed on cards than when they viewed the same material online.

The research strongly suggested that greater emotional processing is facilitated by physical material than by virtual, which should help to develop more positive brand associations. The real experience is also internalized, which means the materials have a more personal effect, and hence should aid motivation.

Direct Mail can be highly visible

Coupons and leaflets can reach a mass audience. The example below shows the results achieved by one retailer that switched the majority of TV spend into leafleting. Awareness of the leaflets was higher than TV ad awareness had been; almost 50% of respondents had noticed them.

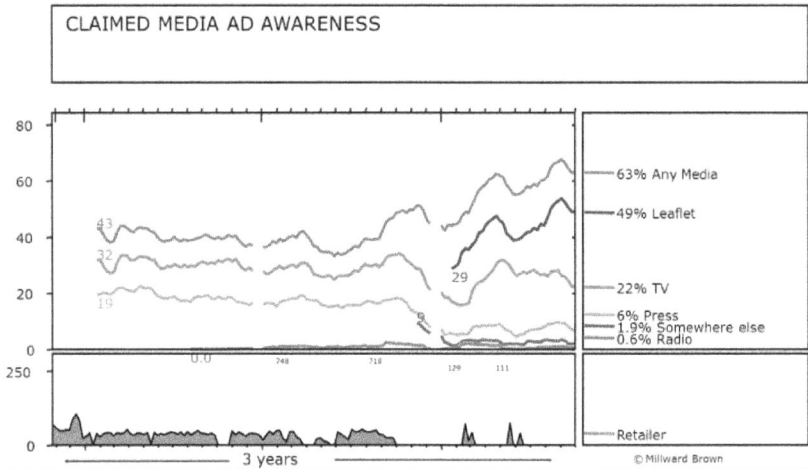

CLAIMED MEDIA AD AWARENESS

63% Any Media
49% Leaflet
22% TV
6% Press
1.9% Somewhere else
0.6% Radio

Retailer

3 years

© Millward Brown

KANTAR MILLWARDBROWN

Call to action

The retailer leaflet campaign generated footfall as well as awareness; one out of three customers who received the leaflets claimed to make a special trip to take advantage of the offers highlighted.

Building image as well as awareness

A Danish security company sent letters to households promoting their alarm systems. Over the subsequent three days, consumers were interviewed by telephone. The mailing clearly had an impact; communication awareness for the brand was almost twice as high (63%) among those who received the letter compared to those in a control cell (32%). When asked 'Which companies offer burglar alarms to private residences?' 50% of those who received the letter mentioned the brand (compared to 35% in the control cell).

Most significantly, however, the letters enhanced the recipients' opinions of the brand. When asked 'Which gives the best protection for your house?' 21% of those who had received the letter mentioned the brand, compared to 14% in the control cell.

Enhancement through sampling

When product experience provided through sampling takes place in conjunction with communications from other media, a great 'enhancement' benefit can be achieved. This enhancement effect occurs when expectations about the brand experience are set up by the marketing communications and then reinforced by actual trial.

In one carefully controlled and disguised experiment conducted by Kantar Millward Brown in partnership with the agency Fast Marketing, 11.8% of respondents who were exposed to an ad for Fox's Crinkle Crunch biscuits said they would buy the brand next time. Of respondents who received a sample of the brand, 14.6% said they would buy the brand. But among those who both saw the ad and got a sample of the product, the percent saying they would buy the brand next time rose to 19.5%.

Potential to annoy

Direct mail, then, can have a very beneficial effect on brand health. But if it is not managed correctly, it can also damage a brand. For example, aggressive marketing on the back of loyalty programs can aggravate users and in fact do more harm than good.

A credit card brand in New Zealand experienced this problem when, after successfully introducing a new and attractive loyalty program, saw future brand consideration among current users decline.

A review of the tracking data showed that direct mail awareness was very high. A qualitative follow-up revealed that people were bothered by very persistent phone calling that offered further cards, travel insurance and other services. So while the offer was an attractive one, overly-zealous use of the card user database made the member experience become a poor one. Consideration of the brand among card users fell.

Consideration of the brand amongst current users declines

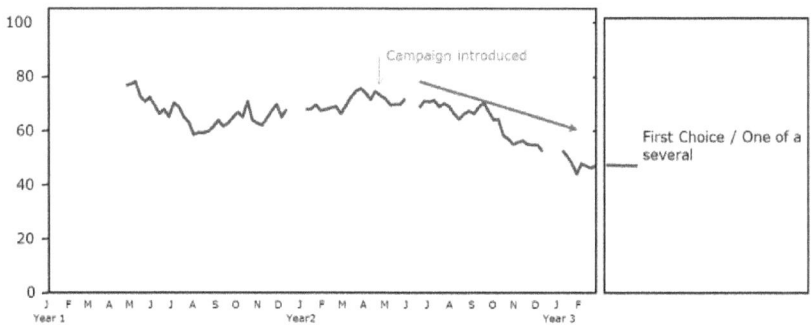

First Choice / One of a several

Tips for effective Direct Mail

Be aware of who uses it

Qualitative research conducted in the UK identified three types of people most likely to use direct mail.

Brand users: Existing brand users will often use coupons they receive as a reward for loyalty.

Bargain hunters: This group consists mostly of females who love shopping, like entering competitions, and tend to keep all coupons.

Organized consumers: Those who are organized enough to keep coupons and catalogues are also likely to make use of the offers.

Groups that show little or no interest in direct mail include: Young families and others who are time-challenged; those who are cynical about marketing; those who are experts on a product category; and those who prefer to conduct their own research.

Make sure it has impact

Direct Mail can easily go unnoticed if the creative does not immediately draw the reader's initial attention. Where possible, make it personal. Address it with an individual's name rather than 'Resident' to increases the chances of it being opened. But if you are addressing named individuals, ensure that your data files are accurate and clean: receiving someone else's mail can irritate, confuse, and alienate people. Once I researched a mailing to a client base where one letter was addressed to 'Mrs Smith (deceased).'

The tone of the mail can affect its impact. While it will not always be appropriate, if the mail seems significant or serious, this can affect impact levels. Consider the attention that people give to things such as invitations, bills, and insurance papers. Mail from the taxman, while generally plain and unwelcome, is almost always noticed.

Make sure it is involving

Direct mail must immediately establish its value. Exposure time is short; interest needs to be generated between the doorstep and the waste paper bin. Consumers are more likely to engage with material relating to a product category that fits their interests; conduct research ahead of time to identify customer needs and establish relevant issues. Aim to provide communication that is simple and enjoyable to read.

Mailings that generate positive emotions such as happiness, safety, security, or nostalgia are more likely to generate engagement. Loud, vulgar, or garish graphics may create a negative image. Direct Mail can fail when it is overly intrusive, when its message is seen to be 'over the top,' when its style is lecturing, hectoring, loud, or incomprehensible, or when there is too much copy with too many messages.

Using imagery from a current TV campaign can be effective. The TV campaign may have built up curiosity that the mailing can capitalize on; equally, the mailing can serve as a reminder of the TV ads.

Seek to extend the processing time of body copy

Techniques that encourage consumers to retain the leaflet for later perusal can be helpful. Offer rewards such as free samples and coupons, information, recipes, or calendars. Designing the brochure so that it acts as a storage place for coupons can also encourage consumers to hang on to it.

Price Promotions: How to Make Them Work for the Brand

Domino's Pizzas success in the UK had been delivered via a promotion-led approach, aligned to menu/door-drop delivery cycles. But as competitors copied this approach, growth stalled. After a lot of customer research, the brand changed strategy and launched a brand-building campaign focused on special occasions and events. The campaign generated £230m of incremental revenue.

Price promotions can be highly effective in boosting short term sales. But encouraging trial isn't the same as building brand loyalty, and price cutting can actually be damaging to brand equity. So, to make price promotions work for your brand in the longer term, you need to be clear about your strategy: what you are aiming to achieve, and when the promotion should end. In addition, you should consider supporting the promotion with brand building advertising, to ensure consumers appreciate what makes your brand distinctive — not just the savings it offers.

The most powerful influence in-store

In many parts of the world, marketers give priority to price promotions over media expenditure. While their popularity varies across countries and across categories, price promotions can be the most powerful in-store influence on purchase.

In recent years, growth in promotional activity has been fuelled by retailer power, but there are also many reasons why the marketing team might consider promotions, including: attracting new (or lapsed) consumers; volume/stock clearance; to hit sales targets; to match competitive promotions; or to squeeze out a new market entrant.

Promotions can be very successful

Promotions can undoubtedly generate increased usage and sales. For example, sales modelling for one petrol brand revealed that brand image advertising produced a short-term sales return of £2,000 per GRP, while a TV-advertised promotion produced a short-term sales return of £11,000 per GRP.

They can be particularly useful in new categories, or for new brands with a genuinely superior product experience. The following example shows that while the advertising is generating brand awareness, it is the promotion that is generating trial.

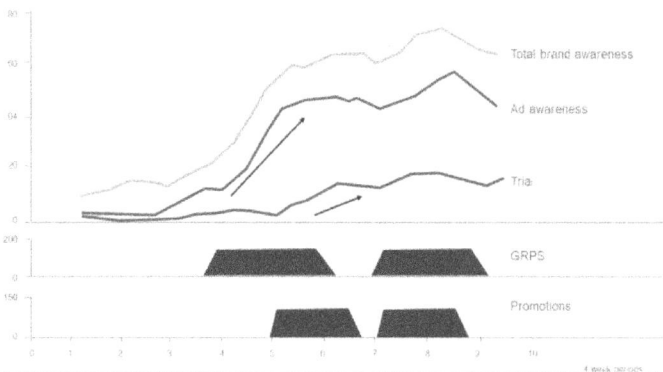

Promotion generates trial

KANTAR MILLWARDBROWN

Promotional pitfalls

However, there are pitfalls associated with promotions. In Japan, for example, the shampoo category is fiercely competitive and worth over US$1billion per annum. When a new brand was launched into the category, awareness built quickly, but trial lagged. In response, it adopted a series of price promotions over a two-year period. Trial built as a result — but regular usage did not follow.

Adding in value share to the picture revealed what had happened. During the first six months, the price cuts helped to build trial and increase value share. After this, trial continued to grow, but value share was in decline. In the final period, trial reached its peak and value share continued to decline. What benefit were further price cuts delivering for the brand? They had helped take the brand to a wider market, but real loyalty didn't build. Further analysis showed the brand had failed to build a distinctive position.

A second example further illustrates this point across a whole category. In the UK, an OTC category was in growth. However, as a result of a price war, the total volume sold on promotion increased by 15% across all brands across the season. The result was that value was driven out of the market.

At the same time, brand equity declined. Loyalty declined from 81% to 55% in one year.

Making the most of price promotions

Two examples from India help point the way to a successful strategy. One food brand that was promoted for three months, supported the promotion through mainstream media. From quarter one to quarter two, claimed 'buy most often' rose from 28% to 31%. But by quarter three, after the promotion ended, this had dropped to 22% — 6% below the pre-promotion level. The most likely explanation was that people had been buying stocks of the product to store for future use.

Meanwhile, another food brand in a different market also supported a price promotion through mainstream media. From tracking data, the proportion claiming to buy the brand most often increased from 16% to 20% from quarter one to quarter two; but, crucially, the increased level held at 19% for quarter three. The difference? This second brand also introduced a brand building campaign with significant spend.

Overall, then, while price promotions can undoubtedly stimulate short term sales, they also have the potential to erode short-term margins and long-term equity. To avoid these pitfalls, and make the most of price promotions, it's important to limit their use — and, when they are employed, to provide brand building advertising support.

Using Consumer Promotions to Benefit the Brand

When I was a boy, Curly Wurly, a chocolate coated caramel bar, offered a promotion; send off a number of wrappers and they'd sent you a glow-in-the-dark skeleton. That skeleton hung in my bedroom for years, and still forms part of my mental associations with Curly Wurly.

Consumer promotions can be an effective marketing tool, and when used well, can build equity. But successful promotions need to be simple, offer a real benefit, and be communicated clearly.

Promotions are a common means to market brands. Free gifts, games and other reward programs have been around for years. These can be very successful, particularly for children's brands, but it is essential to be clear on your strategy. The benefit of most promotions is a short-term sales response rather than equity building.

Promotions are well positioned to adapt to the digital age. Some mobile phone networks have made strong promotions a feature of their brand experience. One promotion for a snack brand targeted at 6- to 11-year-olds required participants to text details from the pack to see whether they had won; this was illustrated by an accompanying TV ad. The promotion was understood, and 20% claimed to have participated — a good result given that a high proportion of this age group did not own a mobile phone. The campaign boosted perceptions that the brand was cool, and usage measures improved.

Using promotions to build equity

While it is rare for them to do so, promotions that are part of a well-established, ongoing campaign theme can build brand equity. One new snack brand, using an established campaign theme, introduced a scratchcard promotion for four months. Awareness of the promotion peaked at 15%, trial levels increased sharply during the promotion. The brand's equity also grew, although the effect was short-lived.

Promoting the promotion

Consumers need to be made aware of the promotion. One confectionery brand ran an annual promotion. One year it centred on glow-in-the-dark figures. An accompanying TV ad was engaging and impactful but failed to communicate the figures. Awareness among adults was very low, but even among children, who are more likely to notice promotions, only 20% recalled the figures from the advertising, so participation was lower than in previous years.

In-store support

Some promotions depend on in-store support. Because this support cannot be guaranteed, promotions awareness can be affected. For example, one premium Chinese juice brand was not supported with TV, as other market-leading brands were, but relied instead on promotion as one of the key marketing activities to grow the brand. It launched two promotions to generate a higher level of trial, Lucky Draw and Buy X Get Y. But these promotions failed to generate an increase in sales; only 1% claimed to have participated. Analysis showed that there was low awareness mainly because less than a third of the stores carrying the brand supported the promotion.

Conveying the benefits of the promotion

Another promotion failed because its appeal was not properly conveyed. Developed for a children's cereal, it was very well received in qualitative research, and, of those who received the promotion, 65% rated it as an exciting new idea — higher than any other promotion monitored in the category. Following the advertising, two-thirds of the target audience were aware of the promotion. However, take-up was weak. Analysis showed that while the advertising had conveyed the name of the promotion, its key benefit was taken in by just 19% of the audience.

Keep it simple

When it comes to promotions, simplicity is key. Analysis from one cereal market showed that awareness was more likely to convert to interest when the promotion was in the pack, than if it had to be sent away for.

In-Packs exceed Send-Offs in both awareness and interest

Cereals - Children

	Awareness	Interest Conversion
Average In Pack	63	44
Average Send Offs	57	31

In general, children have a higher opinion of promotions than adults. In one category the average 'excellent' rating was 19% for children, 11% for adults. But a simple, well-publicised promotion with a clear benefit can be appreciated by any audience.

Capitalising on Word-of-Mouth

First Direct was formed in 1989 as the UK's first telephone banking service. Customers were delighted with the service they received. Along with many others, I was at the receiving end of enthusiastic praise from people who had joined. Spotting this trend, their ad agency ran a campaign showing customers praising the service in unusual circumstances. In was very successful – in part because it chimed with experience.

Brands can generate a positive buzz about themselves with highly enjoyable and involving marketing activity. But it is hard for marketing activity to build advocacy; conversations with family and friends are far more likely to be influential. The extent of these conversations varies considerably by category, but, as ever, excellent product quality can generate advocacy.

Information on web sites is more likely to be negative than that received from friends and family; but understanding how information passes from site to site can help guide marketing activity.

Buzz and Advocacy

While Word of Mouth (WOM) refers to all the communication about brands that takes place on a consumer-to-consumer level, it is useful to separate this communication into two types, according to their content: Buzz and Advocacy. Buzz reflects interest in something new, cool, different, or provocative, and forms a social currency, encouraging 'pass-along' from one person to another.

Advocacy is word-of-mouth communication — positive or negative — focused on a brand and its merits. Advocacy is more likely to sway brand choice in the short term.

Buzz

Buzz can help keep a brand salient and familiar, and advertising can be a useful source for generating buzz. Analysis of the Kantar Millward Brown Link™ database shows that the types of advertising that consumers are most likely to talk about are those that are considered enjoyable and involving.

Talkability: Enjoyment and Involvement

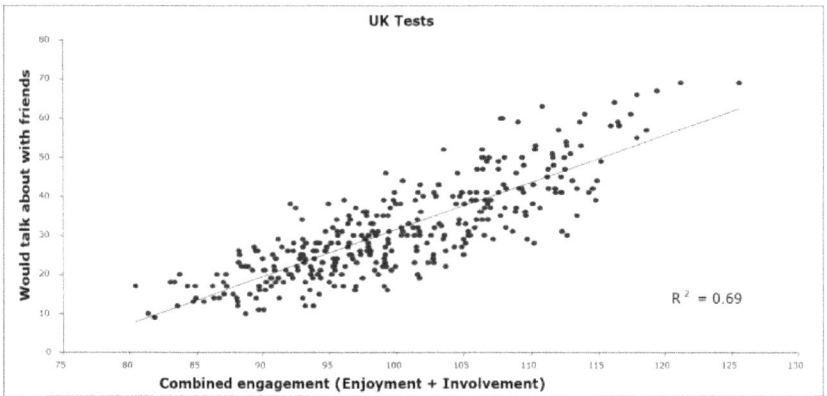

KANTAR MILLWARDBROWN

However, Buzz does not automatically generate sales. One recent ad in the U.S. for whisky was hugely enjoyed, and generated a lot of buzz, as it was designed to do. However, brand imagery was also meant to improve, but didn't. Internet search data from Google Insights revealed that the searches were to do with the ad and the actress featured in the ad; searches for the brand itself were much lower.

Advocacy

Word of Mouth is one of the key channels by which people absorb information about brands, along with more formal news channels and the Internet. In a study in the U.S. and the UK, covering six categories (digital cameras, mobile phones, holiday destinations, car insurance, cars and household cleaning products) one in four people reported choosing a brand solely because of a recommendation received from a personal contact. Similarly, after receiving negative comments about their original choice, 15-17% of shoppers changed their mind and bought a different brand.

Despite the rise in online activity, people are still much more likely to make use of brand recommendations from personal contacts such as friends, family or colleagues than those read online. Data from the same research showed relatively few people (around 10%) used informal sources of online information (chat rooms, blogs, online message boards and online contacts) to guide their last purchase decision in these categories. The majority of shoppers turned to friends, neighbours and colleagues for advice.

Even when it comes to saving money, consumers prefer the advice of friends and family over financial professionals.

Around the world, friends and family come before the experts...

Who would you turn to for advice or information about saving some money each month?

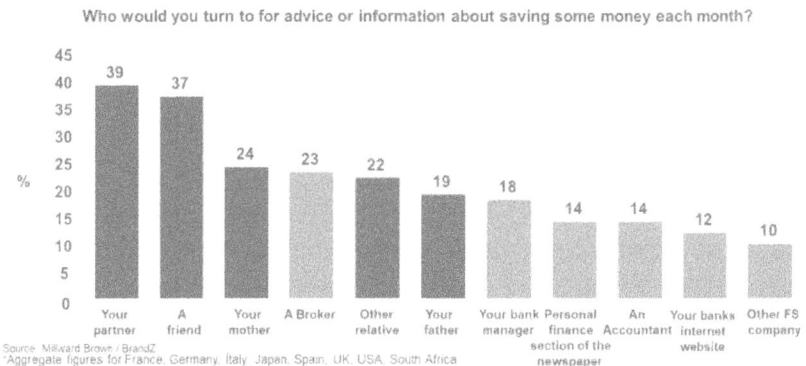

Source: Millward Brown / BrandZ
*Aggregate figures for France, Germany, Italy, Japan, Spain, UK, USA, South Africa

The reason for this is clear. Information from personal contacts is more likely to be trusted: it is considered more convincing and relevant than independent reviews or informal online sources.

Personal contacts are almost twice as likely to be given as the sole reason for purchase as informal online sources.

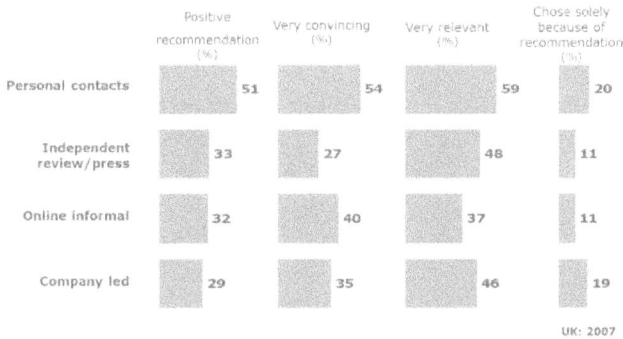

	Positive recommendation (%)	Very convincing (%)	Very relevant (%)	Chose solely because of recommendation (%)
Personal contacts	51	54	59	20
Independent review/press	33	27	48	11
Online informal	32	40	37	11
Company led	29	35	46	19

UK: 2007

KANTAR MILLWARDBROWN

So, although the web is full of personal opinions and comments about brands, more traditional WOM sources continue to have a greater influence on the choices consumers make.

Nonetheless, online comment can be influential. An exploration of online news and consumer-generated content (such as blogs, forums and Twitter) about the UK energy sector revealed that conversations tended to gravitate towards a few broad themes, including discussions about the latest deals, venting anger about customer service, and discussing marketing activities.

Differences by category

The strength of influence of WOM will depend on the category you are operating in. In the U.S., when choosing car insurance, 64% of people discussed the decision with friends and family and 16% used 'informal' online sources to help them make a decision. Whereas for household cleaning products, these figures drop to 39% and 4% respectively.

Personal contact is far more important for car insurance than OTC medicines

Q9. Thinking about the last time you were considering choosing a .., from which of these did you receive advice or information? Please select all that apply.

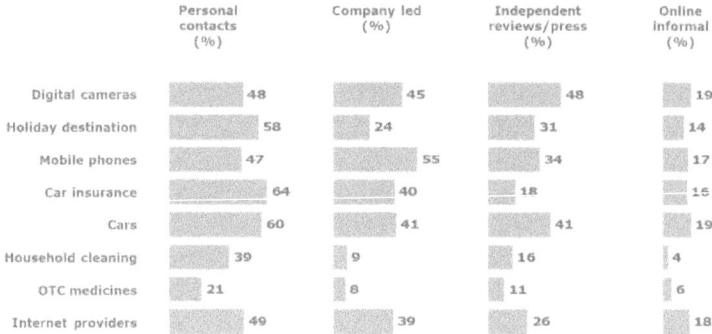

	Personal contacts (%)	Company led (%)	Independent reviews/press (%)	Online informal (%)
Digital cameras	48	45	48	19
Holiday destination	58	24	31	14
Mobile phones	47	55	34	17
Car insurance	64	40	18	15
Cars	60	41	41	19
Household cleaning	39	9	16	4
OTC medicines	21	8	11	6
Internet providers	49	39	26	18

KANTAR MILWARDBROWN

US: 2007

Some categories are inherently in a better position to capitalize on WOM. Baby products, such as diapers and baby food, are very likely to be recommended; as are soft drinks and beer. At the other extreme, credit cards and insurance are far less likely to be talked about.

Diapers is the category with the largest global advocacy

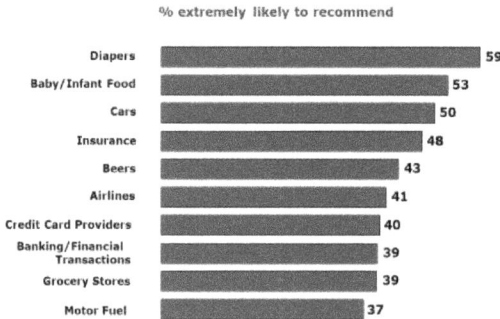

% extremely likely to recommend

Diapers	59
Baby/Infant Food	53
Cars	50
Insurance	48
Beers	43
Airlines	41
Credit Card Providers	40
Banking/Financial Transactions	39
Grocery Stores	39
Motor Fuel	37

But even within categories, some brands are better able to leverage Advocacy than others. This example from the UK haircare market shows that the level of conversations about brands is related to the familiarity of the brands; but brands like Dove, with its Campaign for

Real Beauty, and John Frieda, with products generating high levels of consumer satisfaction, received a disproportionate level of positive mentions.

Which brands get more than their 'fair share' of positive consumer comment

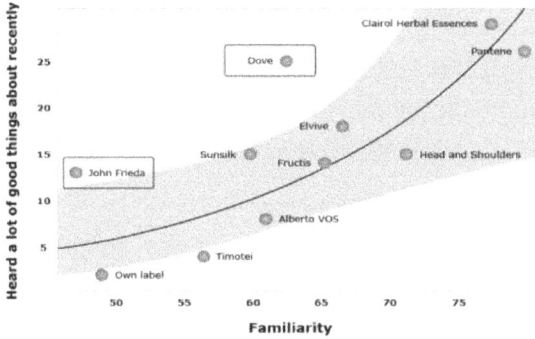

The dark side

While moss marketers like to focus on the positive potential of WOM, it also has a negative side. Informal online sources are more likely, compared to others, to be seen as giving recommendations of *which brands to avoid.* People use internet forums as a means of venting their frustration over poor service or product quality. Of those who had used online communities, online contacts and blogs, 45% said they received negative brand recommendations from them. This compares to 28% who received negative recommendations from personal contacts and 30% from independent reviews. And a consumer is just as likely not to buy a brand as a result of a negative comment read online as a negative recommendation from a personal contact.

However, negative publicity does not always translate into negative conversations. Sometimes the story is not important enough; sometimes the category interest is too low. A large U.S. energy company had been in the news for a series of transgressions. When a more significant event took place this oil company received a substantial amount of negative PR on a national basis. The conversations taking place among the key target audience were quantified and it was found that they weren't as negative as the brand team had feared. Conversations around the brand actually netted out on neutral ground. Negative PR doesn't always overwhelm consumers' conversations — some conversations during these times can actually be positive. The client was reassured, and rather than airing a campaign designed to address the criticisms head on, continued with their traditional advertising, reminding consumers of the good things about the brand.

How Effective is PR?

When Walmart bought the UK retailer Asda in 1999, Walmart was experiencing some strong negative publicity in the US for some of its practises, and there was potential for these stories to reflect on Asda. Instead a very strong PR team filled the media with stories about the great prices that would result from the takeover, which proceeded smoothly.

PR can be a highly effective brand-building tool. In the eyes of consumers, it can carry greater weight than other types of marketing communication, being seen as independent and hence more credible. As with advertising, the degree of impact achieved through PR can vary considerably. But in some categories, it can not only raise awareness but also have a significant impact on sales. Correspondingly, the effects of negative PR can be substantial — though if properly handled, the brand usually does recover, and often very quickly.

The value of PR: a more credible form of communication

PR can play·an important role in the marketing mix. It can supplement and augment advertising; it can educate the target audience; and it can do this through different and potentially more targeted channels.

PR works not only within the marketing mix; for some brands, it can be the major form of marketing activity. Brands such as Aston Martin, and Ferrari do not advertise to any great extent.

Specifically, PR is unique in terms of perceived credibility. The media coverage it generates is seen as independent, and the messages conveyed are regarded as being largely free of the spin that is commonly associated with other marketing communications. This is equally relevant for both positive and negative PR.

Positive PR: from raising awareness to closing the sale

Positive PR can be a valuable tool for any brand — but its importance becomes increasingly significant in automotive and service industries. It works well with brands which are inherently newsworthy (e.g. with a general appeal or aspirational characteristics). In the example below, it is clear how awareness of this automotive re-launch gained significant momentum before the start of advertising activity.

Awareness of Re-launch

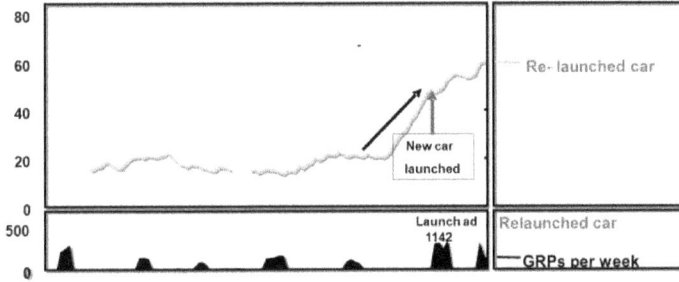

Purchase intent generated by PR can convert directly to sales. In this example, a new financial organization was launched with a major PR push, as well as other marketing activity. Sales modelling highlighted the contribution that PR made to sales during the initial weeks.

Contribution of PR to sales

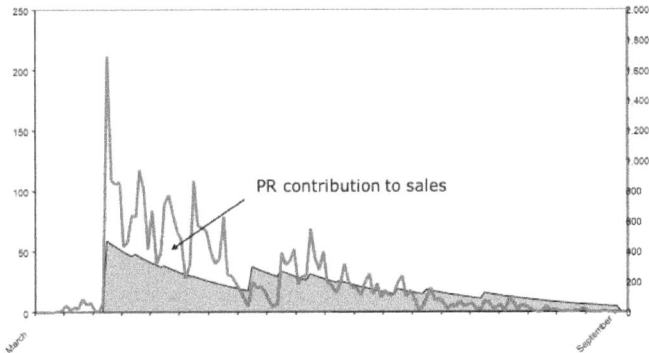

PR can work particularly effectively when it links into other media/marketing activity. Specifically, PR can be used very successfully in connection with sponsorship, maximizing return on the deal by generating stories around the business relationship.

Negative PR: moving to minimize the impact of bad news

Negative PR generated by bad news can have an even more significant effect.

The brand in the example below received a fair amount of negative PR, though this was heavily outweighed by positive PR. Nevertheless, consumer response was far more likely to have been affected by the bad news.

Negative PR can have more weight

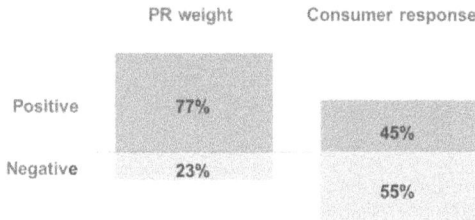

KANTAR MILLWARDBROWN

While a brand can be damaged by negative PR, the effects can be relatively short-lived. One bank became synonymous with news stories about branch closures, profits and 'fat cat' executive pay levels, as a major new advertising campaign pushed the bank's credentials through its size of business. Even in this extreme case, perceptions of the brand personality recovered in the following two years to the same levels as before the negative PR:

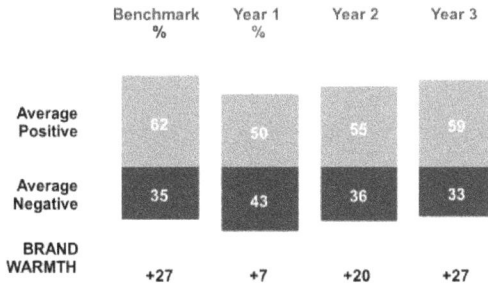

Personality warmth recovers in Year 3

	Benchmark %	Year 1 %	Year 2	Year 3
Average Positive	62	50	56	59
Average Negative	35	43	36	33
BRAND WARMTH	+27	+7	+20	+27

On the other hand, this major automotive brand suffered from two publicized recalls, and showed no signs of recovering.

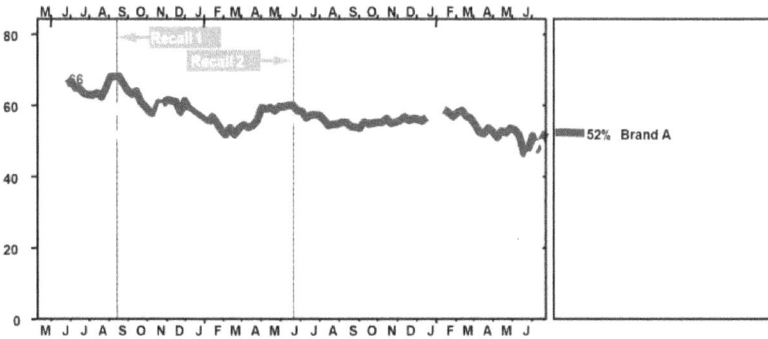

Overall opinion not recovering

The lasting effect of negative PR can depend to a very large extent on how the company responds. Trying to ignore bad news stories, or retaliating inappropriately, can make the problem worse; whereas, with a more considered response and an acceptance of corporate responsibility, the negative coverage may soon lose impetus.

Capitalizing on Social Media

Recently a friend, unhappy with a meat pie he'd bought, complained about it on Twitter. Within hours the brand's official channel had apologised, offered a full refund, and the tweet ended with a personal comment saying he was disappointed because he'd been looking forward to trying the new pie. It was a great response to a negative situation.

With the tremendous growth in the use of social media, brands have wrestled with how best to capitalize on it. However, the way consumers view online social networks means that the normal rules of marketing do not apply; the emphasis needs to be on dialogue and a sense of community. Fan pages can be used to build brand equity, but some pages do this better than others. The nature of social networks is dynamic, and marketers need to recognize that they require active involvement and a willingness to take the good with the bad.

The sociable brand

Social strategies will differ for different types of organizations with different needs; for some, having a presence in social networks will be essential, while for others, it will only be one relatively small part of the marketing mix. But the strategies do need to fit in with the overall brand strategy.

Why do consumers use social networks?

This desire to be involved in social media is understandable but in order to make best use of this medium, companies need to understand it. What really draws people to social media? Kantar Millward Brown Firefly global qualitative research has highlighted several drivers. First, it's about connectedness and belonging. Second, it's about entertainment and diversion. Third, it's about control: control by users and for users. After all, the users are the engine that drives social media and its unique appeal.

The specific activities at the core of social networking have emotional meaning as well. Every post represents a need to be recognized and acknowledged by those around us. Every comment left or shared is, in part, a way of seeking validation. These underlying emotional factors — a sense of control, belonging, entertainment, validation, and recognition — all shape the ways in which consumers react to brands in social media. Marketers should keep these factors in mind as they attempt to engage consumers.

But there are many different social networks, and it is worth understanding their differences. For instance, Facebook is appreciated as a means of keeping connected with family, friends and old acquaintances, while Twitter is more appreciated for information about current events and popular culture. Other smaller, more specialized networks are aimed at particular audiences and emphasize sharing reviews, issues, problems and solutions.

Advertising on online social networks

Given attitudes towards social media, it is perhaps not surprising that, in general, consumers do not respond well to the idea of advertising on social networks; it is far less acceptable than TV advertising.

However, since consumers are now spending so much time on them, online social networks clearly represent an opportunity for advertisers. But brands need to ensure their creative is relevant to the social environment for it to be effective. For the major social networks, this environment is likely to be oriented toward connectivity, entertainment, and fun.

Beyond advertising on social networks, how else can brands legitimately build a social presence? Currently many consumers report that brands can be viewed more or less as 'foreigners' or 'outsiders' in social media circles, insincere at best or trying too hard to be hip and cool at worst. Unless brands are genuinely committed to building real relationships and sharing the space with consumers, they may end up as the slightly odd guy, in unfashionable clothes, who's standing by himself at the party, hoping someone will talk to him.

The importance of fan pages

Gaining fans should be a priority for many brands, since it's a route to enriching relationships with already loyal customers (since those are the customers most likely to become fans). In general, personal contact is a far greater influence on purchase decisions than informal online sources although sometimes recommendations, reviews, and shared experiences posted on specialized networks carry significant weight. Nonetheless, even the general online sources can be useful. In a project for the World Federation of Advertisers, 3687 fans across 24 fan pages were asked how those pages made them feel about the brand when they visited. 43% reported that the brand became more appealing. Analysis suggests that the main drivers in generating brand appeal are stylish design and fun content. Fans reported that their opinions of the brands had improved since they became fans: 49% reported 'loving' the brand more, and 49% were more likely to buy it.

Most popular pages

From BrandZ data Kantar Millward Brown created a global ranking of the brands with the most followers among relevant category users. Category matters. Four out of the top six brands were from categories connected with technology, and the categories with the highest levels of fandom across the whole world were IT software, IT hardware, communication providers, and mobile phones. This isn't surprising; consumers of these categories are more likely to be savvy web users and more likely than others to embrace social media as a source of brand information.

Among non-tech categories, some are more likely to be topics of discussion than others. For instance, the category with the largest level of global advocacy is diapers. Cars came in third in terms of advocacy.

Other categories, such as motor fuel and detergents, are much less popular topics for discussion, offline or online. Consumer just don't make emotional connections with certain types of products, and that makes those categories less relevant for advertisers looking at social networking. The barriers to gaining fans are significantly higher for such categories.

Brand Personality is another factor that correlates with fandom. Brands that have more fans tend to be seen as particularly creative, trustworthy, and desirable. A brand that has this kind of personality might find it easier to attract fans.

Country differences

While social networks are a global phenomenon, there are social and political factors which affect how they are viewed on a regional basis. China is an interesting case because the government tightly controls the flow of information. The Chinese were quick to embrace social media but have yet to fully experience some of the applications and platforms. For example, access to Facebook is difficult. They have other social networks that serve the same end, but they feel left out of the global conversation without the ability to use Facebook. They often have friends and colleagues who live and work outside China and know what's available — and what they are missing. State controls on sites like Facebook run counter to the freedom they believe is inherent in social media.

India also has a strong desire to fully join the global community on social media but for slightly different reasons. Indians had a well-established platform, Orkut, but it did not evolve fast enough to keep up with what people were looking for from social media platforms. It felt 'dated' and too rooted in the region, and more specifically, the developing world. More and more Indians moved to Facebook as their primary social network. Orkut closed in 2014.

Ten tips for making best use of fan pages

Taking findings from a range of projects, both qualitative and quantitative, here's a set of tips for you to consider to help improve your fan pages.

1 Give the consumer a degree of control. This cuts to one of the core issues surrounding social media — it is controlled by users, for users. Often companies are reluctant to relinquish control of conversations about their brands, but pages that edit or censor consumer interactions seem out of place on a social network.

2 Be interesting. When looking at brands' pages, people want to see something new, fresh, or different — not a rehash of the same information they can get on a brand's official corporate homepage. They don't want to be 'sold to' in the traditional sense — they'd prefer to be wooed or courted. One fan page used a variety of innovative apps and slick, stylish content. It achieved a high rating, and strongly increased perceptions of the quality of the brand.

3 Be trustworthy. Be open and honest. Transparency is key for brands in social media and is the most critical factor in building trust. Consumers perceive that most brands would rather hide behind policies and procedures than own up to their failings or shortcomings. They don't trust and respect brands that do not post both the good and the bad on their fan pages.

4 Talk like a friend, not a corporate entity. Consumers want brands to communicate in simple, informal, conversational language. They don't want a bunch of technical corporate-speak; the tone should be clear, light, fun, informative, and unbiased.

5 Offer deals. Fans like to see their loyalty being rewarded. Though this is not the only reason they sign up to a page, they do often have some expectation of getting something in return. While discounts and coupons are in vogue for brands in social media, they are not a sustainable model; consider other 'exclusive' things like special editions or downloads.

6 Offer contests. Fans appreciate contests as a way of interacting with their brands. These do not necessarily need to be major events; they can also be regular, simple challenges that offer relatively small rewards. One very popular fan page, for a premium brand, ran frequent contests and giveaways. Rather than undermine value perceptions, these efforts built perceptions that the brand was worth paying more for.

7 Provide news. One major reason consumers become fans is to get information about new products; fans value information about a brand. But, tonally, this must appear as news, never as advertising.

8 Keep it lively. Sites with more frequent posts by the brand tend to have better overall ratings. Of the pages covered, no page posting less than 15 times per month was rated particularly well. However, posting too frequently can alienate fans; over-posting is one of the major reasons that consumers 'unlike' or 'hide' brand fan pages. So the key is to find a rhythm appropriate to the nature and style of the page.

9 Create a sense of community. Social networks are about community, so it is no surprise that the fan pages that are growing are those where fans post comments. This makes intuitive sense. It is up to you to start the chain reaction. People never go to empty restaurants; you need to create a dynamic, lively, and fun environment. One fan page scored particularly highly in terms of building a community among its fans. It has managed this by making the brand itself less of the focus, and instead facilitating conversation among fans.

10 Be true to the brand. How you best build appeal will depend on your brand personality and objectives. To decide what will work best for any individual brand, the key is in developing distinctive content and tactics to deliver your brand strategy in a way that will appeal to your target audience. One brand whose page strongly increased brand appeal uses the brand's character as the personality for the page. This entertaining approach not only helps bring the brand to life, but respondents reported sharing some of the status updates with friends, they were so entertaining.

AUDIENCE KNOWLEDGE

Do Men and Women Respond Differently to Ads?

Recently I saw an ad showing a geeky man in a lift with a glamorous woman. The guy clearly found her beautiful but didn't have the courage to even speak to her. The men I showed it to found it funny. But the women I showed it to were uneasy at the predicament of the woman alone in a lift with a man who they felt posed a threat. The two groups had very different responses to the ad.

At an overall level, there is little difference in the way men and women respond to advertising. The following chart looks at key measures (enjoyment, active involvement, branding, news, credibility, difference, and relevance) for U.S. English TV ads for which the test sample consisted of both men and women; there is little difference in the scores given by men and women.

Men versus Women: no real differences

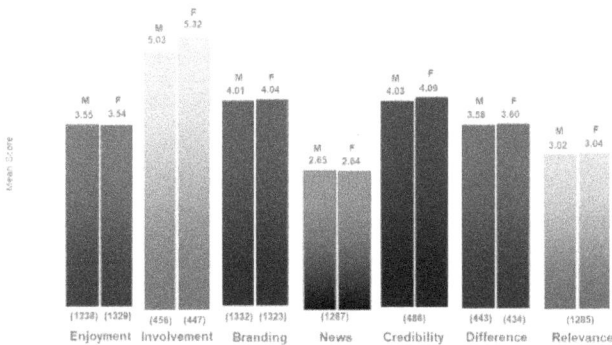

Measure	M	F	Sample sizes
Enjoyment	3.55	3.54	(1238) (1329)
Involvement	5.03	5.32	(456) (447)
Branding	4.01	4.04	(1332) (1323)
News	2.65	2.64	(1287)
Credibility	4.03	4.09	(488)
Difference	3.58	3.60	(443) (434)
Relevance	3.02	3.04	(1285)

KANTAR MILLWARDBROWN

Similarly, looking at emotional responses generated by advertising, the overall pattern between the sexes is similar.

301

Comparison of male and female –
positive emotions

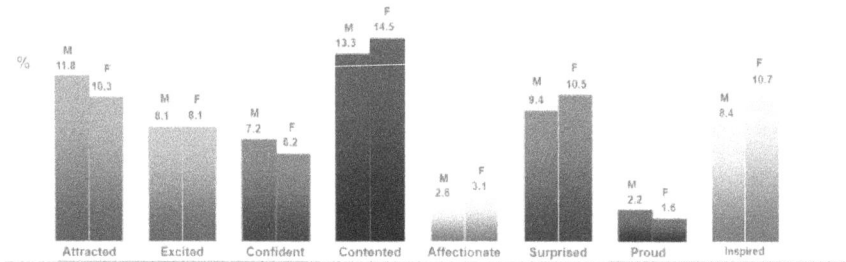

%

M 11.8
F 10.3
Attracted

M 8.1 F 8.1
Excited

M 7.2 F 6.2
Confident

M 13.3 F 14.5
Contented

M 2.8 F 3.1
Affectionate

M 9.4 F 10.5
Surprised

M 2.2 F 1.6
Proud

M 8.4 F 10.7
Inspired

KANTAR MILLWARDBROWN

Men and women enjoy different things

However, behind these averages, it is clear that there are real differences in the types of ads that are enjoyed by men and women.

A set of 1200 U.S. ads that had been tested among samples which included both males and females was taken. The ads that were in the top 10% for each group on enjoyment were explored. This analysis showed that men are more likely to enjoy humorous ads — particularly those involving spoofs. (However, it is worth stressing that there are also many humorous ads that do perform well among women).

HUMOUR	Male %	Female %
Funny	47	28
Light hearted	36	38
No Humour	17	34
Spoof/Parody in ad	12	2
Base (ads)	(114)	(135)

Enjoyment

A Spanish ad that featured a humorous scene in a slaughterhouse provides an example of humour that appeals more to men than women. Men better appreciated the intended black humour and it kept their attention. However, the somewhat violent nature of the ad put off the female target, who in general did not enjoy the ad.

Women on the whole are more likely to enjoy ads featuring a slice of life, or children — but these aren't hard rules.

Response to sexual imagery

Ads that feature sexual imagery can also elicit distinctly different responses from the two sexes. Some ads are enjoyed by both sexes, but for different reasons. A deodorant ad featured a girl preparing for a date while her boyfriend is coming up in the lift. It was an entertaining ad that performed well overall, but men and women found different parts interesting. Women followed the main elements of the story, while men showed peaks of interest only when the woman appeared in her underwear.

Other ads may actually alienate women. For example, one German ad for a chocolate brand targeted at young adults featured a teacher behaving in an erotic, flirtatious manner in front of her young adult class. Responses to the ad differed substantially by gender. Men enjoyed the woman's behaviour, while women increasingly lost interest as the ad progressed, as is illustrated by the interest trace below.

German Chocolate ad

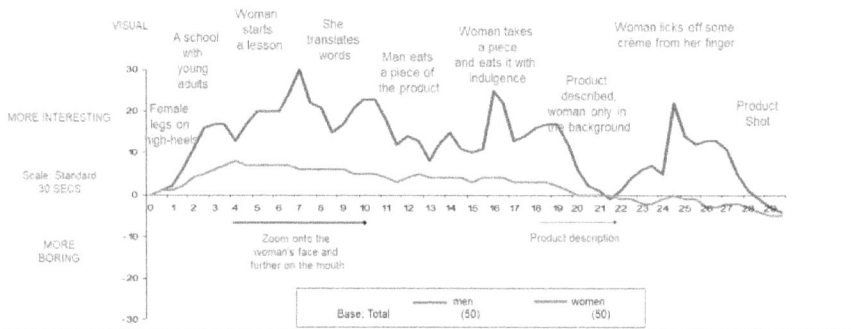

More than twice as many men as women said they would enjoy watching the ad (52% versus 24%). Over half of the men liked the woman in the ad while only 14% of women did. Almost a quarter of the women disliked the ad for being sexist or erotic. Given that women were an equal target for the brand, this represented a major problem.

So while at an overall level there may be no differences in responses to advertising between the sexes, there are clearly differences in response to individual ads, particularly when humour or sexuality are involved.

Successful Routes for Advertising to Children

I once monitored the launch of a kid's food brand. The product was substantial and aimed at older children. The advertising, which featured cartoon characters, was very impactful. The launch was hugely successful — supplies could not keep up with demand. But after the initial rush, sales dropped and the product ended up being delisted. Research showed that the cartoon advertising had mainly appealed to younger children, who found the product just too big. Older children didn't associate with the cartoon style.

While much advertising is aimed at a broad spectrum of children, it should be recognized that there are wide differences in cognitive and emotional development between younger and older children. Children pay more attention to adverts than adults, particularly when they include jingles, cartoons, humour, and elements borrowed from popular culture. This generation is internet-savvy and can appreciate interactive campaigns.

Emotional needs

Research by Kantar Millward Brown showed that kids go through four basic stages of emotional needs. These overlap because different children progress at different rates.

The Nursery stage (up to 4 years) is characterized by a safe, cosy, warm, nurturing environment. Parental guidance is essential at this stage. Toward the end of this stage kids learn to shift their play style from playing side by side to sharing playtime activities with friends.

The Playground stage (ages 3–10) is where pleasure, excitement, exploration (with mum and dad) and discovery take place. It is also a time where kids become aware of advertising. Initially, when kids first understand that advertising is something that shows things you can have, or ask mum to buy, they take everything at face value, but within six months they learn that sometimes advertising doesn't tell the truth.

The Street Corner stage (ages 9–12) is when kids start to develop a sense of identity and peer groups gain increasing influence. While children can adopt a rebellious stance at this point, it tends to be a safe stage, likely to be demonstrated by their choices in fashion and music.

The Underground stage (ages 13 or over) is about being different, and is rarely a place where adults are allowed to venture, although some brands can exist there.

Cognitive development

When targeting children under 10 years old, messages need to be fairly direct, and time should be presented in a linear way. In the U.S., an ad was aired showing a schoolboy who acts as though it were the weekend on a weekday, because of his breakfast. The ad starts with the boy at school, then flashes back to show him breakfasting at home, and finishes with him back at school. More than one in five found the ad hard to understand. While the children could play back most elements of the story, they did not understand its progression. As a consequence only 6% got the message that you could now have a weekend-breakfast taste during the week.

Under-10s prefer a happy story, one that is amusing, exciting or adventurous; a simple, complete story with a playful or imaginative mood. At the younger end of the spectrum, children enjoy slapstick comedy and simple verbal jokes.

Older children are better able to cope with more complex messages, and tend to prefer more intricate situations, with a realistic mood. As they grow older they are more likely to appreciate double entendres and complex lines, as well as cynical humour. For example, one German cereal brand introduced a campaign aiming to bring kids into the brand with a character who was designed to be a 'friend' of the kids. The ads encouraged the children to become part of his world and his adventures. Six- to seven-year-old children had problems understanding the idea, older children did not.

Children notice more

Children pay more attention to advertising. In general, advertising has three times the impact among kids as it does among adults. They also show greater appreciation of advertising and remember it for longer. Similarly, they recall more detail, as the next example shows.

Kids recall advertising detail better than adults

	Children	Adults
The boy gets out of bed	37	17
Goes to the kitchen	12	6
Tries to take BRAND	37	25
The boy is transformed into a 'monster'	42	34
He says "I want BRAND"	24	3
He begins to eat BRAND	24	11

KANTAR MILLWARDBROWN

Additionally, in countries where advertising is still relatively new, children can more readily assimilate it into their lives than their parents. Research in China suggests children understand advertising better than their mothers.

Successful routes

A wide variety of advertising styles achieve success among children. To take a few examples:

The use of jingles and slogans helps generate impact. In Mexico, a bubblegum brand launched a gum with a liquid centre. Four ads were developed and researched. The storylines were found to be hard to understand; as a consequence brand linkage and communication were weak. The variant name was not noticed, and if anything, the respondents associated the ad with the parent bubblegum brand. A completely new ad was created which gave a full description of the product, and integrated the brand name into a song that later became a ringtone. Branding and communication improved markedly, and the brand went on to a successful launch.

Some of the most impactful ads make use of established branding devices, which become the 'hero' in an action story. Some of the most successful ads feature the animated branding device saving the brand from a 'baddy'.

Humorous ads can be very successful: over 80% of the most impactful ads involve humour. 'Black' humour (with characters getting hurt) can be particularly popular among older children. One of the highest-scoring ads tested featured a granny being fed to lions — although this was never aired. An ad launching a confectionery brand showed the sweets being used to make a little figure who then moves around and interacts with a pair of hands. Eventually, the figure gets annoyed with being played with and bites the hands. The ad was hugely impactful. Within eight weeks the brand achieved 80% aided brand awareness and 41% trial, despite distribution problems.

Another route that can be successful is to link your brand to aspects of popular culture. One ad that was developed for a U.K. confectionery brand targeted 8- to 15-year-olds using a popular song. It was highly impactful; ad awareness peaked at 81%. The ad conveyed its key message well, and claimed purchase rose from 5% to 22%. Through its use of the hit song, the brand was viewed as 'cool'. However, it is also worth noting that when the ad ran for its third burst two years later, the song was no longer appreciated, and the ad suffered as a consequence.

Cartoons can be particularly effective; 52% of the most impactful kids' ads use cartoons (compared with just 20% of the least impactful). One brand's launch advertising used 3-D animated characters and was somewhat darker and more mischievous in tone than most children's ads. TV ad awareness peaked at over 60%, with 40% of recallers saying the ad made them want to ask their mum and dad to buy the product for them. Within weeks, over 15% of the target audience were claiming to eat the brand most weeks.

In terms of casting, it is worth noting that children see those two or three years older than themselves as role models.

Get interactive

In many parts of the world, today's youth are web-natives; the internet is as much a part of their lives as TV was in their parents' youth. Many brands are capitalizing on this with fun, interactive web sites. This interactivity can extend to mainstream advertising.

In the U.K., one brand used an interactive TV advertising campaign. The first ad in the campaign ended with the brand character in trouble. It prompted children to vote for their favourite out of a choice of endings shown on product packs. The follow-up ad showed part of the first ad as a reminder, then the ending that had achieved the most votes. The advertising was enjoyed and appreciated, and had a positive impact on brand metrics.

The need for a strong product

As with adult brands, strong advertising cannot make up for a weak product. One brand was launched using well-known cartoon characters as the advertising vehicle. The ad was enjoyed, with two-thirds describing it as one of their favourites, and it generated a strong interest in trial. After three months, awareness had reached 73%. However, after a successful launch, trial levels soon dropped off. Research revealed that the product simply did not live up to the great advertising.

Targeting the Over-50s Market

When I first wrote about the over-50 market, I had yet to reach it. Now that I'm well within in, I feel more strongly than ever the benefits of understanding the older generation.

This older market can provide great opportunities for many brands; roughly a third of citizens in Europe and the U.S. are over 50 years of age. In developed markets this group tends to be relatively prosperous, and are open to new ideas. Since they tend to be heavier media consumers, they can be reached more easily than many segments; but in terms of tone and content, communications need to be carefully targeted for this audience.

Finances

In many markets, the over 50s are, overall, relatively prosperous. TGI analysis shows that in the U.K. over 45s have approximately 80% of all financial wealth. In the U.S., over 55s control around three quarters of financial wealth. Not surprisingly, then, the over-55 age group accounts for approximately half of all spend on food, drink and household products in the U.S.

Attitudes

In general, with age comes a sense of increased confidence. Membership of a 'tribe' becomes less important, and a sense of identity is more likely to come from within. Consequently, older people are not a homogenous group. Health, wealth and lifestyle attitudes also play a role. Some prioritize holidays, some prefer to lead a quiet life at home, entertained by the TV, some seek new experiences, while others aim to become influential within their communities.

In China, qualitative work reveals that older Chinese consumers, having spent many years bringing up their children, start re-looking at their lifestyles after retirement. They begin to spend more time on their interests and hobbies, 'bettering themselves', and (in the primary cities) learning PC skills. Nonetheless, they seek social belonging and attend gatherings with people their own age; travelling through China it is not uncommon to see groups of older people performing Tai Chi in parks. One major difference with Western economies is the respect and reverence in which the older generation is held in China.

In Brazil, changes in the law have resulted in greater facilities for the over 50s: special lines in public services, special features in toilets and showers, and special seats in public transport. There is a growth in the number of gyms catering for mature consumers.

Attitudes to brands

While there can be an assumption that older people are 'set in their ways', this older target can be experimental users of new offerings. A study conducted by Firefly Kantar Millward Brown in Australia suggests that those in the over-55 age group are as open to new opportunities and experiences as the younger targets. Endorsement of the statement, 'I am adventurous and will try new brands and products before anyone else,' was 21% for the under 55s, and 22% for the over 55s.

Similarly, a report by Kantar Millward Brown (Focalyst) in North America revealed that older consumers are about as likely as younger consumers to experiment with different brands (67% for 18–41 year olds versus 61% for 42–59 year olds). Their analysis also suggests that brand loyalty is primarily a function of product type, rather than the age of the consumer. Of the ten categories studied, seven had nearly identical levels of single product loyalty across age groups, the exceptions being cars and airlines (where the older group were more likely to be loyal) and music and video players (where the older group were less likely to be loyal).

This willingness to experiment should not be surprising. There are several major life-changing experiences this generation can go through, all of which can stimulate changes in their buying behaviour. These include children leaving home, retirement, paying off the mortgage, loss of a spouse, and inheritance from parents.

They are also just as likely to shop around. Analysis of developed markets shows that within food related categories, there is little difference in brand loyalty amongst the over-50s age group than for those aged under 35 years (who are typically assumed to be the experimenters/early adopters).

Naturally, loyalty varies by category. According to the Focalyst report, while 39% of U.S. Boomers feel 'It doesn't matter which company I use' for cruise lines, this drops to 7% for banks.

Among the over 50s, there is often a desire for luxury, quality, and self-indulgence. There is also a greater need for, and hence interest in, health-related products. In China the cost of medical care is high, so health tonics are popular.

Media consumption

A benefit of advertising to this target group is that they tend to be heavier consumers of traditional media. Nonetheless, they are not averse to new technology: 50% access the internet daily and this age group makes more purchases online than by mail and telephone combined. This acceptance of new technology reaches even further; over a third of U.S. consumers aged over 60 are connected to the internet.

Advertising content

Like any advertising, when targeting the Boomer generation, ads that demonstrate a genuine understanding of the targets' needs, not just their date of birth are most effective. Focalyst analysis in the U.S. shows that the over-50s population is more likely to find advertising in general to be insulting or condescending.

In many respects, the older generation respond to ads similarly to their younger counterparts. However, there are differences.

Qualitative feedback highlights the need for advertising to reflect a lifestyle that is dynamic, active and optimistic. The over-50s are aware of the problems associated with aging and prefer to see it portrayed in a positive light. For example, an ad for an incontinence product was tested in two edits. In one, the emphasis was on the lack of confidence of the sufferer, while the other focused on the confidence she felt by using the product. The latter version was preferred.

In Colombia, the leading incontinence brand adopted a new strategy, of educating the consumer about incontinence, as well as demonstrating the practical and emotional benefits of using their products. This resulted in a major change in attitude towards the category.

Research in Mexico explored the appeal of a range of positionings, to understand how this group related to their age. While the concept 'the road travelled was worth it' had some appeal, it was dismissed as suggesting closure — the lack of a future. Similarly, the message 'You've met your commitments, now you owe nothing', also portrayed the view that no one was expecting anything of them anymore. The idea of enjoying your achievements resonated better, as did 'now is the time to enjoy life' (although it had the implication that life has held no enjoyment until now). Coupled with this, ideas suggesting that 'now is the time for you' hold an invitation to pamper as a reward for sacrifices made, and were well received. In general, the research found that it was better to present the past in a positive way, but to acknowledge that a future still exists. There was also appreciation of the value of knowledge and experience gained.

Qualitative research shows that, as with all advertising, engagement is key, and relevance remains crucial. Shared history and life stage events can create meaningful connections. For instance, one common problem faced by many in this age group is reigniting love once the children have left home, but this is a life stage problem not often acknowledged or discussed. Another factor, common to over-50s around the world, is that they like to see old age portrayed as a happy phase of life.

In some Asian countries, such as China, the family plays an important role, and grandchildren in particular are viewed as the emotional fulfilment for this generation.

The over-50s market is more likely to appreciate familiarity (familiar music and slogans that had been used previously for a brand/campaign) and nostalgic style ads. Animals and children are more likely to make involving and enjoyable viewing. Two thirds of the over-50s age group in North America feel that today's advertising is too 'weird' to resonate with them.

Humour is not seen to be as appealing to the older target as to the younger generation, although this could be due to the nature of the humour in the ads. Qualitative feedback shows that humour specifically targeted at this generation can be appreciated.

The rule of thumb seems to be to avoid stereotypes; instead play to this generation's sense of intelligence, wisdom and confidence.

Nonetheless, it needs to be recognized that in many parts of the world, this generation has spent most of its life being exposed to advertising, and established associations can be hard to shift. For example, in one study in the U.K., three-quarters of older consumers remembered advertising for the ice cream brand Cornetto — advertising which had not been on air for 12 years. It is likely to be particularly hard to shift perceptions of the brand for this group.

What Role does Marketing Have in Business-to-Business Markets?

The longest presentation I ever gave lasted about six hours. It wasn't intended to last anything like that long, but this was the first research data the brand manager had seen on his brand and he was keen to get as much insight from the data as possible. This was for a business-to-business computer software brand, and the team fully appreciated the importance of the brand.

Brands have a valuable role to play in business-to-business markets, but there are several key differences from consumer markets which need to be considered when planning any campaign. The differences relate especially to the decision-making processes, particularly in large organizations.

It is generally recognized that in consumer markets, a strong brand is in a better position than a weak one to maximize its performance, take advantage of marketplace events, and grow shareholder equity. But when it comes to large business purchasing decisions, it is common to question what role marketing plays.

Business-to-business is different

Marketing will not overcome product or service shortcomings. Reliability is a major driver in business-to-business markets, because it provides peace of mind for the decision maker. Marketing can help to reinforce the impression of reliability but will not compensate for its absence.

Branding can simplify purchase decisions. It can give the product or service a visible presence in a market, and clarify the relevance of the brand in a category, helping to get it into the consideration set. Marketing can also create the perception that the brand is an acceptable choice. Additionally, it can enhance experience of the brand, by highlighting positive product experiences.

Business-to-business branding is, in this sense, no different from any other branding activity, but there are important differences from general consumer marketing. With business-to-business brands, the corporate brand tends to be more visible than the product brand. This can influence where marketing spend is allocated.

There is generally a smaller target audience, leading to more targeted communications. This affects the choice of media. There also tend to be longer-term contracts, resulting in a greater emphasis on pricing, and a greater scrutiny of details. Decisions tend to be based more on functional benefits than, for example, when a consumer is buying a tin of baked beans. So in terms of spend, positioning and media, business-to-business is different.

Nonetheless, in millions of smaller organizations, and for low-budget items, the decision-making process tends to be very similar to that for consumers. Even in companies with up to 25 employees, most decisions are made by the owner. Here a mass of information from many sources, including advertising, is likely to coalesce into overall impressions that offer short-cuts to decision-making.

In larger organizations, decision-making is diffused among different functional areas for different types of purchases. For example, IT infrastructure, such as computer equipment and networks, might be purchased centrally, while IT-enabled applications, such as sales force management systems, are more likely to be purchased by functional areas such as the marketing department. Even when decisions are made by specialists, they are likely to have to justify them to non-experts. And often, employees who are not explicitly identified as decision-makers play a role in their company's choices. Failure to deliver on the benefits (for instance, poor mobile phone performance) filters up through complaints and can eventually lead to a change of vendor. In choosing software for company intranets, there can be pressure, even up to senior levels, to use Google or Facebook solutions, because they have good internet reputations. So even in large organizations, the views of non-specialists can be important.

The drivers of decision-making

For service brands, there are massive differences in the drivers of brand health between users (for whom their experience of using the brand is key) and non-users (who will be more reliant on communications). The extent to which individuals working for the brand can build relationships with their customers and put together advantageously priced packages will often be crucial in bonding customers to the brands they use. Clearly it is also vital to offer the right products or services, with sufficient capability to deliver what customers need (at the right scale and over the right geographical area) in order for people to put together the right packages or deals.

Professional business customers are generally more focused on functional benefits and less on loyalty than smaller businesses and consumers, and this bias grows with the size of the organization. In one financial market, the average 'first-choice' consideration score for customers for their current supplier averaged at 63% for businesses turning over under £1 million a year, but fell to 52% for those turning over more than £15 million. Similarly, the relationship between satisfaction with current experience and first-choice consideration is not direct. In larger organizations there is less commitment to current suppliers and more willingness to explore alternatives.

Relationship between satisfaction and consideration is not direct

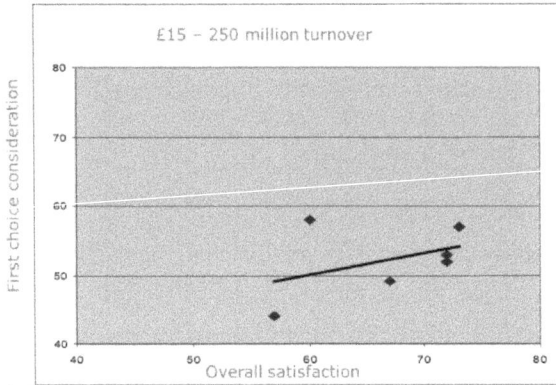

£15 – 250 million turnover

There are many factors at play here. The needs of larger companies are more complex, and they are more likely to, for example, use more than one bank. In larger organizations, there is an increasing disconnect between the user of the product or service, and the decision-maker(s). There is also a tendency for the number of decision-makers to increase: major decisions need to be ratified by a number of people. In these situations, the decision-makers are more likely to try to make choices based on needs, and the deals and capabilities offered by each competing supplier. It is these processes that weaken the relationship between consideration and satisfaction.

But even where you might assume that functional benefits determine brand choice, other factors are still important. Here's an example from what is often assumed to be a highly functionally driven market, the pharmaceutical industry. Loyalty to brands among specialists is not solely driven by price and functional elements, and in one particular market with little product differentiation, modelling shows that loyalty is strongly driven by popularity.

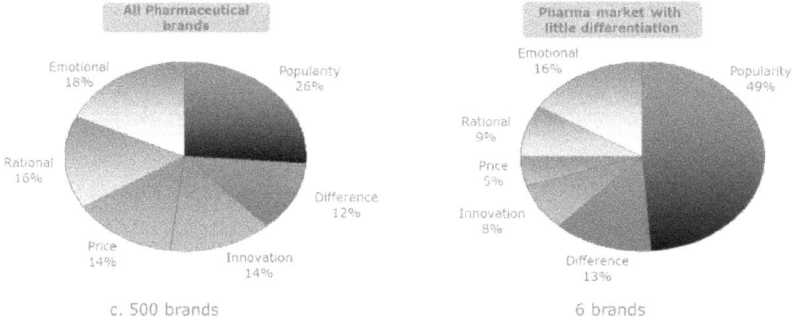

All Pharmaceutical brands

Emotional 18%
Popularity 26%
Rational 16%
Price 14%
Innovation 14%
Difference 12%

c. 500 brands

Pharma market with little differentiation

Emotional 16%
Popularity 49%
Rational 9%
Price 5%
Innovation 8%
Difference 13%

6 brands

KANTAR MILWARDBROWN

As another example, technology firms are increasingly realizing that design is important: how the product looks and feels can drive perceptions of functionality and innovation.

Decision makers are also influenced by impressions arising from experience, and from the network of influencing relationships which affect feelings about brands and companies. When making decisions they are subject to the same kinds of pressures and influences as everyone else. Of course they have expertise, and a need to maintain their professional reputation. But they also have moods and emotions, and mixed feelings towards the people they are dealing with. The pressures and stresses that arise in their working lives also contribute to the decision-making process.

One additional factor affects brands that straddle the consumer and business-to-business environments. The reputation of a brand in one sector is likely to influence its reputation in the other. One telecoms company had a poor reputation for its consumer service. Ads for its business products and services were treated with a lot of scepticism because business professionals did not believe the company could deliver in the business environment either.

The value of a strong brand

Branding can influence business-to-business decisions. A good example is IBM which holds a strong position in the business IT solutions market. While IBM is undoubtedly strong on functional elements, the brand is also very well-known and is seen as a leader. This helps to make it seem a safe choice in areas that are tricky for non-specialists to evaluate. These aspects will have contributed to the growth of the brand.

Similarly, the Marriott hotel chain in the United States is a very strong brand among business professionals. A detailed exploration of the equity of the brand shows that not only is it strong on functional strengths, such as facilities, size and cleanliness of rooms, and quality of food, it also conveys emotional values, and a sense of leadership.

How best to market to business professionals?

Business professionals are people, and they respond to advertising in as such. They notice and remember advertising and are more likely to pay attention to advertising that they enjoy or appreciate. All the main media can be employed successfully to reach this audience, but it should be understood that business professionals have a personal appreciation of advertising, as well as a professional view.

Typically business professionals deny (at least in public) that they are influenced by advertising, as indeed do almost all consumers! However, that is not the case: they do retain associations and imagery from the advertising they encounter.

Business professionals notice advertising. In this example from a financial market, the two leading brands both have higher ad awareness among their business targets than among general consumers, particularly for newspapers, posters and direct mail.

Business users are more aware of (mainstream) secondary media

In which of the following places have you seen, heard or read anything about ...recently?

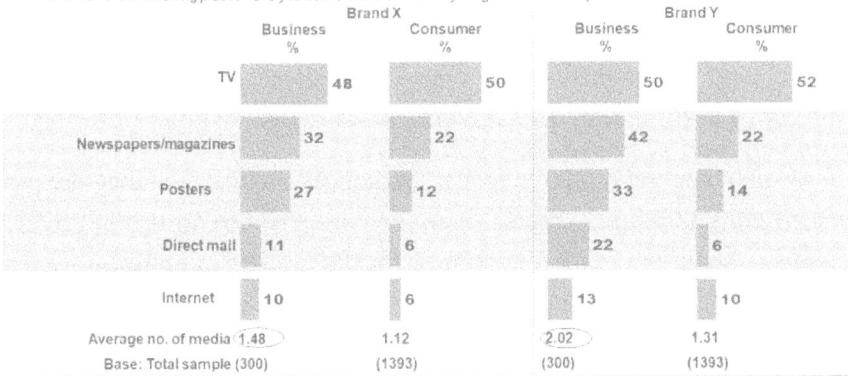

	Brand X		Brand Y	
	Business %	Consumer %	Business %	Consumer %
TV	48	50	50	52
Newspapers/magazines	32	22	42	22
Posters	27	12	33	14
Direct mail	11	6	22	6
Internet	10	6	13	10
Average no. of media	1.48	1.12	2.02	1.31
Base: Total sample	(300)	(1393)	(300)	(1393)

KANTAR MILWARDBROWN

Ads don't just do things to business professionals; business professionals also do things with ads. Through advertising — and other communications as well — they make themselves familiar with the options available, and build up a landscape of organizations and services which they view as suitable in particular contexts. They attach character, meaning and associations to these brands, absorbing not only their practical offerings, but also their imagery and 'personality'.

Reactions to advertising

Professionals' reactions to advertising depend on two aspects: their professional roles, and their personal characteristics.

Sometimes ads are treated as a negative intrusion. Business professionals often want to reject the implied attempt to influence their decision making. However, they do acknowledge that ads play a useful role in keeping people informed.

An individual's personality and outlook will also influence their appreciation of advertising. Many people enjoy good ads. They can brighten the chore of reading professional publications, and provide amusement and pleasure, in contrast to the serious articles. On the negative side, ads are sometimes found irritating. Some ads are simply ignored. This is especially true of ads that are perceived as boring and unimaginative, or over-complicated and confusing, or if the visual presentation does not clearly draw out the point of the ad.

It is also apparent that business audiences notice ads that are not specifically targeted at them, since they are also consumers in a wider context. So all the market messages for the brand should be consistent in their broad positioning, regardless of the target.

Print

Print advertising is often a primary medium of communication between a business-to-business company and potential purchasers. Business professionals typically have access to a variety of different magazines and newspapers targeted at their sector. These are often read only superficially and out of a sense of obligation; professionals need to keep up-to-date and watch out for information of specific importance to them. The time spent on ads and the attention paid to detail are both minimal. To be effective, ads must be designed to function in this context of selective attention and pressure to scan the publication as quickly and efficiently as possible. However some business titles are designed to be lighter and more appealing, and are read during leisure time.

One advantage of print media — in the business just as in a more general context — is that the reader has control over the medium. They can take additional time to consider an ad (or an article) that they find new, interesting or intriguing. In contrast, material that comes across as familiar or boring attracts little or no attention. General learning shows that print ads tend to 'wear out' after around three exposures. It may take one or two 'opportunities to see' before real exposure to an ad takes place: That is, the individual registers the ad, and takes time to absorb it. The corollary is highly important: If someone has already seen an ad a few times but not paid attention to it, it is highly unlikely that they ever will; and if they have paid it attention once already and absorbed it, they will not bother to do so again.

There comes a point, then, when providing more and more opportunities to see the same ad is a wasteful exercise. What is needed is a new 'twist' in execution and/or message to draw attention again.

Online

The web can be an ideal medium for communicating with business professionals, who usually have ready access to the internet at work. While there are major issues with spam, the internet can be a great, cost-effective vehicle for well-targeted direct communication. The web offers the ability to target your audience. The web also allows for a large amount of information to be communicated where appropriate. Few companies do not have a web page. As well as conveying details of the offering, they can also convey the brand's character and personality through the use of imagery, including video.

Television

For reasons of cost and targeting, television is not commonly used for business-to-business advertising. When it is used, it is often used badly. The chart below contrasts the performance of business-to-business TV ads with consumer TV ads in the United States. They perform weaker on all key dimensions except Involvement; (but this stronger score reflects what can be described as a 'negative involvement' — the ads are more likely to be viewed as irritating and unpleasant).

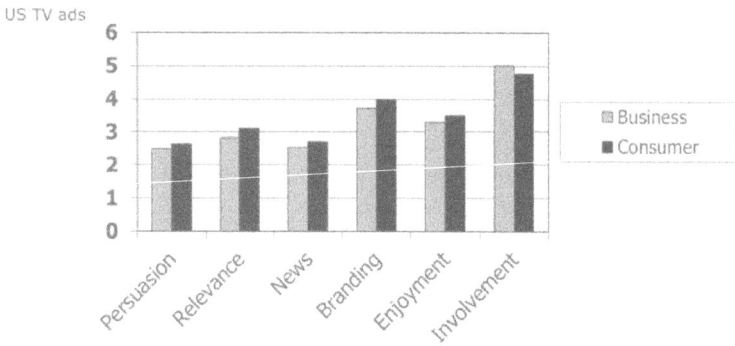

US TV ads

KANTAR MILWARDBROWN

This should not be taken to mean that TV advertising cannot be used for a business audience; there are examples of successful business-to-business advertising which show it can be effective. But higher income, higher social class respondents — those to whom such advertising is often targeted — tend to be more critical of advertising in general.

Customer relationship management

While not viewed as part of the advertising budget, customer relationship management (CRM) has a major role to play in building the brand relationship with the consumer. Experiences with sales people and pre- and post-sales interactions can really colour perceptions of the brand. This encompasses many dimensions, both practical (such as problem solving, the provision of information, and access to events, forums and workshops) and emotional, (including respect, friendship and a sense of partnership).

One project among a business audience highlighted that business professionals could be segmented into six groups, based on aspects such as their interest in their job, their need for social recognition, their interest in new developments, and their balance between team work and working as an individual. Their requirements for a CRM program varied considerably by segment. While business-to-business companies tend to view CRM programs as serving their own needs, this research acts as a useful reminder that customers can also find them useful, when they are appropriately positioned.

Another project illustrated the importance of this relationship when the right balance is found. It reported that if a respected contact moved to a new company, the business was likely to follow. Individual relationships can be more important than the brand.

Postscript

Ten Things I've Learned in Thirty-Five Years

Here are my top ten research tips from researching brands and advertising over a long period.

1. When interpreting data always go back to the questionnaire to check what you actually asked your respondents.

2. When you come back from holiday, you're going to be swamped with emails. It's horrible, but on the other hand, if everyone got on fine while you were away, it would probably tell you something worrying about your role....

3. When assessing advertising persuasion is one interesting and sometimes useful metric. But it represents only part of any evaluation, its relevance depending upon the strategic goals of the advertisers. It is hard to get a strong persuasion score without what consumers will see as news. *Most successful advertising works without news or persuasion.* I put that in italics because it might just be the most important sentence in the book.

4. People like reading lists.

5. Correlation is not causation. Too often I've seen presentations where the core analysis is based on some form of correlation, and the researcher has assumed causation. The result is that probably the client has acted on misleading advice.

6. This is particularly relevant when looking at the relationship between brand images and consideration. Gordon Brown showed years ago that people's attitudes to brands changed after they started using them; so that often, usage 'drives' both future consideration and images. This thinking may be so old that it is new to some people.

7. It is also particularly relevant when people think of assessing the effect of advertising by looking at brand measures among those claiming to be aware of the advertising v those claiming not to have seen the advertising. This is almost certain to result in misleading recommendations.

8. The long-term effects of advertising are often far greater than the short-term effects; and are not simply the accumulation of short-term effects. They are hard to measure and harder to predict; but that is not an excuse to focus only on the short term.

9. Look for findings; but mistrust them. That's easy to say, but hard to do. When you see what looks like an interesting pattern in the data, **stop** and ask yourself what else might be causing the pattern. Questionnaire change? Data error? Charting error? An alternative explanation for a correlation?

10 Data is nothing without intelligent interpretation. People are our most important asset. Treat them fairly and with respect, train them well and do what you can to help them enjoy their work.

Lightning Source UK Ltd.
Milton Keynes UK
UKHW010754081119
353113UK00002B/35/P